THE

BOOK OF

CATHOLIC AUTHORS

(Fourth Series)

Informal self-portraits of famous
modern Catholic writers, edited
with preface and notes

by

WALTER ROMIG

fully illustrated by portraits

WALTER ROMIG—PUBLISHER

979 Lakepointe Road
GROSSE POINTE 30, MICHIGAN

WALTER ROMIG,—PUBLISHER

also issues

The Guide to Catholic Literature
The American Catholic Who's Who
American Catholic Convert Authors
Negro Catholic Writers

PRINTED AND BOUND BY THE ABBEY PRESS, ST. MEINRAD, IND., U.S.A.

To

JOHN WILLIAM ECKENRODE
founder and director of
THE NEWMAN BOOKSHOP

PREFACE

The increasing demand for this series can be regarded only as a command for its continuation. Hence, while this fourth series is going through press the manuscript of the fifth is in preparation.

The secret of the popularity of the series evidently lies largely in the fact that being autobiographical it brings you both the personality of each author as well as a generous specimen of his writing style.

Also by now it has been proven that the principal purpose of the series is being achieved, namely, that these genial, informal but informative autobiographies of distinguished Catholic writers are leading more and more readers from an author's sketch to his books.

Those who desire greater detail in factual biographical data are referred to the volumes of *The American Catholic Who's Who,* each of which includes biographies of more than seven hundred notable living Catholic writers, and those who want more material on any or all of the author's books are referred to *The Guide to Catholic Literature, 1888-1940,* its first permanent supplement, *The Guide ..., 1940-1944,* and its second, *The Guide ..., 1944-1948,* which is scheduled for publication in June, 1948.

To all who have shared in the making of this series I express my thanks.

WALTER ROMIG

CONTENTS

of the first four series of *The Book of Catholic Authors*, with the number preceding the name indicating in which series the author's chapter is to be found.

RUDOLF ALLERS

THE LIFE OF A MAN WHO WAS AND IS MAINLY ENGAGED IN study, research, and teaching is likely to be, on the whole rather uninteresting. There are no exciting events, no adventures, no unexpected turns of fortune the like of which one encounters in the biographies of soldiers, explorers, statesmen, or also of the leaders in business. The only things which to know might be of some profit to the reader are details of intellectual pursuit; perhaps one may learn something from another man's experiences, although I am not sure that this is really the case. But the mere facts of life are surely unimportant. Since this essay is, however, meant to be autobiographical, I shall first briefly indicate these facts.

Born in Vienna, Austria, in 1883, the son of a physician and of a mother stemming from a family of scientists. Having finished secondary school, I studied medicine at the

University of Vienna and received my M.D. in 1906. During the last two years previous to the study of medicine I had devoted much time to work in a chemical laboratory, and while interning at the General Hospital in Vienna, I continued such work.

My chief interest, however, was psychiatry, and I was fortunate in securing the position of an assistant at the Clinic for Nervous and Mental Diseases at the German University of Prag. (Then, there were in this city two universities which had branched off from the old one: a Czech and a German school.) In 1909 I went as an assistant to the Clinic of Mental Diseases at Munich, where I became instructor in psychiatry in 1913.

During the first World War I served as surgeon in the Austrian army under a very outstanding man and learned quite some surgery. After the war I was offered the position of an assistant at the Institute of Physiology at Vienna, with the particular function as head of the department of sense-physiology and medical psychology. I became an instructor in psychiatry in 1927, and practiced psychiatry while carrying on researches in the laboratory. The study of psychology, and not less that of the problems of my clients, besides a certain interest I had always felt, led me further into philosophy, and finally, in 1934, I received my Ph.D. from the Catholic University at Milan.

A book of mine, *The Psychology of Character*, had been translated into English in 1930, and I had written *The New Psychologies* in English myself in 1932. These books had attracted attention somehow and, during the summer of 1937, I was invited to join the faculty of the Catholic University of America. Since the beginning of the second semester in 1938, I have held the position of professor of psychology in the School of Philosophy.

Perhaps it is worthwhile to ask what factors have proved, so far as I can see, most helpful in my work. It seems to me that these factors are of three kinds, and they determine in truth everyone's life and career. They are two personal factors and one which is impersonal: talent, interest, and opportunity.

A man is not responsible for his talents, but he is for the use he makes of them. He is not responsible for the opportunities which chance or destiny offer him, but he is for making the best of them or for neglecting them. He has to find out what gifts he possesses. Nothing seems to me a greater obstacle in life than to take for granted that one can do one thing and not do another. Only experience can teach us that. Usually it is believed that overrating one's capabilities is the greater danger; but if one does so, he will, if he is of a somewhat sensible mind, realize it rather soon. There is a greater danger in not undertaking a thing because one feels sure before hand that one cannot do it. Many people lead a life poorer than it need be, one below the intellectual level they might attain, simply because they believe that certain things are "not for them." A student encounters difficulties in mathematics and he concludes immediately that he is not gifted in this subject; another finds it difficult to acquire a foreign language, and he is sure that he had better leave this study alone. It seems to me that, on the whole, every average normal person is able to achieve an average success in all average fields. The demands made in any field whatsoever on the level of secondary or even of college education are absolutely average. To be sure, one will find one thing easier and another another. But it does not follow from this that they are also unable to do the things which they find difficult. Nor does the existence of such difficulties prove that the corresponding talent is missing. Such a talent exists often as a mere disposition or, in the terminology of philosophy, as a mere potentiality; and it has to be actualized by practice. One cannot say how long it will take to effect this actualization. A study which

seemed hard at first may soon become easy simply because
the actualization of the hitherto dormant potentiality has
proceeded far enough.

Although one is not responsible for one's gifts, one may
be responsible for one's interests. The worst attitude to
assume is that of the fox who, because he could not reach
them, claimed that the grapes were bitter. Things are interesting by virtue of their nature, and there is in truth
nothing void of all interest. Our interests are more or less
restricted by the limitations of human capacity, but this
does not justify our frowning on things with which we cannot be occupied. The often heard phrase: "How can a sensible person be interested in this or that?" indicates neither
a superior nor a practical mind, but rather one which is
narrow and petty. It were wiser to say that one regrets
not being capable of appreciating such an interest.

This is an age of specialization, or concentration, as they
call it. The general idea is that it is never too early to begin
specializing in this or that. I believe that this is a great
mistake. As I see it, the manifold interests I experienced
in my life have been one of its greatest assets.

I was appointed to the assistantship at Munich because I
had a good training in biochemistry; but this training also
proved valuable later since it enabled me to understand and
to evaluate the importance of science and scientific metho-
dology for humanity and for the philosophical understanding of reality. Necessity made me a surgeon and when the
war ended I ceased to be a surgeon; but the surgical technique I had acquired enabled me to carry out experiments
in the field of nerve-physiology. Because I had been a phy-
siologist and experimentator I knew how far this line of
research may lead to understanding the fundamentals of
human nature. This experience enables me to evaluate the
usefulness and significance of the so-called biological ap-
proach in psychology, or rather, to recognize how little it

actually signifies. Likewise, as a psychiatrist I can discern
the boundaries of abnormal psychology and the danger of
introducing too much of it into normal psychology, education, and other fields.

I can claim, of course, no merit for having been offered
the opportunities. But opportunity is not all. One must
avail oneself of it. I gratefully admit, however, that I was
very fortunate regarding opportunity. First, that I grew
up in an intellectual and stimulating atmosphere, among
books and among people of a high standard. In a family
where everyone reads it is but natural that a child be interested in reading.

And after opportunity, encouragement is necessary.
Many parents seem to feel that reading more than is demanded by the school is a waste of time. This is not true.
It is often in a book that a person finds the first indication
of what he would like to do in life. Reality is too rich to
be experienced within the boundaries of an average existence. The fullness of reality enters our lives through the
printed word more often than in any other way.

I think that the acquaintance, by means of books, with
parts of existence and reality one cannot, in view of the inevitable narrowness of the individual life, personally experience, is the needed compensation for the growing
specialization and departmentalization of modern life. The
more 'vocational' our training becomes, the more the development and growth of our personalities suffer. And this
does damage eventually not only to the individual but to the
nation, even to mankind.

This danger threatening human personality is particularly great when the vocational training is scientific or tech-
nological. However important science and technology be for
the improvement of living conditions, they are essentially
alien to things of a strictly human nature. The human factor disappears in science; even when man himself is made

the object of scientific inquiry, he is, so to speak, dehuman-
ized. In dealing with our fellowmen in social intercourse
and in the manifold forms of human relations, we are all
agreed that man must be considered as endowed with a
unique dignity. But when science inquires into the nature
of man it forgets all about this unique dignity and treats
him just as one thing among others. By its very nature
science must do this. But there are other sources from
which we may gather a knowledge of human affairs. These
sources are principally literature, art, and history.

It may seem strange that one trained mostly in medicine
and psychology should advocate the extensive study, or at
least reading, of literature and history and a good acquaintance with art in every sense of the word. I have already
remarked that no one's life is rich enough to encompass the
whole of human experience. Take the practical psychologist.
Neither the case-histories he finds in his textbooks nor the
individuals he meets can acquaint him with all the varieties
in human nature. The case-histories, moreover, are necessarily short and rather lifeless. The persons the poet or
novelist present are much more alive and varied. I have
found that I have profited much in my understanding of
human problems by an extensive acquaintance with literature.

The world has become very small. Distance has disappeared. There is no longer any place one might call far
away. The news of what happens in every corner of the
world reaches us immediately and influences our lives. We
are forced to concern ourselves with foreign nations, their
activities and their attitudes. Without a knowledge of history we are utterly unable to understand either.

History also teaches us that, while life and its conditions
are continually changing, some essentials remain forever
unchanged. We speak confidently of everlasting values, of
moral principles which are valid always and everywhere.

But how can we convince others that we are right? Pure philosophical speculation impresses but a few. But history furnishes proof for the many.

History also makes us aware of the absolute uniqueness of every human person. Science, even the social sciences and anthropology, cannot do so. As Aristotle said, science deals with generalizations. In history, as in the vision of the poet, human persons appear as unique individuals.

One of the basic causes of our present world state is the ignorance of things strictly human. We have fallen prey to the idolatry of technology. We believe that there is a right technique for everything, and that we need only find it and learn it. Hence the success of the books which profess to tell you how to be or to do everything. But this is wrong. An infallible technique exists only in regard to events which repeat themselves in an identical manner. But every man is unique.

This uniqueness of the human person forbids also that any man's life be set up as an example to be imitated. We may strive to imitate the virtues a great man displayed, but we cannot imitate him. If we try, the result is a caricature, and we are acting a role which is not our own.

One may learn techniques from others, but not the inner attitude in regard to things and problems and tasks. There is no such thing as a 'technique of life' to be employed indiscriminately by everyone. Hence, one person's life cannot teach much.

Is there a technique of research? I do not mean, of course, the mere technicalities, the experimental procedure, the mathematical formula, the collection of references, and such like. I mean the inner attitude in regard to research. I do not think that this is something one can teach, in the true sense. One can only awaken the propensity for it in a person. The teacher can make things interesting; and the

more things he makes interesting, the greater his service to
the pupil.

For the rest, there is little I might say. Not more, perhaps, than this: it is eminently necessary to pay attention to
little things. Research and study proceed step by step. One
should know as much about one's subject as possible. But it
is equally essential that one remain conscious of the wide
frame within which every little thing or problem or achievement becomes significant. An emphasis laid exclusively on
the detail, the mere fact, the immediate object of inquiry,
leads to the loss of a broad understanding, leads to a frag-
mentary view of reality. On the other hand, by overempha-
sis on the all-encompassing frame, one runs the risk of being wrong in the factual foundation of one's ideas.

The best a scholar and writer has to give is contained in
his work as an author and a teacher. His work is more important than his biography. While one does not compare
one's work with that of the great men of past ages, the relation, on however small a scale, remains the same. The
message that one has to convey, the view to suggest, the
position to defend, they are all in the work. The work alone
counts. It is the fruit by which we shall be known.

EDITOR'S NOTE: Dr. Allers' preference of his books over his biography
is understandable in one who has written such significant volumes as
The Psychology of Character, Macmillan, 1931; *Practical Psychology
in Character Development*, Sheed, 1934; *The New Psychologies*, Sheed,
1933; *Character Education in Adolescence*, Wagner, 1940; *Self Improvement*, Benziger, 1939; *The Successful Error* (Freudianism),
Sheed, 1940; and *Sex Psychology in Education*, Herder, 1937.

EUGENE BAGGER

I WANT TO BEGIN BY PAYING MY DEBT OF GRATITUDE TO A BOY named Carl Mayer. He is not a boy today if he is alive (which I doubt), but a man of fifty-four like myself; but he was a boy when I knew him, having shared a desk with him for six out of the eight years of *gymnasium*, as high school was called in my native Budapest, capital of the then flourishing kingdom of Hungary. Well, it was not exactly high school, but rather an amalgam of high school and college. We had eight years of Latin and four of Greek and six of universal history; we also had a little algebra and geometry and physics and natural history, but the scientific side of the curriculum was not considered very important. Having been around a good deal since, I know today that that Hungarian high school gave about the best secondary education to be had anywhere in the world. They did not teach us Latin and Greek as thoroughly as they do in the so-called public schools of England, such as Eton and Harrow, and they did not teach mathematics so well as they do in France, and they did not teach "useful" subjects at all as they do in America. But they did give us a thorough grounding in European culture, with proper stress on its Catholic and Roman origins; and they impressed on us that without understanding mankind's past one cannot understand its present, and is apt to grow too optimistic about its future. However, even our excellent drilling in history contained no prevision of and provision for the emergence of Hitler and Stalin, and to this extent the realistic outlook which it inculcated was almost as much off the mark as is that overconfidence in an inevitably bigger and better tomorrow which characterizes American education.

Now this boy Carl Mayer did not know what an important part he was playing in my life; nor did I know it myself at the time. His contribution consisted in sitting next to me in class. He was a Catholic boy. My parents were Jewish. They were not orthodox Jews and not even "practicing" Jews. My mother believed in God and used to pray, but I do not think she had any clearly defined theological doctrine. I do not know exactly what my father believed in, for he died before I got around to discussing religion with him; but I think, in retrospect, that he believed in the natural law and in honest, upright conduct, and lived up to his belief. He was a lawyer, and he belonged to a coterie of lawyers and business men who ran the municipality of Budapest, a large city of 800,000 people in those days. All my father's friends had grown rich out of city politics, but my father died a poor man when I was nineteen. That's why I had to give up the academic career which I had dreamed of, and got myself a job on a newspaper. So, for the next twenty-five years I was a journalist.

However, I must get back to Carl Mayer. I had a very quick brain and an excellent memory, and when our masters explained something in class I got the whole of it in the

first five minutes; so when they went on explaining I was
bored, and sought to amuse myself by books held under the
desk. I used to borrow books from this Carl Mayer, and
among others he lent me his textbooks on religion, including
the New Testament and the Catechism and a little volume of
Catholic apologetics. All this was news to me, and very
wonderful news. It told me what I was eager to know
about God and man and the universe. And so at the age of
fourteen I decided to become a Catholic. I began becoming
one by raising my cap to the priest who came around twice
a week to hold classes in religion for the Catholic boys. In
Hungary it was the custom to greet a priest with the beautiful words, *Laudetur Dominus Jesus Christus* (Praised be
the Lord Jesus Christ). Peasants and townspeople said in
Hungarian, but schoolboys said it in Latin, and the priest
answered, *In sempiternum, amen* (Forever and ever,
amen). After I had greeted Father Molnar in this way
a few times, he began to wonder why a little Jewish boy
should do this, and eventually he asked me why I did it. I
told him; and the upshot of it was that at the age of seventeen I was baptized a Catholic. I have often thought since
that if my neighbor in class had been a Protestant or Jewish
youngster this might not have happened at all; though of
course the grace of God might have found another way. So
now you see why I feel I owe a great debt of gratitude to the
boy Carl Mayer, and why I include him, and also Father
Molnar, in my prayers. I don't know whether they are alive
or dead; if the Nazis did not kill them when they overran
Hungary, perhaps the Russians did later; as they killed my
young sister and two nephews.

At the age of twenty-two I came to the United States. I
had learned to speak English at home when I was ten years
old, and I decided then and there that English is the greatest
language in the world. How I figured this out as a little boy
I do not know, but I still think that I figured rightly.

French is more precise and more elegant, Spanish more brilliant and more sonorous, Italian softer and more tuneful;
but for power and depth and richness of expression, nothing
beats English.

A few days after my landing in New York I took out my
"first papers," and five years later, in 1920, I became an
American citizen. By then I was an editorial writer on the
New York Tribune. A little later I went to Europe for the
New York Times. I had heard that the imperial archives of
the old Austrian Empire (which was destroyed by the Allies
after the first world war, to the greater glory of democracy,
as they thought, but really in the event to the benefit first of
Hitler and then of Soviet Russia) had just been thrown
open to public research. So I rushed to Vienna to get a
scoop, and got it, and wrote some articles for the *New York
Times* about the private life and public policies of the old
Emperor Francis Joseph, and then extended these articles
into a book. I thought then that it was a very good book;
but I don't think so any longer, for I had been very hard on
the old Emperor, and today I know that he was entirely
right in his determination to maintain the Catholic Haps-
burg Empire as a bulwark against Prussian and Russian
imperialism, even though he went about it in the wrong
way. So I herewith tender my apologies to Francis Joseph;
some day I may do this at a greater length.

In the spring of 1927 my book was finished and the manuscript mailed to my publisher in New York. So I left Vienna and went to the South of France for a little vacation of
six weeks. I stayed for six years.

Now this was an odd thing to do for a man of thirty-five
who had made a fair start in his profession but was still
a long way from a landfall. My friends told me I was an
"escapist," hiding out from life in a private world composed
of books, pipe-dreams, and the pinewoods and mimosa
groves of the Provencal coast; and in my not infrequent

moments of discouragement I was inclined to agree with
them. Yet I knew in a dim way at the time, and know quite
clearly today, that in throwing away my chances of "making
good," I was not a deserter from reality but a conscientious
objector. I could not bring myself to believe that "success,"
as the world understands it and measures it in terms of
money, is the highest aim of life; I refused to regard everybody's war against everybody else for self-aggrandizement
as a holy war. I was determined to take time out to *think*.
I believed in those days that I could resume my career,
which I had dropped, in my own good time and on my own
terms. But things do not work out that way, as I discovered
when I eventually returned to New York in 1940, after sixteen years spent in (practical people would say, wasted on)
reading books in France, England and Switzerland. Today
I am sure that my choice, which practical people called fool-
ish, was fundamentally right.

In my autobiography, *For the Heathen Are Wrong,* I told
at length the story of how I, in that Provencal retreat, had
drifted into, rather than taken up, the study of philosophy;
and how, after years of weakened faith and intellectual bewilderment, I eventually read and thought myself back into
the Church which I at the age of seventeen had entered
without sufficient preparation. I am, I need hardly say,
very sorry that I ever lapsed, not, indeed, into formal apos-
tasy and aggressive disbelief, but into the fog of intellectual
uncertainty and moral indifferentism; and I wasted a lot of
time groping my way back to Truth through the maze of all
the false doctrines whereby modern man has betrayed his
reason to his pride and lust for power, and has sought to
justify or "rationalize" his usurpation of the place of God
as the master of life, the maker of all law, the measure of
all things, and the final cause of the universe. Yet, in another sense, those years through which I wandered back to
the Faith by the devious path of exploring its maninvented

substitutes were not wasted. They meant, rather, a kind of spiritual ordeal and cleansing, imposed by Providence. A convert like myself may be in a better position than the "born" Catholic, and the faithful who have never wavered, to appreciate the blessed privilege of belonging to the Church, of being freed by the truth of Our Lord. Such a prodigal son may not only see but *live* the meaning of the Psalmist's words: "The measuring lines have fallen to me in pleasant places ... mine inheritance is pleasant to me ... with him at my right hand I shall not be moved." Again, a Catholic who has come by his faith the long and hard way is rather like the officer of military intelligence who was caught in enemy territory at the outbreak of war and tried to make good use of his opportunity to learn all about the enemy's ways. One of the weak points in the armor of many Catholics, even of some Catholic thinkers, is that they apt to underestimate the power and scope of consistent intellectual error in history, looking mainly for wrong dispositions and laxity of will as the explanation of the evils rampant in the world, not having seen from the inside, as it were, the working of that malice of the human reason which lies at the bottom of it all. Such Catholics come to imagine that some of the worst evils of our time may be remedied by methods of compromise, by coming to terms, in regard to this urgent practical problem or that, with the secularist enemies of the Faith. A convert like myself who has done time, so to speak, on the wrong side of the frontier is less likely to drop into such self-confident error. To his mind the fundamental, irreconcilable opposition between Catholicism and the modern world is ever present. He cannot be what Father Furfey and others have called a Catholic conformist, that is to say, a Catholic who is eager to minimize the difference between him and his non-catholic environment, who wants to be "just like everyone else," who, in other words, wants to possess all the supernatural advantages of

being a Catholic and still feel perfectly comfortable in a
world which hates and scorns the supernatural. Now the
convert cannot be a conformist Catholic for the simple reason that if he had had any tendency to conformism he would
not have become a Catholic. He is a convert, not in spite
of but *because* of, his realization that the Catholic ideal, to
quote Father Furfey again, "so gloriously supernatural in
character, is opposed by the whole ethos of the modern
world; for a basic dogma of contemporary civilization is the
complete denial of the supernatural. Having rejected the
grace of God, men tend toward a state of mental confusion
in which even the principles of natural morality are ob-
scured." Now the convert who entered the Church by the
gate of Catholic philosophy knows the inside story of that
mental confusion, for he has escaped from it. Speaking for
myself, I agree entirely with Father Furfey when he says
that "Catholics must break sharply and clearly with the
modern world." They must pay that price for the inesti-
mable privilege of being the children of God; and the convert is not likely to forget about that price, for he has
already paid it. He has chosen for his motto the words of
Saint Paul: "Be not conformed to this world, but be transformed in the newness of your mind."

EDITOR'S NOTE: Readers of Mr. Bagger's *Francis Joseph, Emperor of
Austria, King of Hungary* (Putnam, 1927) will appreciate the mental
and spiritual maturity he attained between the writing of it and his
writing of *For the Heathen Are Wrong* (Little, Brown, 1941 and in
England, Eyrie & Spottiswoode).

MAURICE BARING
(1874 - 1945)
by Anne Fremantle

THERE ARE SIX GREAT POWERS, THE THEN DUC DE RICHELIEU
said, in the mid-nineteenth century: England, France, Austria, Prussia, Russia, and Baring Brothers. Maurice Baring
was born the eighth child of the first Lord Revelstoke, head
of this great banking house, and he was also nephew of the
famous statesman, Lord Cromer. Seldom has any human
being been so lucky in the outward circumstances of his
whole life. He has himself described, in perhaps the most
fragrant of all his sixty-four books, *The Puppet Show of
Memory,* his perfect childhood. His family had been English
for more than a hundred years (the Barings descended from
Pastor Frantz Baring, minister of the Lutheran Church in
Bremen) without ceasing to be European.

As a child, Maurice was taken to all the good foreign
plays, many of the Italian and German ones, and was introduced to European literature as early as to English. Chérie,

his French governess, not only solidly grounded him in the French classics (at six he knew the whole of the last act of Victor Hugo's "Hernani" by heart), but gave him a life-long devotion to things French—to the shops of Paris, and the toys. Ah, if governesses but realized their power to make or mar international relations! A great diplomat once admitted his lifelong dislike of Germany probably stemmed from an odious Fraulein; and much of pre-1917 Russian distrust of England arose from the conduct and conversation of "Ces Meess."

So exquisitively sensitive was Maurice (his first memory is of his delight in the brightness of a large bird with yellow and red plumage) that he would gloss over Agincourt for fear of hurting Chérie's feelings, and play up Fontenoy, and he refused to recite in French at lunch before a French visitor, because he feared the latter would suffer from his English accent. This perceptiveness was never blunted or impaired: as he lay dying, he gently apologized, to the younger members of his beloved Lovat family as they gathered for Christmas, for dying at such an inconvenient time.

Maurice adored Eton, and then essayed both Cambridge and Oxford—he preferred the latter, because it was more like Eton, and it was there that he made lifelong friends with Hilaire Belloc. Then, after "ploughing" repeatedly— in arithmetic—Maurice escaped through the Foreign Office examination. His diplomatic career proceeded "according to plan"—he was sent *en poste* to Paris, Copenhagen and then Rome, all plums. Yet Maurice was already, for all the bubbling gaiety, the practical jokes and the boisterous high spirits that made him the gayest of companions, a serious person. Vernon Lee, one of those strange "Englishmen Italianate" (though she happened to be a woman) who knew and understood Maurice better than most people, wrote to him: "I suppose it takes such a spirit of heroic pity as that little book [a volume of verse] breathes, to be as funny as you are, Maurice." And for "heroic pity" the diplomatic service has little use. "Poor dears, they lead such sheltered lives," a sailor uncle of mine said of his two Foreign Office brothers. Maurice's life, for all the warmth and love and comfort of it, and in it, was not to be sheltered.

The stage was his first love, and he and his brothers and sisters spent all their nursery and schoolroom days acting. Sarah Bernhardt was one of the great influences in his life, and his drawings of her, made when he was seven (they serve as illustrations to *The Puppet Show of Memory*) are inspired. At Eton he had won the Prince Consort prize for French, and in 1899 he published his first book, called *Hildersheim*, after the little place where he tutored in German. It is a collection of four pastiches in French on current French authors and is tremendously admired in France. His gift for languages was miraculous, a real "gift of tongues." Not only was he a superb translator—his renderings of Pushkin and of Lermontov are unique—but he could write in the languages he knew: some seven really fluently, no less idiomatically and comfortably than in English. When he lay dying he said the rosary in some of the tongues he loved: French, Russian, Spanish, German, Latin.

He made many experiments in drama, some in prose, some in verse. "The Black Prince," "Gaston de Foix," "Manfoy, Duke of Athens," "Mahasena," are the least unreadable of the poetic dramas; "The Double Game" and "His Majesty's Embassy" the most plausible of his straight plays. Vernon Lee said of his verse-plays, "they are like Handel opera; three or four divine airs in pages of dull recitative." They read like bad Stephen Phillips, and he was no such great shakes. All the plays lack conflict: it is not until he began to write novels—the first published when he was thirty-seven—that Maurice Baring learned how to internalize conflict, to reincarnate it.

His poetry is also tremendously uneven. Much is medi-
ocre, much tepid and trivial. Then suddenly he will sing
true. He is at his best in laments: his poem for Lord
Lucas; his dirge for HMS *Tiger*, about to be broken up, his
verses for his dead nephew, Charles Spencer, are his high-
water marks. T. E. Lawrence, writing to him in 1928 about
the latter, speaks of his "exquisite ear for the syllables of
grief" and adds "it's ever so queer; quite half its lines are
plain prose, and the whole of it is poetry."

> I do not need you changed, dissolved in air
> Nor rarified
> I need you all imperfect as you were.

Desmond McCarthy has called him "an author whose
pockets were never empty." But he was late in finding an
audience: he wrote to Vernon Lee in 1920, "I have a public
of three. You used to be a fourth."

In July, 1901, after a visit to Sarah Bernhardt at her
country place, he went to stay with the Benckendorffs—
whom he had met in Copenhagen—at Sosnofka, their home
in Russia. Instantly he fell in love with the country and the
people (in spite of having his pocketbook, passport and
other such necessities, stolen on the train). He then and
there resolved to study Russian, to write about Russia, and
to give up the diplomatic service.

The stage, and Sarah, had been his first love; Russia was
his second. And there were hints of it, too, in his childhood:
a picture of Saint Petersburg on the nightnursery wall; a
love of Tolstoy, whom he was so surprised to find was a
Russian, writing about Russian people. Dickens, Maurice
had thought of as English; but it never occurred to him that
the characters in Tolstoy had a country—or rather, that
they could have any country of which he was not a part.
His third love—for every man's heart is threecornered—
was God. It is given to very few people (and fewer artists)

to have their loves so tidy and so integrated, flowing each
out of the other, not contradicting, but complementing each
other.   For many artists, as they proceed through the
forest, in the woods become tree. This Maurice never did.
Together with his exquisite capacity for appreciation, his
tuning-fork sensitivity of ear, he had, too, that detachment
which is a natural quality of the type of human being of
whom Sir Philip Sidney was the prototype for all time, and
Maurice a sparkling example. And Philip Sidney's goodbye
to Stella might have been Maurice Baring's to life: *Splen-
dide rerum valedico nugis*—splendidly I bid farewell to all
the trifles of things.

He went to Manchuria to cover the Russo-Japanese war
for the *Morning Post* in 1904, and in October, 1906, took up
his duties as *Morning Post* correspondent in Saint Petersburg. He remained in Russia until the end of 1907 and saw
almost the whole of the 1905 revolution. He went also twice
to Turkey—once for the *Morning Post*, to see the Young
Turk Revolution of 1909, and in 1912 for the *Times*, to cover
the Balkan War. In 1914, he was in Russia as usual for the
summer, came home to be attached to the infant RAF and
was throughout the 1914-1918 war in France, at RAF headquarters. His account of these years, a continuation of *The
Puppet Show of Memory*, is like a Seurat picture of a Goya
subject: a mass of pointilliste detail adding up to one of the
grimmest imaginable of war books.

In 1912 he went around the world, and after 1918 he took
up his traveling again. In 1921 his first novel, *Passing
By*, was published; it was followed by *Overlook*, and *A Tri-
angle*—more novelle than novels; then came *C, Cat's Cradle,
Daphne Adeane, Tinker's Leave*, and seven more, including
the lovely reconstruction, *In My End is My Beginning*, an
account of Mary Stuart's last days told by the four Marys.
His last two books were an anthology, *Have You Anything
to Declare?*, and a book of Russian lyrics (1943).

In his various Russian books he repeatedly tries to
analyze for the reader the reasons for the greatness of the
Russian people; and the source of their particular charm
for him, particularly in *What I Saw in Russia,* an *Outline of
Russian Literature,* and in the long book of Russian history
of which far the best chapter is that on Religion in Russia,
at the end.

He faces bravely the faults of his beloved people: here is
a passage from *The Puppet Show of Memory*: "The *advo-
catus diaboli* had a strong case. He could have drawn up a
powerful indictment, not only against the political conditions, and the arbitrary and uncertain administration, but
also against the character of the people; he could mention
the moral laxity, the extravagant self-indulgence, the lack
of control ... Russia, he would say, was a nation of inef-
fectual rebels under the direction of a band of corrupt and
timeserving officials." But, he goes on, "perhaps the secret
of the whole matter is that the Russian soul is filled with a
human Christian charity which is warmer in kind and in-
tenser in degree, and is expressed with a greater simplicity
and sincerity, than is to be met with in any other people."
And elsewhere he writes: "Somebody once prophesied a few
years ago that in the future the Americans and Russians
would carry everything before them, because of their sheer
warmth of heart." This was written nearly twenty-five
years ago.

His account of the Russian Church—for all his enthusiastic descriptions of the singing—is pretty grim: "All
minor public servants and soldiers when they go to confes-
sion receive a ticket from the verger to say that they have
received absolution, and the pope keeps a list of those who
go to communion. People who do not go to communion run
the risk of being considered politically unsound. Many
people pay to be on a list from year to year stating they
have received the sacraments when they haven't." This con-

dition was like that of Ireland during the days of the anti-Catholic Penal Laws, when the public reception of the Anglican sacraments was obligatory. Yet, he concludes, "Religion in Russia, whether believed or not, will always remain a part of patriotism, and as long as there is a Russian nation, there will be a Russian religion at the core of it." Perhaps one of the most illuminating incidents in all his books is his account of a long religious conversation with Nazarenko, one of the peasant deputies to the Duma, who could not understand an Englishman believing in God.

Even before his novels, Maurice wrote superb accounts of action. He had what Vernon Lee called "a dry, bony style, which looks like no style at all," and a superb English power of understatement, which was made articulate and was transformed into an art by his study of Russian authors and by living in Russia. An artist never creates *ex nihilo*: he functions like the magpie, not the spider. He has to impose order, and, curiously but also naturally, he prunes and pares best where he has the richest material from which to make his selections. The extreme economy of Chekhov, as of the Chinese, is rooted in plenty, not in penury. In Baring's case, add a most sensitive ear and palate, and it is little wonder that, as Vernon Lee (again!) wrote of him, "the whole subject of Russia seems exactly to suit your strange, rather musical than literary talent."

"I was holding up a man who had been terribly mangled in the legs by a bayonet. The doctor was bandaging him. He screamed with pain. The doctor said that the screaming upset him. I asked the man to try not to scream, and lit a cigarette and put it in his mouth. He stopped immediately and smoked, and remained quite still—until his socks were taken off. The men scarcely ever had socks; their feet were swathed in a white bandage, a kind of linen puttee. This man had socks, and when they were taken off he cried, saying he would never see them again. I promised to keep

them for him, and he said 'Thank you, my protector.' A
little later he died."

Maurice Baring's account of his conversion might have
been written by Andre Maurois's immortal Colonel Bram-
ble: "On the eve of Candlemas, 1909, I was received into
the Catholic Church by Father Sebastian Bowden at the
Brompton Oratory: the only action in my life which I am
quite certain I have never regretted." Yet the first letter
quoted by Dame Ethel Smyth from him—written in January, 1900—had begun, "I wish we were all born Roman
Catholics."

It is as a novelist that Baring was most Catholic: his
novels are all and every one of them concerned with the relation of the soul to God first, and secondly with the relation
of souls—and bodies—to each other. It is possible to argue
whether any novel can be Catholic, whether fiction can bear
the weight of so tremendous a primary fact; it is also possible to doubt whether any novel can not be Catholic and be
a novel at all: for human beings exist only in terms of that
first relationship, and if it is not faced, none other is valid.
But it is impossible to question Baring's position as one of
the great Catholic novelists: he is of the stature of Mauriac
and of Bernanos, and the French consider and are devoted
to him as such. The two best current English Catholic
writers—Graham Greene and Evelyn Waugh—both owe a
tremendous lot to Maurice Baring's courage. If today the
Catholic novel has not only been accepted but is admitted as
the best and most serious type of fiction both in England
and in France, it is due, in England, greatly to Maurice
Baring. He himself acknowledges how profoundly Saki's
The Unbearable Blessington moved him; and his debt to the
Russians, especially to Turgeniev, is patent and acknowl-
edged in every novel he wrote.

Vernon Lee has once more put her finger on the reason
why Maurice Baring was not even greater than he was. She

is discussing Proust. "Of course he's a great writer. Those sort of sticky people often are. The brisk, fresh energetic type is usually too energetic to put all energy into good art, worse luck. Art gets the *ténébreux*, the *ronflants*, the *Slimy Toves* ... Stenhal! There's a man so brisk, so clean in perception and movement, so full of breeze and sunshine, that he wrote only two—at most three—novels, and spent his time at dozens of useless things," did "dozens of useless things."

Maurice Baring, too, played splendidly with trifles. At the Paris Embassy, he and a colleague had a battle of ink-pots that lasted until there was no red nor blue nor black ink left in the Chancery, and they had to buy the ambassador a new carpet. Once he was sent by Baring Brothers to Moscow to negotiate a loan for some tramways, "or at least," writes Dame Ethel Smyth in her biography of Baring, "to watch the proceedings. He sat like the Mikado in the hotel and refused to see a soul, whereby he got the reputation of being an inflexible Lord of Finance. After two days someone informed him that the other side had at last consented to the terms insisted on by Baring Brothers, and Baring presided at the ensuing banquet." In 1924, when staying at Beaufort Castle, he found Lady Lovat's driving license and filled in the space left for endorsements and collisions with such items as

    August 1 collision with train
    August 2 collision with perambulator
    August 3 collision with donkey-cart

When, with infinite trouble and after paying a heavy fine, she procured a second license, he immediately did it again.

It was to the Lovat's he came for the last five years of his life, and he died cherished by their love and care. His house was badly bombed, all his books were destroyed, and he himself was terribly shell-shocked by enemy action in 1941. He remained a complete invalid, unable even to sign his name.

He died very peacefully, and is buried in the small Highland churchyard, between Simon Lord Lovat and Hilaire Belloc's little godchild, Rose. "Just the three of them there, beneath the great elm," writes the priest, Father Austin McGuire, who celebrated the Requiem Mass.

Meeting Maurice, one might be put off by the pear-shaped, pendulous body and bald head, by the nervous laugh, the childish jokes. But then, suddenly, he would say something full of astonishment, of the wonder he had kept and "we all" have lost, and one would be humbled by his presence. His best epitaph is the anonymous prayer with which he concluded his anthology:

Et à l'heure de ma mort soyez le refuge de mon âme étonnée et recevez la dans le Sein de notre miséricorde.

EDITOR'S NOTE: Our thanks are due *The Commonweal* and Miss Fremantle for permission to include this chapter in The Book of Catholic Authors. Still in print in this country are Baring's largely autobiographical collection of essays, *Lost Lectures* (Knopf) and his ever-popular anthology, *Have You Anything to Declare?* (Knopf). It is likely that other titles are still available from publishers in England.

FATHER BRICE, C. P.

IT WOULD BE INTERESTING IF I COULD SHOW THAT GOD HAS prepared me from the beginning for literary work. That would be a fine build-up for my books. But I am not so sure that I shall be able to establish proofs.

Certainly there was no preparation in my early years. I was born in St. Louis, too late to greet the century, and a year too late to see the World's Fair; at which time, too, the radio did not bring the daily ball games, although the cheering now and then reached our home from Sportsman's Park.

The first World War interrupted my education at St. Augustine's, where I might have become sharp in German subtleties; and perhaps it was already too late, as I joined the fourth grade at Holy Name, to learn the spontaneity of Irish wit. In my early teens, after the lessons in school, it was my duty to help my father in his meat shop, where knowledge of human nature and practical affairs might be imbibed pleasantly, while the vigor for youthful mischief was exhausted. I was good at numbers, I remember, but not the kind that add up to figures of speech; and my pleasure in reading was due more to boyish hunger for the novel and exciting things rather than to a desire for literary ability. I must honestly admit, I fail to see how these years prepared me for the homeliest of fine arts.

When I was about thirteen, rheumatic fever caught up with me. Probably I was a sorry sight, lagging behind and limping with rheumatic pains like an ancient. The injury to my heart kept me in bed for many months; and because I wished never to be the worry of truant officers, I succeeded in missing the entire last year of grade school without causing them the least apprehension. (There are still times when I feel that someone will ask to see my diploma.) That, surely, was no preparation for anything.

Reaching sixteen in spite of rheumatic fever, I took a business course and worked for a time as a stenographer; long enough at any rate for my fingers to become nimble with shorthand and typing. The shorthand has fled from my mind, but facility in typing remains as a handy key to speed. During this period a love for literature and drama made itself felt, with more than passing emotion, I believe. But whatever attraction I experienced in this direction I was ready to spurn, as I heard the call to a religious life with the Passionists.

Education for the priesthood, and for Passionist missionary work in particular, comprises indeed a training toward lucid thinking and clear expression. But while, on the one hand, the study of English literature taught me the noble office of words, on the other hand, philosophy and theology gave me not so much facility as caution in exposition; and I learned what I have since found strongly stressed in the mystics: the inexplicability of divine things.

In 1939 ill health caught up with me again, and has not since lost the pace. Ordination was, certainly, a consolation; but the career of missionary life for which I had prepared became impossible, and writing scarcely suggested itself. Previous to this, I had made the bowing acquaintance of St. John of the Cross. A rather stiff bowing it was; and I was hardly disposed to speak in his behalf. On the contrary, I felt my whole unified being drawing more closely together in antagonism toward his uncompromising attitude. Afterwards his double-edged doctrine divided me against myself and the duel-elements in my nature compelled me to grip a pen, to parry his advances, then lunge at the sixteenth century mystic. It was a mortal combat, the more painful marks of which were not carried over, as a mercy to the reader, from the blotches and disorder of the original manuscript to the clean, smooth pages of *Journey in the Night*. I soon found myself on the defensive. Every book, no doubt, is the reflection of situations or problems that once perplexed an author; mine perhaps more so than many others; and as a result I took up writing, no less for myself than for potential readers.

Unaware of any specialized preparation for authorship, I nevertheless set about unravelling the knots in the dazzling chain of thought in John of the Cross. Possibly I was surprised to find that one link fitted into the next; or that the sheen of his arguments was but a quality of their steel; or that the whole chain was such a unity of principles as to lend strength and beauty to each link. In any event, one of my first impressions—which has not failed to be a lasting one—was that we of the twentieth century, terrified by the prospect of an explosion of some vague sort, have run away from, and lost sight of, a mine of purest gold. Our modern attitude is the more paradoxical in that we eulogize Teresa of Avila, and idolize Therese of Lisieux, although their spirituality is essentially the same as that of the master of the *Dark Night*.

I abhor the slightest tendency toward the view that St. John of the Cross, having settled himself complacently in his poetical craft, cut himself adrift from traditional spirituality, like some *mistico* lost on the Mediterranean Sea. In *Spirit in Darkness* I endeavored to show—and in this I claim no originality—that the darkness of St. John's poetical *Night* is merely that darkness which is necessarily proper to the very nature of faith. With regard to the obscurity of faith, tradition is one with St. John. Without denying that there are differences in the temperament and style of the classical spiritual writers, I contend that the study of their essential unity would be profitable to many in our times. As a step in this direction, I pointed out in *Teresa, John and Therese* certain similarities between John and his co-worker of Avila, and, what is more striking, the influence of John on "Little Therese" of our own day, as also the apparent ease with which she assimilated his doctrine, at the age of seventeen and eighteen. But all this is beside the point...

We were speaking of specialized training for writing. Whether it be an interesting observation or not, I have failed to prove that I am prepared to write. As for beginning to prepare myself now at the eleventh hour, that is out of the question. It is already too late. And I prefer to write.

EDITOR'S NOTE: Brice is Father's religious name; his family name is Zurmuehlen. His books, all published under his name in religion, and all published by Pustet, are: *Journey in the Night* (1945), *Spirit in Darkness* (1946), and *Teresa, John and Therese* (1946).

JOHN GILLAND BRUNINI

ONE OF THE MOST DISCONCERTING QUESTIONS A NEW ACquaintance can ask me is, in any form, "What is your occupation?" This question was sprung on me on one occasion when I was in thought far removed from my surroundings. The truth came out in my unpremeditated reply, "Sometimes I wonder." It would be so simple, indeed satisfactory, for me to be able truthfully to answer doctor, mechanic, bricklayer. I could, of course, say that I am a poet. But then I have never particularly wanted to be considered merely as a poet. That conjures up pictures of garrets or cellars, in neither of which I have ever lived or desired to live. Nor would I consider as a compliment the statement that I look like a poet, for I would go to the extreme of patronizing a face-lifter to avoid looking like a poet,—at least what is popularly but erroneously considered the proper appearance and attire of the male poet.

I could say that I am a critic. But that needs explanation,
—a critic of what? That need for explanation has always
dogged me. "Brunini" is pronounced to rhyme with "Houdini"; it isn't "Bernini" and there is *no* "m" in it. "Gilland"
is pronounced with accent on first syllable which is like a
fish's gill. I always use it, because, my father also being
John, everyone in my family (if they don't call me "Brother") and all in my native town call me by my middle name.
I wouldn't answer to it by any one associated with my post-college life.

If I were to say that I am a Southerner by birth, I would
meet the inquiry, "What's happened to your accent?" (Bits
of it are still extant, or so I'm told.) There have been frequent occasions when introduced to Italians they have
promptly flooded me with a rush of sentences in a language
which, when I could interrupt their display of enthusiasm
on having met a compatriot, I must explain I do not understand. If my vis-a-vis is not too disappointed, and indignantly wants to know why, with such a surname, I do not
understand Italian, the answer can only be found in circumstances for which I am not particularly responsible.

Those circumstances must then be the burden of these
comments about a person who has been dragooned into
being autobiographical, a practice which for many reasons
he does not relish. If from the details a reader can provide
me with the succinct, final answer to the question that so
often bothers me, I will be grateful. Perhaps better than I,
he can determine the salient pattern of a rather diversified
life.

There are two common denominators in the lives of all
men: they are born and, if not dead, they will die. I am not
dead, save perhaps in some of the metaphorical senses. But
I was born in Vicksburg, Mississippi, on October 1, 1899,—
a date which I find convenient in recollecting my age (which
I am over-inclined to forget), since it makes me precisely

three months older than the century. I used this yardstick
once when at twenty-eight, I got into an argument with a
friend who at twenty-seven insisted he was older. When I
prevailed he accepted defeat by protesting, "You are certainly remarkably well preserved,"—a statement I would
today hail less hilariously and more appreciatively.

In geography classes Vicksburg is cited as one of Mississippi's "leading cities," a term which is not quite accurate.
It is a town in population smaller than many metropolitan
suburbs. Vicksburgers occasionally are called "hill-billies"
—the town is a succession of hills and hollows—but they
are neither farmers nor urbanites. My paternal grandfather
and grandmother did settle on a farm some miles to the
north in 1854. They were driven into the town by the arrival of Sheridan's army to join with Grant in the Siege of
Vicksburg and possibly had Alexander Brunini, who partici-
pated in that siege, long survived the war he might have
been called an "unreconstructed rebel." My maternal grandparents also began on a Louisiana farm, but shortly after
the war transferred to Vicksburg.

I have a theory about my father which I have never
tested. It is that he was so determined on being an American that he could not compromise by learning Italian. In
any event, he knows nothing of the language and it was
never spoken in my home.

This was one of very definite discipline. There were eight
children born to Blanche and John B. Brunini, of which I
was the second. Discipline was unquestionably in order.
I still deprecate some of the limitations visited upon us, but
adulthood has taught me the value of much of the regimen.
I recall in particular one item—the last reason we could
urge for permission to do any one thing was that all the
other children were doing it. Perhaps this argument, which
I have long since repudiated, tended to keep the family a
close unit. Even when we were separated, my parents have

kept us all well-knit to them and to each other—our jocose
appraisal is that we live in regard to the others "in a gold
fish bowl." A large family for growing children is a rather
wonderful thing—it is even more unique when the ties are
preserved throughout life. Not all eight children survived;
the firstborn, my sister, died at sixteen, the third boy in
infancy. The six—four boys and two girls—shared many
common experiences. The boys were all primarily educated
by the Brothers of the Sacred Heart, the girls by Sisters of
Mercy. The four former—this was determined for us before we were born—took A.B degrees at Georgetown University; the two girls at Trinity College, also in Washington.

My father, made a Knight of St. Gregory by Pope Pius
XI because of his devoted service as attorney for the Diocese
of Natchez (which comprises the State of Mississippi),
hoped that two of his sons would join him in the practice of
law. Being the firstborn, I was obviously elected. He also
wanted his second son. Instead, he got the second, Alex,
and the fourth, Edmund. Joseph, instead of going for law,
attended North American College in Rome where he was
ordained, later took Canon Law at Catholic University, and
is now practicing that form of law as Monsignor Brunini,
Chancellor of the Diocese of Natchez. I am the only son not
a lawyer. I have often wondered first had my father not
been so insistent and second had he not taught me to use
my own will, if I would have practiced law. The idea is a
rather fascinating "might-have-been," but not a regretted
one.

Instead I wanted to write, and New York was indicated
as that place where I could best do that and meanwhile support myself in some allied job. In 1919, however, New
York did not seem particularly hospitable with jobs of the
kind wanted. I got on the bottom rung of the ladder in the
shipping business, and shortly after ascended three or four
rungs to take charge of all the incoming freight brought

into the port by the United Fruit Company. I grew a mustache to make me look old enough for this responsibility. It made me look younger and disappeared as soon as I could show it off to the family.

I had a theory at the time: it was that one should not remain in any one position longer than four years (not too bad a theory for a young man until he has found his level). Anyhow, after four years I resigned from the U.F. and sneaked into the newspaper business by a back door. There were four years quite thoroughly mixed in experiences during which time I was a reporter—covering everything from murder trials, missing girls and coal strikes to railroad disasters, submarine sinkings and dirigible wrecks—a radio critic, feature editor, automobile editor and yachting editor among other almost forgotten "asides."

In 1928, I joined *the Commonweal,* where as the junior on a brilliant staff, I was called on to try my hand at anything around—editorials, theatrical criticism, book reviews, advertisements, circulars, proof-reading, make-up, editing copy, clipping, and what-has-the-editor-today?

In that period I began what has been usual with me since —I spent more time at the office than at home which normally for me has been but a place to sleep. I wrote—in the off-time. Of the many unpublished items, I can only say that editors were correct in rejecting them but with, ahem!, a few exceptions. Definitely the few poems of those rejected have long since been destroyed.

During the early days of the depression—it hit *The Commonweal* and me—I knocked around doing too many odd things to admit classification. In 1932, the year in which my book of poems, *The Mysteries of the Rosary,* was published, I became associated with the Catholic Poetry Society of America, then in its infancy. The nameless position I first held has since become crystalized in the title of Executive Director—a title which rather haunts me, as does Secre-

tary. I have been one or the other, oftentimes both, in one
connection or another ever since. "Chief cook and bottle
washer" would be a more accurate description. The Society
in 1934 launched *Spirit: a Magazine of Poetry,* and I became
its editor. I have held down that desk ever since. Meanwhile, without any particular solicitation on my part, I
somehow got involved in what might be humorously referred to as "public affairs." I don't just know the word to
describe these activities—"impresario" would state too
much, but is a pointer. It all began with my being "secretary" to a committee which arranged at Radio City Music
Hall a mammoth commemoration in 1933 of the opening of
the Holy Year. It took me into the avocation of staging
public dinners—or breakfasts, lunches, teas, anything in-
volving food (I'm considered a good cook but on such occasions I really do not officiate in the kitchens)—then lectures, forums, symposia, congresses, campaigns, and pa-
rades.

When the New York World's Fair was being projected I
was enlisted to handle all religious participation and shortly
thereafter in 1937 became Executive Director of the Temple
of Religion, and Secretary of its Board of Directors. Before
the Fair's opening I shuttled back and forth between an editorial office, in the Empire State Building and headquarters
in Flushing Meadows. Those years defy description: I
came to the conclusion, having to deal with people of every
form of religious belief and disbelief, that there are more
near-insane among the religious cults than in the field of
poetry.

Shortly after the advent of the second World War, I was
heavily immersed at various offices of Civilian Volunteer
Defense. Despite the fact that I held a certificate testifying
that in 1918 I had completed training as an officer at Platts-
burg (for me, no commission, but the Student Army Training Corps back at Georgetown, because I was not old

enough), Uncle Sam in 1942 didn't want me even as a private. Seemingly the Army valued gall bladders, and I had lost mine together with my vermiform appendix in 1928. The Army was also unimpressed by the fact that three years before Georgetown had awarded me an honorary M.A. (I paid for it, at that, for the occasion was a Sesquicentennial Commencement and I wrote and read the commemorative ode). After a physical, I was listed as 4-H and turned my interest to salvage as Manhattan chairman for the first great scrap metal drive; then Manhattan Director of Neighborhood Defense Councils; finally, at City Hall as Executive Assistant to the CDVO Chairman of Greater New York. Again in the "public" field, in 1945 I took over as Executive Director—oh yes, also as Secretary to the Board of Directors—of the Park Association of the City of New York, and so "to date," as biographical notes explain. I am neither executive director nor secretary, but a garden variety member of the Municipal Art Society, the Legal Aid Society, the New York Federal Grand Jury Association, and the Lotus Club.

In the literary field over the past twenty years—I should not be asked "how" because I could not explain—I have continued writing. This has been of varied nature: short stories, articles, reviews, editorials, poems. For the Catholic Poetry Society, I have edited, and managed all details of publication, two collections of poems from *Spirit*: in 1939, *From the Four Winds;* in 1944, *Drink from the Rock.* When occasions arose, I have done unclassifyable work for publishers. I have also done my share of public speaking and have never been able to understand why a speaker should be intimidated by and fumble before a "mike," when there is no stony-faced audience to stare him down.

In 1943, I began *Wheron to Stand,* subtitled "What Catholics Believe and Why," to which Cardinal Spellman wrote the Introduction. If a delegation of Cardinals were to wait on me tomorrow and ask that I write a book of similar nature, I am now quite sure I would flatly refuse. *Whereon to Stand* was begun altogether too blithely. During the three years when its writing was in progress I developed quite a passion for gardening, in which I am assisted occasionally by a four-year-old nephew who reels off names—salpiglossis, pachysandra, lupine, broccoli, escarolle and strawberries—as fluently as I do.

He has yet to share my enthusiasm for swimming, bridge and the opera, but with a little more encouragement will join in that for the theatre. His mother, my younger sister on whose Long Island place the gardening, vine pruning and other activities of the husbandman go forward, does not think too much of my piano playing. But then, I taught myself to read music, have never taken a lesson, and have only recently again had access to a piano. I really do not think I am too old to learn.

EDITOR'S NOTE: In 1932 Macmillan published Mr. Brunini's *Mysteries of the Rosary*, and in 1946 Harper issued his *Whereon to Stand*.

GEORGE CARVER

I'VE WANTED TO WRITE, IT SEEMS TO ME, EVER SINCE I learned to read—at the age of five, sitting on my grandmother's lap, with *Hamlet* as a textbook. How many reams of paper I covered in those early days only my grandmother, again, who supplied the paper, and I knew. It was a long road—is still a long road. In fact, even now whenever anything of mine appears in print I am completely surprised.

Like many another whose gift is so slight as to warrant its exercise more or less as a hobby, I aimed at college teaching. After attending the University of Alabama, the University of Chicago, and Miami University, I joined the English staff at the Pennsylvania State College and came under the tutelage of Fred Lewis Pattee, one of the first critic-historians to recognize American literature's coming of age, and of A. Howry Espenshade, in those days one of the most distinguished rhetoricians.

Soon, however, came the first World War, and I was off to France and, after the Armistice, to Germany where, while serving in the Army of Occupation, I was able to continue my studies. Just before entering the army I had sent off a war-inspired story, "In a Moment of Time," to the old *Stratford Journal*. I had no idea what had happened to it until one night the mail caught up with us in a captured dugout and I received a letter from the late E. J. O'Brien, who had seen the story in the *Stratford*. The fatigue, the trench rats, and the rumble of distant gunnery all disappeared as I read, by the flicker of a one-inch candle, Mr. O'Brien's flattering request for autobiographical items to be included in his *Yearbook of the American Short Story*. "In a Moment of Time" was my first public—though quite restricted—appearance.

Upon my return, I went to the University of Iowa as a member of a notable department. There I came to know John T. Frederick, Percival Hunt, Edwin Ford Piper, Frank Luther Mott, Ruth Suckow, Hardin Craig, and the late Thomas A. Knott, who was to become editor-in-chief of *Webster's Dictionary*. Wanting very much to cultivate whatever small gift I had, I soaked up as much as I could of the atmosphere thus provided; and in a short time interested William Marion Reedy in my second story, "About the Sixth Hour," which he published in his redoubtable *Mirror*. Soon, too, the group of young writers clustered about *The Midland*, among the chief "little magazines" of the 1920's, took me in. Mr. Frederick, the editor, liked one of my things, "The Scarlet One," well enough to include it in his anthology, *Stories from the Midland* (Knopf, 1924).

All this was stimulating, to be sure, but I was not getting anywhere in particular. I had married in the meantime and had a small son, Robert. In the hope of augmenting my meager instructor's salary, I collaborated with Dr. Knott and Mr. W. S. Maulsby, then in the School of Journalism, on a textbook. The habit thus started became confirmed to such a degree that to date I have published nine such books, only two of which, however, do I like: *The Catholic Tradition in English Literature,* and *The Stream of English Literature.* Upon this latter volume, the late Sister Mary Eleanore, C.S.C., of St. Mary's College, Notre Dame, and Miss Katherine Bregy, author of *Poets' Chantry* and *Poets and Pilgrims,* collaborated with me.

To my marriage, referred to a moment ago, I cannot pay sufficient homage. Not only do I owe to it much happiness, but I also owe to it my Catholicity. In fact, it is to my wife, Eve, and to her late mother, Mary Bradley Schultz, to whom I am indebted for my present interests and for my way of life. I had been brought up a Presbyterian in a family of Puritan descent; and while I had enjoyed going to Sunday School and treasured the "Golden Text" cards, religion had lain but lightly upon me. Upon my marriage into a Catholic family, however, I learned much that hitherto had remained undisclosed to me and so became a convert—and at no cost to my relationship with my own people.

Then, because of my expanding interest in things Catholic, I began to contribute reviews and articles to *The Commonweal, America, The Sign, The Magnificat,* and to various other Catholic publications. An article in *The Commonweal,* "Gnats and Camels," later reprinted in the *Boston Transcript;* one in *America* called "A Certain Politician"; a short story in *The Sign,* "Bread and Soul," reprinted in Mary Curtin's anthology, *Pilgrims All;* an article about Cardinal Newman in the *Journal of Religious Education;* and a little essay titled "Blessed are the Light of Heart," which appeared in *Magnificat* are, I think, the best of my short things. In connection with the *Magnificat* essay came one of the greatest satisfactions I've had: a short passage from it was quoted by Sister Mary Clare, S.N.D., in one of the Paulist Press pamphlets, *What is a Nun?*

In 1924 I came to the University of Pittsburgh where I have remained ever since, teaching and writing—with an occasional lectureship at Seton Hill College, Greensburg, Westmoreland, County, Pennsylvania, a small but distinguished school for young women, and one richly Catholic in atmosphere.

Several years ago, Father Joseph Husslein, S.J., of St. Louis University, suggested that I prepare something for inclusion in his Science and Culture Series, issued by the Bruce Publishing Company of Milwaukee. At the time I was engaged in writing a book about biography as a literary form, stressing the men and the books that had contributed notably to its development. The work had grown out of a course I had been giving in the subject—one of the few such courses, I believe, given in the United States. Father Husslein fell in with the idea that this work be my addition to his Series, with the result that my *Alms for Oblivion* was included in it, with a foreword by Father Husslein.

The theme of the book is that biography, like the drama, music, and painting developed from a need of the Church and was fostered in the shadows of her Altar. *Alms for Oblivion* is my only ambitious attempt so far. I hope it is to be neither my best work nor my last.

Why does any one write? Most persons who do, I think, look upon writing as a means of self-realization—if fortune and prestige follow, so much the better. But these last, I have long been convinced, are only incidental. Note how many of the great writers in English have been non-professional. If one has the Faith, however, besides his gift, small though that may be, he increases his satisfaction by discharging a moral obligation in making the one serve to promulgate the other. Hence, I should like one day to write a book of sufficient worth that it would help me to share the happiness of my life experience.

EDITOR'S NOTE: Perhaps one of the reasons for Dr. Carver's preference for *The Catholic Tradition in English Literature* (Doubleday, 1926) and *The Stream of English Literature* (Heath, 1930), from among his nine textbooks is that they deserved and received a wide general reader interest as well as appreciative classroom use. His *Alms for Oblivion* was issued by Bruce in 1946.

REV. DANIEL A. CASEY

IT'S A LONG WAY FROM A CRADLE IN TIPPERARY, EIRE, TO AN editorial chair in Kingston, Canada. It began on July 18, 1886, and ended on March 13, 1916.

The ninth of a family of ten, Daniel Aloysius Casey was blessed with parents whose proudest heritage was the living faith characteristic of the Irish people. The example of an elder brother in the seminary and a sister in the cloister turned his thoughts to the priesthood and the foreign missions. Entering All Hallows College, Dublin, in September, 1903, he was ordained for the diocese of Peterborough, Ontario, on March 11, 1910. Assistant in turn at St. Peter's Cathedral, Peterborough; Campbellford and Bracebridge; and pastor of St. Paul's parish, Norwood, Father Casey was invited by Archbishop Spratt of Kingston to accept the editorship of *The Canadian Freeman* early in 1916. At that time, Bishop O'Brien of Peterborough had no surplus of priests, but convinced of the worth of the Apostolate of the Printed Word, the zealous prelate did not hesitate in releasing the pastor of Norwood for the vacant editorial chair in Kingston.

Father Casey took up his new posting in the Church's army not without misgiving. True, he had a flair for writing dating from primary school days. Looking back across the years the editor of *The Canadian Register* still vividly recalls the thrill of receiving a checque from *The Irish Independent* of Dublin for a short story in the author's sixteenth year. During college days he exercised his pen when time permitted, the harvest of which is a scrapbook of stories and sketches which he confesses gave him more sense of accomplishment than the recognition of his talents by famous Laval University's conferring on him of the degree of Doctor of Letters.

Shortly after his ordination, Father Casey became associate editor of *The Catholic Record*, of London, Ontario, a weekly with a long and fruitful history in the field of Catholic journalism, then published by his cousin, the late Senator Thomas Coffey. After six years of this apprenticeship, the call came to Kingston and *The Canadian Freeman*. On March 14, 1916, he opened the office door for the first time to find a staff of three and a building on a side street, poor and cramped as a Cottage in Bethlehem, an accumulation of debt and a total circulation of under seven hundred weekly. For a time the going was hard and the future of the paper precarious. Thanks mainly to the apostolic zeal of the saintly Archbishop Spratt, the hand-to-mouth existence of *The Freeman* since its establishment in 1884, gradually developed into vigorous life. But it was the translation of Bishop O'Brien from Peterborough to the metropolitan See of Kingston in 1929, and the incidence of the province-wide controversy over the constitutional rights of Catholic primary schools that put the venerable weekly on the map and prepared the way for a momentous development in the field of the Catholic Press in English-speaking Catholic Canada. Archbishop O'Brien was a prelate of many parts, a man of broad vision who consumed himself in the duties of his apostolic office. Under his direction *The Freeman* advocated a square deal for the Catholic schools with a cogency that the enemy found it difficult to refute, but which, due to the treachery of politicians, just failed of success.

The Freeman's smashing crusade for Catholic educational rights engendered the idea of a Catholic weekly that could rightly claim to speak for the entire Catholic body. After much negotiating and careful planning, the idea fructified in February, 1942, in the birth of *The Canadian Register.* *The Register* is the result of the amalgamation of *The Canadian Freeman* of Kingston, *The Catholic Register* of Toronto, *The Beacon* of Montreal, *The Northern Catholic* of Sault Ste. Marie, *The Observer* of Pembroke, and *The Prospector* of Nelson, B. C. The new paper is highly influential in that, with a circulation approaching the 70,000 mark, it speaks for Canadian English-speaking Catholics from Quebec to the Pacific coast. Thus the four-page, six column *Freeman*, has expanded into the twelve-page, eight column newspaper of today, and the staff of three has multiplied by twenty. The editorial board consists of Rev. D. A. Casey, Litt.D., Henry Somerville, M.A., Rev. S. B. Plunkett, S.T.L., and Rev. J. G. Hanley, B.A.

In addition to his editorial work, Father Casey also cultivates the muse and has two volumes of poetry to his credit: *At the Gate of the Temple,* and *Leaves on the Wind.*

After thirty-five years' connection with the Catholic Press and thirty years as editor of *The Freeman* and *The Register,* Father Casey confesses that he sometimes feels "fed up." But always the cover comes off the typewriter just the same, for, as the veteran editor admits, there's something in the smell of printer's ink.

EDITOR'S NOTE: Just a mite more on those two volumes of poetry by Father Casey: *At the Gate of the Temple* was published by Briggs, in 1914, and *Leaves on the Wind* by McClelland, in 1920. The latter volume bore a foreword by another distinguished Irish-Canadian priest-poet, Father James B. Dollard, D.Litt. (Laval).

CAROLINE A. CHANDLER

I WAS BORN IN FORD CITY, PENNSYLVANIA, ON DECEMBER 7, 1906, an event of which I have no recollection whatsoever.

My pre-school days were notable chiefly by the fact that my family moved about a great deal, which may well account for the "loose foot" I seem to have even to this day.

To go back a bit to my family to explain the moves and what-not, my father belonged to that rapidly vanishing species of people known as "business men." In fact if I say so myself, he was a very good business man. In a sense he followed in his father's footsteps, in that he entered the Pittsburgh Plate Glass Co. (as did his three brothers) right after he finished college and stayed with the company the rest of his life. In a way the Pittsburgh Plate was the family business because my grandfather, Amasa Franklin Chandler, had helped to found the company when it first began back in 1895.

The odd thing about it though was that prior to helping found the Pittsburgh Plate, and thereby becoming a business man, my grandfather was a doctor. As a matter of fact he had first met my grandmother when he was doing post-graduate medical work in Germany and she was "doing" Europe. Perhaps I got my bent for medicine from this paternal grandfather of mine even though I never knew him because he died before I was born.

But to go back to my father—he began on the lowest rung of the ladder in the glass business, the factory, and eventually became an executive in the company. It was during his early days when he was being transferred from one factory to another that we moved about so much. And so in rather rapid succession I lived in Ford City, then in Crystal City, Missouri, then in Charleroi, Pennsylvania, and finally back in Ford City, after which prolonged sojourn, again the family moved and this time we landed in Pittsburgh where we stayed throughout the rest of my primary school days.

Now, although my father was finished with learning the business and permanently settled in Pittsburgh, apparently we really had developed the gypsy instinct in earnest because during the next four years before I went away to school we moved no less than five times and all within the city limits of Pittsburgh (and honestly we weren't jumping the rent)! So from Liberty where I entered in the fifth grade, I transferred to Friendship School, then to Wightman and finally wound up in Peabody High School where I spent exactly one semester.

Whether or not changing schools so many times was responsible for my gradually growing dislike of school I can't say, but I do know that by the time I hit high school I came very close to loathing the whole idea of education. So much so that for the first time in my life I tried the primrose path of going AWOL from school a couple of times and, until

mother caught up with me, thought I was a very smart and
daring gal indeed. It only took a few firm parental words
and actions, however, to show me the error of my thinking
and ways and so there ended rather abruptly my brief
career in "hooking" school.

I guess my temporary rebellion must have disturbed my
mother and father more than it did me, because when the
fall of 1921 rolled around I found that I had been entered
in a convent school not far from Pittsburgh, by name, Mt.
Aloysius Academy. Here again I shall have to go back to
the family momentarily to say a word or two on my religious background. My mother came from a long line of Episcopalians and my father from an even longer line of Presbyterians, not a few of whom had been clergymen (at least
one in each generation since the Chandlers had first settled
in Massachusetts in 1634). In spite of this rather formid-
able religious ancestry, we were not in the least a "religious" family. We managed to get to church on Christmas
and Easter but aside from those two high spots in the year,
our church-going or any other pious observation was just
about nil. Which in itself might perfectly well explain why
my mother and father felt no compunction about sending me
to a Roman Catholic school, except for the fact that it would
be only a partial explanation of their attitudes on religion
(and other things as well). If I had to choose a single at-
tribute that I liked best in my parents, I would unhesitating-
ly pick their complete lack of prejudice—religious, racial,
social and moral—which seemed as natural to them as the
air they breathed. Whatever else they did or did not give
me, I shall be forever grateful to them for bringing me up in
an atmosphere as nearly free of prejudice against one's fellow man because his color or "isms" were different as I
think possible in this not-too-perfect world. In fact, on the
contrary, it was from my parents and particularly my father, that I developed a distinct preference for people with

other ideas, other cultures and other *mores* very early in life. Perhaps this too was just another manifestation of the gypsy instinct, but whatever instinct or drive it sprang from, it, like my loose foot, has stayed with me ever since. For which I am grateful because it has always made life more colorful, delightful and decidedly much more fun in every way.

I spent three years at Mt. Aloysius, and I must say they were three of the happiest years of my life. When I graduated in 1924 with highest honors, in all honesty and fairness, I must explain that the only reason I did so was because of the superb teaching of the nuns plus the wisdom of their ways with wilful children. Thanks to them I developed a yen for the things of the mind and the spirit that is as unquenched now as it was then.

Next to college—briefly as a freshman and half a sophomore at the University of Pittsburgh for eighteen months, then as a transfer to Barnard College in New York, from which I graduated in 1929 with an A.B. and Phi Beta but most important of all a sense of loss at leaving such a swell place.

Right here I must insert a brief but momentous parenthesis which simply states that in September, 1929 I entered the Catholic Church.

In the fall of 1929, like Tom Brown, I went to Yale. Unlike Tom, however, I came, I saw and Yale conquered me, for if my three years in the convent school were the halcyon ones of my adolescence, my four years in medical school were the halcyon ones of what the statisticians are pleased to call my young adulthood. I never worked so hard in my life and I never had so much fun. Than which I can think of no better combination. I got my M.D. in 1933 and the only thing which mitigated my regret at leaving medical school was the fact that I was given an internship in pedia-

trics in the New Haven Hospital which meant that I stayed
on in New Haven for another year.

In my odyssey the next port of call was Boston, to which
I came as a research fellow in pediatrics in the Harvard
Medical School in 1934. From that time until I left in 1939,
the foundation of my post-graduate medical training was
firmly laid under the tutelage of two uniquely gifted and
brilliant men in their fields (pediatrics and bacteriology)
namely, Dr. Kenneth Blackfan and Dr. Hans Zinsser.

After 1939, the years began to go by very rapidly and so
I can only hit the high spots from here on in. I came down
from Harvard to Johns Hopkins in 1939 to work on rheumatic fever and I stayed on until the spring of 1943. If it
had not been for the war, I am quite sure that I should not
have budged from Hopkins because, again, I was lucky
enough to be apprenticed first to Dr. Helen Taussig and
second, to Dr. Perrin Long. As it was however, the war
changed everything and so in April, 1943 I left Baltimore
to join the staff of the Children's Bureau in Washington to
work on a special project chiefly concerned with the war
effort. After a very productive eighteen months, I finished
that assignment, and from the Bureau moved on to the
United States Public Health Service where, commissioned as
a Surgeon in the Reserve Corps, I worked in the Tuberculosis Control Division until shortly before V-J Day. And so
ended the war years.

Now I am once more back in Johns Hopkins as an Assistant Professor of Preventive Medicine under the same Dr.
Perrin Long under whom I worked before and because of
whom, I should like nothing better than to spend the rest
of my days in the present status quo. I am also on the
staff of the Johns Hopkins Hospital as an Assistant Pedia-
trician.

Which brings us up to here and now and just about to
the signing off place. Only since all orthodox autobiogra-

phies conclude with the personal tastes, idiosyncrasies, whims and things-better-not-said of the autobiographer— here goes: In music, my favorites and Bach, Beethoven, Brahms and equally boogie-woogie; in art, I have a yen for Giotto, Cimabue, Romanesque architecture, from which I skip over the Renaissance lightly and wind up with Tou- louse-Lautrec, Gauguin and Van Gogh; in literature, prac- tically anything and everything because it *is* literature; in sports, swimming, horse-back riding and sailing; in politics, the New Deal brand of democracy. As to idiosyncrasies I would far rather be a little late for a play, concert or foot- ball game than a lot early; as to whims I'll take onions and garlic anytime; and as to things-better-not-said—no com- ment.

EDITOR'S NOTE: For teen age girls who like their fiction fast moving but clean and informative, Dr. Chandler wrote *Susie Stuart, M.D.*, in 1941, *Susie Stuart, Home Front Doctor*, in 1943, and *Dr. Kay Win- throp, Intern*, in 1947. These stories are included in the Dodd, Mead series of "Career Books."

REVEREND GEORGE THOMAS DALY, C.Ss.R.

I WAS BORN IN MONTREAL, QUEBEC, ON SEPTEMBER 5, 1872, OF a French-Canadian mother and an Irish father. My parents were devout exemplary Catholics.

I received my elementary education in Sarsfield School, Montreal. In 1885 I started my classical course at Montreal College. After three years, in 1888, I left for Belgium to join the Redemptorist Order. After my novitiate and religious profession in 1891, I finished my classics and for seven years I studied philosophy and theology. In 1898 I was ordained. In 1900 I returned to my native land, and for twelve years was engaged in educational work in the Preparatory College of the Redemptorist Order in Ste. Anne de Beaupre. While there I wrote for several French magazines. Among other articles I then published was a series of historical studies of the nineteenth century. These appeared in *La Nouvelle France* of Quebec. I wrote under the pen name of Fra Angelico.

In 1902 I was appointed parish priest of St. Ann's in Montreal. While there I was asked by the Catholic School Commission to write an essay on "The Educational and Social Value of the Kindergarten."

In 1915 I was transferred to Regina and there became pastor of the Cathedral, under Archbishop Mathieu. This contact with the West gave to my life a new orientation. The great religious and social problems of this part of Canada, then in the making, touched me profoundly, and awakened in me a great desire to write on them. I felt the need of awakening in our Catholic population a sense of responsibility. For problems are solved only by those who know them and grasp their far-reaching consequences for Church and Country.

In 1918 I became a missionary, stationed at St. John, New Brunswick. This gave me time to write the books I had planned. The first book was *Catholic Problems in Western Canada* (1920), respectfully dedicated to the Catholic Hierarchy of Canada. In this book I treat of the religious, educational, and social problems of the Church beyond the Great Lakes. This first effort of mine met with a very understanding reading public, particularly in clerical circles. Some seminaries adopted it as a manual in their Study Clubs.

Pursuing the idea of awakening our Catholic public to the need of action for the happy solution of our religious problems, I wrote *Catholic Action* (1937). This book deals with Catholic Action as the expression of a fuller life of the Church, as an intelligent participation in her corporate existence. To lay bare the obstacles with which it has to contend; to outline the principles upon which its ultimate success depends, was the purpose of my book. Catholic Action is considered here more as the "corporate" action of the Church than that of her individual members.

A Trumph in Decoration (now out of print) was a brief outline of the principles which govern the art of church decoration and of their exemplification in the interior decoration of St. Patrick's Church in Toronto. This work had suggested my essay.

My Father is my latest publication. This is the life of an exemplary Catholic layman, of an ordinary business man, but lived in an extraordinarily Catholic way. There is nothing spectacular in his way of life. Yet it is profoundly religious.

The scope of this book is well expressed in the Introduction written by Archbishop (now Cardinal) McGuigan: "In these days when the Church looks to a sanctified laity for leadership and for the radiation of Christian principles, this life of a practical devout Catholic layman, as head of a good Catholic home, should be an inspiration to many others."

For the last twenty-four years I have been associated with the Sisters of Service, a missionary society founded for the home-mission field. To every issue of its quarterly magazine, *The Field at Home,* I have contributed an editorial. This association also promoted the writing of several booklets: *Call to Service, Ten Years in the Master's Service,* and *A Coat of Arms.*

EDITOR'S NOTE: Macmillan, of Toronto, published Father Daly's *Catholic Problems in Western Canada,* in 1920, and his *Catholic Action,* in 1937. The Catholic Truth Society, also of Toronto, issued his biography of his father, *My Father,* in 1945.

MAUREEN DALY

MAUREEN DALY, AUTHOR OF THE POPULAR NOVEL, *Seventeenth Summer,* and a book for teenagers, *Smarter and Smoother,* youngest writer to have a story chosen for the *O. Henry Collection of Best Short Stories,* reporter, columnist, and book reviewer for the *Chicago Tribune,* joined the staff of the *Ladies' Home Journal* in July, 1945, as associate editor and editor of the monthly Sub-Deb page. She has made her reputation by simply putting down in fiction form her own recent memories of teen-age hopes, experiences and frustrations.

Born in Castlecaulfield, County Tyrone, Ireland, on March 15, 1921, Maureen was the third of four daughters. When she was two years old, her parents, John Desmond and Margaret Mellon (Kelly) Daly, moved to the United States, where they made their home in the small town of Fond du Lac, Wisconsin. Maureen attended the public grade school

and St. Mary's Springs Academy there, from which she
graduated valedictorian. Her childhood was "pretty routine," to quote Miss Daly, "but very happy to look back on.
My whole family was always interested in books and reading," she says, "but it was a teacher of English who first
encouraged me in writing."

When she began writing stories, Miss Daly has revealed
"it was not ambition but inhibition that spurred me on. I
had a kind of shyness which often kept me from talking
about what I thought and felt, but it seemed natural and
easy to write those same thoughts."

Maureen's first short story, "Fifteen," a simple episode
about a first date which took place and was written when
she was that age, won fourth place in *Scholastic Magazine's*
nation-wide high school short story contest held in 1937.
While previously her ambitions were somewhat aimed at the
field of nursing, now she decided to take up writing in
earnest, resulting in new and greater triumphs the following year. "Sixteen," which was written while waiting for a
telephone call that never came, took first honors in the next
Scholastic contest. "It wasn't meant to be a short story at
all, but rather I just wanted to get the experience down on
paper to relieve the tense, hurt feelings inside of me."

Soon after the first publication of "Sixteen," letters began
to pour in from teachers and students all over the country.
Seven years later, she was still getting fan mail from "Sixteen" readers. Harry Hansen, literary critic, chose it for
reprinting in the *O. Henry Collection of Best Short Stories
for 1938*, making Maureen the youngest author ever to be
represented in that well-known annual. *Redbook* magazine
reprinted the story as its "encore of the month," resulting
in another flood of fan mail. Since then "Sixteen" has appeared in many smaller magazines and newspapers, and has
been presented in play form many times over the radio,

making its bow originally on a nation-wide broadcast by Northwestern University, later given in the East, in Chicago, and in Wisconsin. It has just recently been adapted for amateur dramatics on the actual stage. Numerous textbooks and anthologies have also included the story, and through such publicity, several requests came in from leading magazines for more of the author's work. Miss Daly responded, and many of her other stories have been published in the *Ladies' Home Journal, Cosmopolitan, Woman's Home Companion, Redbook, Mademoiselle, Writers' Digest,* and a number of other magazines and newspapers. She has written some 105 short stories in her brief career.

In 1941, while still a senior at Rosary College, in River Forest, Illinois, Maureen submitted the first fifty pages of her first novel, *Seventeenth Summer,* in the national intercollegiate competition for the Dodd, Mead Intercollegiate Literary Fellowship Award, the first one of its kind to be offered. This fragment was the unanimous choice of the judges for the $1200 advance against royalties, which made it possible for a beginner to complete a first novel. It is the story of a boy and a girl who have fallen in love for the first time. Discussing it, Maureen says: "When you get older, I believe you lose accuracy in remembering all the funny quirks and sadnesses and happiness you go through in adolescence. It is a wonderful and a very important time. It was still so much a part of me that I felt I could write of it with truth and sympathy." Published in April, 1942, the novel is now (December, 1946) in its twenty-fifth printing and is still a best seller with teen-agers and adults alike.

While finishing her full-length novel was one of Maureen's chief ambitions in those last years at Rosary College (another ambition was to find herself among those glamorously present at the Notre Dame prom), she still found time to hold down a job as columnist and book reviewer for the

Chicago Tribune, edit the school literary quarterly, *Rosary College Eagle,* write a column for the campus newspaper, and keep up a high scholastic average. Majoring in English and Latin, she was the first junior ever to edit the *Eagle.* "It *was* hard," she says, "but my grades were good and I had a wonderful time."   .

Her four-times-a-week column for teen-agers, "On the Solid Side," started in 1941, was later syndicated to more than a dozen newspapers. Hundreds of letters a month came to the columnist, asking for advice. A collection of these articles, titled *Smarter and Smoother,* was published in 1944 and has since gone into its eleventh printing. Maureen has kept in close touch with the teen-age point of view, and in this book gives pointers on high school manners and ethics, and their relation to those in later life.

After her graduation from college, Miss Daly continued her column and also was a police reporter for the *Tribune* in 1942-43. She declined an offer to go to Hollywood as a screen writer because, she said, she was not ready for that kind of work. Maureen and her talented eighteen-year-old sister, Sheila John Daly, shared a private office in Fond du Lac. When Maureen moved to Philadelphia to become associate editor of the *Ladies' Home Journal,* the mantle of the column editorship fell on Sheila, who has herself recently written a book, *Personality Plus!* Before this, in December, 1944, Maureen had done "Meet a Sub-Deb" for the *Journal's* "How America Lives" series.

Some idea of Maureen's working methods may be gathered from her statement: "It took me months longer than it should have to finish *Seventeenth Summer* because I was too soft with myself. I did a lot of rewriting, and the parts I rewrote aren't as good as the parts I just knocked off very fast. I'd make myself a stint—so much a day, about eight typewritten pages, and on a slip of paper I'd make a few notes of what points I wanted to make in those eight pages. But writing takes a concentration and discipline I am only now learning to impose on myself."

EDITOR'S NOTE: Dodd, Mead published both of Miss Daly's books: *Seventeenth Summer*, in 1942, and *Smarter and Smoother*, in 1944. A point Miss Daly missed is that she is also in frequent demand as a lecturer. And, as one who has heard her, I might add that she does herself proud in that field, too.

CATHERINE DE HUECK

BELIEVE IT OR NOT, BUT WRITING IN THE FIRST PERSON SINGU-
lar does not come easily to me. In fact, if memory does not
fail me, in all the fifteen to twenty years of writing articles,
I have written only two dealing with the pronoun "I". But
I guess if I put my mind to it, I can produce a few autobiographical notes. So here goes.

I was born (of all places!) in a Pullman car, in Nijni-
Novgorod on the Volga in Russia. My father, Theodore de
Kolyschkine, was a colonel of the Grodno Hussars, but at
the time of my birth had retired and was connected with in-
surance interests and the diplomatic service. He was the
son of a Polish woman, Pani Lisetzka, and a Russian officer,
Archip de Kolyschkine. My mother, Emma Thompson, was
the daughter of a nationalized Russian-French mother,
Madame Verne, and a nationalized Russian-English doctor.
Perhaps this mixture of many bloods in my own parents,
not to mention my more distant ancestry, that could be

traced to eleventh century Russia, brought to me at an early
age a love for all races and peoples and an understanding
of them, just as my strange birthplace brought with it much
travelling. For in the course of my life I have travelled
the world over except South America and Australia, which
I still hope to see some time in the future.

Besides my half-brother Vsevolod, son of my father's first
marriage (he was a widower when he married my mother),
there were two brothers, Serge and Andrew; my sister Na-
talie, and two other children who died at birth.

My first childhood recollections are trains and boats. For
business took father and us to Constantinople, Athens,
Egypt, Japan, China, India, and most of Europe. My
education was varied, to say the least. I had French, German, and English governesses, and with their help, and that
of travelling, at the age of twelve I spoke Russian, French,
German, Italian, English, modern Greek, Arabic, Finnish
and Polish fluently. And I understood Bulgarian and Ser-
bian. Our Lady of Sion in Ramleh-Alexandrai Egypt gave
me my primary and secondary education, and the Pension
de jeunes filles of Madame Milliard, in Paris, polished it
up. The select Gymnasium of Princess Obolensky, in St.
Petersburg, filled in such gaps as were left, and the University of St. Petersburg (department of philology) made
me, in American parlance, a B.A. holder, with a few credits
missing for an M.A.

A course in English vocabulary at Oxford, and lessons in
journalism, short story writing, and American history at
Columbia, psychology at the New School of Social Sciences,
diatetics at the Boston School of Home Economics, and
nurses' training at the Montreal General Hospital, followed
in quick succession; with shorthand, bookkeeping, filing,
business methods and efficiency thrown in.

What if some of them were extra-mural, they all helped
to satiate my hunger for more and more knowledge. I have

always remembered my father's words: "A year in which one has not learned anything new is a year wasted." I am still learning from the great university of life.

The even trend of my life with my parents was interrupted by my marriage to Baron Boris de Hueck in 1915, when I was just about fifteen years old, having been born on August 15, 1900. The first World War sucked us both into its vortex. I became a nurse's aid and, due to the shortage of nurses, saw front line duty. This service brought me a decoration or two for acts of 'bravery' which I was not cognizant of performing.

The Communist Revolution followed with startling rapidity, nay, seemed to merge directly into the war. It brought pain, suffering and disaster to all, including myself. Many members of my family died from starvation, from persecution and imprisonment. I fled to our estate. But there I was imprisoned and condemned to die from hunger. I languished there for many weeks before being miraculously saved by the chance of civil war then raging, which, for a few days, brought the armed forces opposed to Communism to our part of the world.

England, Canada and the United States were my next destinations. My son, George-Theodore-Mario, was born in Toronto, on July 21, 1921, the year I reached the blessed north of Bataan. It is a little fishing village located on the land of Canada. Poverty being my constant companion, I went to work. I was successively a laundress, salesclerk in large department stores, a waitress, a factory worker, a lecturer, and a lecture manager. Jobs succeeded each other with startling rapidity, raising me ever higher on the ladder of material success ...

But in my heart was a great dream, born in the struggle of war, revolution, and the nearness of death. The dream was to devote my life to God in the Lay Apostolate of the Church. The need of earning money for my family was

passing. Responsibilities were slowly lifted from my
shoulders. I decided to make a clean break with the world
and the ways of the world I intended to leave though re-
maining in its midst. Friendship House was being born in
the soul of a woman who went through hell to find heaven.

In Toronto, Archbishop Neil McNeil gave me words of encouragement, his blessing, his understanding and his help.
He led me finally to give up all other work, sell what I possessed, and, with five other fools like myself, to "take up
His Cross and try to follow Him."

The first Friendship House was opened in Toronto's
slums on Portland street. It soon grew to five houses, serving as soup kitchens for forty thousand "brother Christopher's" (hoboes) a year. These along with food for the
body were given food for the soul. Seven of them are
priests of God today.

We likewise instituted recreational activities for almost
seven hundred children, who thus met Christ the Child, perhaps for the first time in their lives. We had our paper,
The Social Forum, our Catholic lending library, our open
forums, and a whole department of Catholic propaganda,
opposing Communist propaganda in Canada.

Subsequently I was called to New York; and today there
is a Friendship House there, in Harlem. There is another
one in Chicago. There is a ten-room house on a farm near
Marathon City, Wisconsin, which operates as a summer
school for Catholic interracial techniques and a rural apostolate. And there is a training school for staff workers of
Friendship House, in Comberemere, Canada. We have a
monthly paper, *The Friendship House News.* We print and
distribute pamphlets, and send out a monthly letter, on religious topics, to more than a thousand men and women who
wish to know more about the Catholic Faith and the Church.

Somewhere along the way I met "the great Eddie
Doherty," the well known Catholic author and reporter, and

was married to him by Bishop Bernard Sheil of Chicago, on June 25, 1943.

Life marches on happily and, so far, I think I have marched in step with it. My great dream has come true. Friendship House is a reality. And it is growing and spreading continuously. Yet I have found time to write two books: *Friendship House* and *A Cry in the Wilderness*. And hope time will be granted me to write several more.

EDITOR'S NOTE: For Eddie's side of their story see his autobiographical chapter in the third series of *The Book of Catholic Authors*. Books by the Baroness are *The Story of Friendship House*, Sheed, 1946, and *A Cry in the Wilderness*, Sheed, 1947.

REVEREND E. J. EDWARDS, S.V.D.

AT A VERY EARLY AGE I GRADUATED FROM THE SIDEWALKS OF New York. My diploma was conferred on me by a gentle-voiced Sister, my teacher in the parish school, and the ceremony was very informal. At the close of school on a very momentous day, she called me to her desk and handed me my copy-book. "I would like to speak to your mother tomorrow. There is a note for her in your copy-book."

City boys have a wonderful faculty for group organization and there is romantic adventure for them around every corner and in every vacant lot. I had been enrolled some months previously in a group on our block, and while the activities of the gang were fascinating in the extreme, they required no little sacrifice of the hours supposed to be devoted to homework. It was a sacrifice, however, which I had been cheerfully making for a number of weeks, unknown to my parents.

The note from the Sister to my mother did not present any cause for alarm. There are ways to handle matters like these. It would be a simple matter to remove the page from the copy-book. On the way home I went through the book and found the note—written at the bottom of my last composition, or what was supposed to be a composition. The note informed my mother that if she did not appear with me at school the next morning I would not be admitted to class! After that I could not very well destroy the note. In fact, after a good deal of thinking I could not see anything else to do but face the music. I was amazed at the low sort of trick that this seemingly gentle Sister had played on me.

Mother went to school with me the next day, and that was for me commencement day—a lot of things commenced. I began to go straight home from school, I began among other things to write my compositions, and I've been doing it ever since. This is the most recent one.

But though I have learned to submit to it, I do not like it. Writing is still a chore and when I start on a book I think back to all the writing cramps that that one little Sister has inflicted on my mortal career.

There is small excitement in a life devoted to book work. That is, perhaps, why the missionary life attracted me. I did not, however, realize when I determined to become a missionary what a long, long line of compositions and examinations I would have to write before they would consider me fit for the work of the missions. But at long last the years of study were over. I was ordained in 1930, and off I went to the Seven Thousand Emeralds—the Philippines!

I was not particularly taken with any romantic notions about the missionary life, for the years of training were realistic enough, but it did present the enticing picture of active work and freedom from the picayune work of paper and pencil. So they sent me to a small town on the north-west coast of Luzon, Vigan by name, and I settled down to the active (?) work of correcting the compositions of seminarians!

For three years I taught English composition, homiletics and algebra, and as a side line organized a Catholic Club among the boys of the local public high school. There were some six-hundred boys enrolled in this club and the care of them was an absorbing task.

The mission field of Abra, entrusted to the care of our congregation, the Society of the Divine Word, was about a four hours' run into the interior. It was a relief and a pleasure to be able to get up into the mountains and be one with the priests and brothers laboring there. My summer vacations were always spent that way, and the high-lights of those wonderful weeks were incorporated in *Thy People, My People.*

My last vacation in the Philippines, however, was spent in different surroundings, in the small town of Subic, just shores of beautiful Subic Bay. I was alone there, taking charge of things for the missionary who had become seriously sick, and I speedily learned to know the people and to love their simple life. The locale furnished the background for my second book, *These Two Hands.*

On very short notice, the University of Peking was turned over to the care of our congregation and a cablegram from Rome sent me packing off to Peking on a three-day notice. There had been no chance to obtain the needed clothing and I shivered from Shanghai to Peking in very tropical garments. It was late October when I arrived in Peking and found the University struggling along with a doleful shortage of men. My duties began the next morning and were rather varied. Director of athletics, professor of rhetoric, director of the University Press, and editor, circulation manager, proof-reader, and contributor to the magazine *Fu Jen.*

Two years later I returned to the Philippines for the opening of the Colegio San Carlos, on the island of Cebu. For five years I acted as Prefect of boarders, moderator of the college magazine, *The Carolinian,* director of athletics and coach of the basketball team, director of dramatics, professor of religion, college English, discussion and debate. I also played the organ for church services. The school grew rapidly and at the outbreak of the war it had an enrollment of well over two thousand and lacked but one year of engineering to receive its university charter.

Several kilometers outside of the city there was located a leprosarium that housed more than one thousand patients. Once a week I would spend a day there and the experiences and friendships formed at Consolacion furnished the nucleus for *White Fire.*

In 1940, after ten years of missionary work, my health gave out, and after two months in a Manila hospital I was packed home to the United States for a period of convalescence. When the Golden Gate hove into view, I really knew what the poet felt when he said:

> "Breathes there a man with soul so dead
> Who never to himself has said
> When returning from some foreign strand
> This is my own, my native land?"

One really learns to appreciate things by losing them, and distance does not only lend enchantment to the view, it also gives one perspective.

I stepped ashore and went directly to a drug store and got a big, a very big, malted milk! It was a long cherished desire, and after ten years of abstinence I had almost forgotten how a malted milk tasted. I need not tell you that this one was plu-perfect.

My first week at home in New York I traveled far uptown, alone, to visit the halls of my Alma Mater, the sidewalks of the Bronx. Things had changed a great deal, but some of the old landmarks were still there. I went into my parish church and sat down in a pew. There was still the same dark shiny wood of the pulpit and pews, the same altar rail where I had received my First Communion, the large stained glass windows mellowing the hard light of day. My gaze sought out and found one particular window that always used to arouse my boyish wonder at Sunday afternoon vespers. It was of the Blessed Trinity, and the Heavenly Father, a patriarchally bearded figure, was still seated on a prismatic rainbow sort of seat.

It was strangely satisfying to be back in these old familiar surroundings and produced in one a definite feeling of home-coming.

From the church I went to the parish convent, but there I encountered disappointment. The little Sister had written me some three years before and I had the idea that she was still located at this address. Missionaries are notoriously bad correspondents. She had been transferred and I was informed that she was teaching in a small town in Pennsylvania.

A week later I became ill and spent a month in bed. When I could be up and about again I was ordered to a milder climate by the doctors. But before my departure from New York I was approached for advice by a gentleman who had had some amazing experiences. Later on, while in Tucson, this gentleman gave me permission to incorporate his experiences in a book and the result was *This Night Called Day*. The essential details of that novel are factual. The details of plot and dialog and most of the personages, of course, are treated imaginatively.

On the appearance of my first book a copy of it went to a town in Pennsylvania with an appropriate inscription for a certain Sister. I considered it in the form of a retribution for her having launched me on this career of composition that she should now be compelled to read a seventy-thousand word one by the victim of her pedagogical persistence. It was an object lesson of what one little note in a student's composition book could produce.

A new book has been completed and will appear, I trust, sometime this year (1947), and there are others sketched out and waiting for completion. It takes work, a great deal of it, to produce a book, and it requires steady systematic effort and solitude. The rewards of active work are far more readily visible. A writer is necessarily a lonely man, but missionary life has been a good training for that.

EDITOR'S NOTE: Father Edward J. Edwards' novels, all published by Bruce, include: *Thy People, My People* (1941), *These Two Hands* (1942), *White Fire* (1943), *This Night Called Day* (1945).

MAURICE FRANCIS EGAN (1852 - 1924)

by Rev. Matthew A Coyle, C.S.C.

WHEN I WAS A YOUNG MAN, MAURICE FRANCIS EGAN WAS already becoming partly a legend. My elders quoted him and always, as I recall now, with relish. Little quips with just the right pungency—for he shone as a conversationalist —and sometimes epigrammatic splendors, were attributed to him. I knew him by report, although I should have remembered the author of *The Disappearance of John Longworthy* and *The Success of Patrick Desmond*. He seemed to be always nearby but never accessible—a Prince Charming, as Henry Van Dyke later called him, a man of fine culture, with always the perfect sally or tidbit to enliven social gatherings whenever dullness threatened. At one time, however, I had dinner with him but we said not a word to each other. I was one of some forty seminarians in the same dining room and Dr. Egan was seated, of course, at the head table where only our beloved elders heard and enjoyed what was said that day. I did get a chance, however, to observe him, and my impression of him was that he was then in failing health. Shortly after that occasion I heard of his death on January 15, 1924.

Before me as I write is practically all of the literary work of his career, forty volumes. This does not include his contributions to the *Yale Review, Atlantic Monthly, International Literary Review,* and some fourteen other magazines. He was one of the editors of the *World's Best Literature, Encyclopedia of Irish Literature, Knights of Columbus Commission for Examining Sources of American History.* He wrote "ten to fifteen thousand words a week," lectured at Johns Hopkins, Harvard, and was president of the American Academy of Arts and Letters. The University of Notre Dame in 1911 awarded him the Laetare medal for distinguished services as a Catholic.

Sixteen of the volumes before me show him as an author of books of fiction the most notable of which, *St. Martin's Summer, The Vocation of Edward Conway, The Disappearance of John Longworthy,* and *The Success of Patrick Desmond,* were first published in *The Ave Maria.* The *John Longworthy* book published in 1890, has this introductory picture of Broadway:

John Longworthy walked up Broadway, swinging his umbrella rather recklessly. Fortunately, there was not anybody in lower Broadway to be prodded by its gyrating point; for eight o'clock had just struck and, until he came to Fulton street, Broadway was a desert .... He had no need to be in a hurry ... yet he dashed under the heads of the horses of a streetcar that was turning into Broadway ....

Definitely Catholic in tone and treatment, these and other stories supplied edifying fiction for generations of Catholic readers. *The Wiles of Sexton Maginnis,* a later and more popular book, was acclaimed by *The Monitor* as "a new discovery in American literature." The artful intrigues and capers of this playfully deceptive Irishman who "never tells a lie except in the interest of truth," are definitely dated and have slender present-day appeal. *Sexton Maginnis* is Irish stage "stock," the clay-pipe Irishman of a past generation.

Three volumes of verse attest the catholicity of taste and interest in poetry of Professor Egan—*Preludes* and two editions of *Songs and Sonnets*. Six years intervene between the publication of the first and second editions and seven years before the appearance of the last. Only eleven poems are in the 1885 book. These were dedicated to Father Daniel Hudson, C.S.C., and were published "to aid in the rebuilding of the University of Notre Dame." *Preludes* begins with an often quoted line of those days:

> There were no roses till the first child died.

In the 1879 *Songs and Sonnets* are fifty-nine poems and seventy-one in the edition of 1892, a considerable increase in poetical activity, and, of course, all duly copyrighted.

Mr. Egan's verses fall rather easily into convenient groupings, i.e., nature, literary, religious, translations, etc., and are probably as fair an example, despite obvious sentimental qualities, of nineteenth century academic achievements in verse as will be found anywhere. At times the poetical conceits shown are of a much earlier age. The starched, brocaded beauty, with its inevitable manner, is the produce of the age. The "snowflakes" that fell like "frozen tears," and the "fickle zephyrs" yield gracefully at times to

> ... her hood
> Showed golden hair astray that never could
> Even in sin, forget its young design
> To curl like tendrils of a summer vine.

But the carnival that reigned "blithe and jocund" and the poets "who are human birds" and "rainbow-tinted" love are poetic conceptions which stain in no way the white radiance of eternity. The whirligig of time does something to lines like

Sunshine comes and glad birds sing.

and

Ah, my heart is pansy-bound.

Two poems—*Theocritus* and *Maurice de Guerin*, writes
Mr. Egan with easy insouciance in the *Atlantic Monthly* in
1919, did much to bring him literary friends:

> My acquaintance with Theodore Roosevelt began back in the
> eighties. At that time I was editor of a weekly paper in New York,
> and we had some correspondence on social and literary subjects.
> Everything he said was interesting ... he was most deferential in
> considering my opinions, especially in literary matters. I found after-
> wards that this attitude was largely due to his having read two son-
> nets of mine, *Theocritus*, and *Maurice de Guerin*, which he did not
> pretend to understand.

In *Confessions of a Book-Lover*, Mr. Egan dwells effusive-
ly and in detail on the delights furnished him by the characters and work of both *Theocritus* and *Maurice de Guerin*.
Yet while there is absent in his poems that high intensity
of poetical conception and expressions postulated by deep
inspiration there is ever present, deeply and strongly, that
mystical, religious view which gazes at life under the aspect
of eternity.

*Ten Years Near the German Frontier, Confessions of a
Book-Lover, Everybody's St. Francis,* and *Recollections of a
Happy Life* were among his most popular books. Among
his literary criticisms is a slender volume containing six
essays, chief among them being "Some Words About Chau-
cer" and "On the Teaching of English." In the latter he
sagely observes the need of fostering the study of English
literature in our schools as a discipline apart from the mere
study of philology. In his enthusiasm for this newly born
tendency in American schools he does not underestimate the
study of language, but argues strongly for the need to
understand and appreciate the spiritual values in literature.
Surely not a bold thesis today, but yet one that needed a

champion then as it occasionally does now. It is not so long ago that among the uninformed, the teaching of English consisted in an absorbing concern over predicate and subject and a nice regard for the structural differences in sentence and clause. Punctuation too, and grammar, gave, for them, totality to the subject.

Close attention to language, its words, phrases and structures is most important for therein lies the subtleties, overtones and the assurances, if mastered, of correct interpretation. Professor Egan had no quarrel here, but he became impatient with those who saw little beyond these disciplines. He was intolerant of teaching which reduced sublimely spiritual achievements in literary art to mere exercises in philology. And how correct he was in this!

In a career as preoccupied and as varied as Mr. Egan's the central interest is not to be found in his writings but in the man himself. An author, teacher, statesman, the "unofficial diplomatic adviser" of three presidents, Maurice Egan brought to all his activities a political shrewdness and an ardent patriotism that were equaled only by his unique social gifts. Aside from his formal training, his independent reading yielded him the most profit. From his mother came his avid literary interests and from his genial Irish father he inherited his democratic contagiously good humor. High lights in his diplomatic career are concerned with his work in purchasing the Danish West Indies and keeping the American government informed about European affairs as they reached him—senior diplomat—at Copenhagen, "the whispering gallery of Europe." He was appointed minister to Denmark in 1907 and later declined an ambassadorship at Vienna offered to him by both Presidents Taft and Wilson. "He was not only dean of the diplomatic corps," writes Henry Van Dyke, in his introduction to *Recollections of a Happy Life*, but " .. the one to whom all turned for help in difficulties." The story of his success is told in *Ten Years Near the German Frontier* (1919).

Bohemianism in the best sense was one of his endearing characteristics. He was a connoisseur of fine food and wine, and devoted to good music and society. These social traits brought him many friends and form much of the inextricable portions of his last and most interesting work, *Recollections of a Happy Life*, a book which represents him in the sere leaf time of life and reveals all of the charm of his personality.

Dedicated to his friends, the book has twelve chapters of rambling, gay chatter about almost everybody who ever touched the periphery of his life:

Walt Whitman, I remember, was not pleased at my taking up my abode in New York. Curiously enough, we were very good friends, although I was not at all backward in giving my opinion of some of his—excrescences. He informed me that Mr. Edmund Clarence Stedman was going to give him a party in New York and he said: "Eddie is coming to me like everybody else. In fact, Jews and a Catholic like you are coming to me!"

I informed him that I was not coming too close and that I had my reserves. He laughed very much at this audacity and quoted a sonnet of mine which had struck his fancy, but which I thought was quite alien to his convictions. It was *Maurice de Guerin*, and later, through the kindness of Harrison Morris, I found part of the sextet of the sonnet quoted in his *Prose Works*.

Henry George, Mrs. John Drew, Jusserand, President Arthur, Mrs. Surratt, are in the book, also Cardinal Gibbons, Archbishops Spalding, Ireland and Keane. The social behavior of society in South Bend, the teas, comments, and influences of the Studebakers, O'Brien and others are etched in nostalgic detail, as is the stateliness and the political intriguing of society in Washington, D. C. No, South Bend is not *Main Street*, avers Mr. Egan. "Compared to life in New York, the social life in South Bend was what might be called unartificial." How charming, and with what old-

world loveliness is the recall that on New Year's day the
Abbé Sorin, General of the Congregation of Holy Cross,
always "sent to his friends and acquaintances in South Bend
a bottle of Chartreuse or Benedictine and a large cake." His
treatment of university life at Notre Dame, its professors,
priests and Brothers, is both delicate and reverent. There
are illusions to the "dreadfully old horse" that Judge
Howard drove, talk about the dinner jacket "tuexdo," about
dear Brother Bruno and the devotion of South Bend to pro-
hibition—"in appearance." Topics of interest are abundant.

My elders still testify to the vividness and interest of
Maurice Francis Egan as a lecturer and conversationalist.
It is too bad that chronology did not allow Hazlitt to observe
the piquancies of both. Sometimes my informants, seemingly with gracious approval, tell of the employment by the
professor, of the Olympian flourish to make his points con-
vincing. I understand this and can appreciate the diverting
results that surely followed. The political and literary
milieu of such a man would permit it and bring about in his
admirers, I am sure, a "willing suspension of disbelief."
This privilege of the noble fiction, a part of the literary
armor, demands cautious handling. The creative imagina-
tion frequently uses the Homeric trust for the sake of the
picturesque. We know that its motive is to beguile. No
such easy acceptance, however, can excuse its graceless employment by the mind which hopes to create wonderment
by the use of the merely preposterous. In the former, one
observes a literary device that is innocent and entertaining,
in the latter, a phenomenon that may be pathological. At
times Maurice Francis Egan created laughter and friends
by the former.

Henry Van Dyke pays a beautiful and a just tribute to
Dr. Egan when he writes:

I first became acquainted with Maurice Francis Egan in the
eighteen eighties when I became a member of the Authors' club of

New York shortly after his entrance. Many a night, after joyous symposium, we walked home through the empty streets in the wee, sma' hours, talking of the things that make life worth living—faith and friendship, work and poetry. He was a firm Catholic and I an equally firm Presbyterian, but ecclesiastical differences never divided us. No doubt he would stretch the doctrine of "invincible ignorance" enough to give me a good hope, and certainly I made the doctrine of "prevenient grace" include him. Always, through the long years of our friendship, he was the same cheerful, loyal, and serviceable man. In poverty and in what writers call wealth, in sickness and in what men of high-strung temperament call health, in lodgings and in a palace, he grew and was unchanged.

Maurice Francis Egan was a valiant and Catholic man of letters at a time when our country and our Catholic people sorely needed such leadership. His associations with *The Ave Maria* cover a span of happy and fruitful years. His reviews, essays, and stories published in the magazine helped to establish him as a writer of importance. No task seemed too humble or great for his undertaking. He would lecture to students on table manners or to the faculty on Dante or "Intensive Farming," and in the next hour be gossiping with the great or near-great about some daring adventure, political or social, of the moment. His friends were many and influential, but he never lost the common touch. Probably the only quarrel Father Hudson, his friend of many years, had with him was over his penmanship. He found it difficult to decipher.

Outstanding statesman and literary man of his time, Maurice Francis Egan lived to see more than half of the nineteenth century unfold before him. An inspiring teacher and friend, a writer and political figure of keen outlook, he was at the same time, and always, gallantly Catholic and Catholic too at a time it was not popular to play the role. One quarter of the twentieth century was about to end when death brought his indefatigable and liberally Christian life to a close at the goodly age of seventy-two. Well might Matthew Arnold have been proud of him as an apostle of sweetness and light as were his contemporaries; and well too may the same author's lines be attributed to Professor Egan.

But be his
My special thanks, whose even-balanced soul,
From first youth tested up to extreme old age,
Business could not make dull, nor passion wild:
Who saw life steadily, and saw it whole ...

ROBERT FARREN

BIOGRAPHY IS IN MANY RESPECTS MUCH MORE IN NATURAL accord with the Christian virtue of humility than is autobiography.

The first person singular pronoun is full of opportunities for vainglory and even the fact that some of the Saints—Augustine and Teresa of Avila, for example—have written "their own stories" is no excuse for any lesser person to write his or hers. To make one other point, Augustine and Teresa wrote quite certainly for the love of God and the edification of their fellow-Christians and it would be presumption on my part to claim that these are my unmixed motives for writing. Still, in so far as it is Catholic, any man's writing will, under God, serve His purposes, and to that extent should be made known. Salving my conscience with this consideration, and hoping that it suffices, I will tell you something of myself as a writer and trust that I may do so modestly.

I was born in Dublin, Ireland, on April 24th, 1909, and have lived there ever since, except of course for holidays in other places. I was educated in St. Mary's National School, St. Patrick's Teacher's Training College, and the National University of Ireland. I have a degree in Scholastic Philosophy from this University.

The things which chiefly influenced my career have been three: the first, that I was born a Catholic; the second, that during my boyhood and youth the Irish War of Independence was fought and the Irish Free State, Eire, consisting of twenty-six of the thirty-two counties of Ireland, was established; the third, that I knew from a very early age that I wanted to be a writer.

The first of these need not be elaborated. Of the second and third I may say a few words.

The beginning of the last phase of the Irish War of Independence was the Insurrection of 1916 which, notably! was led in great part by poets: Padraic Pearse, Joseph Plunkett and Thomas Mac Donagh. The insurrection was followed by a long drawn war, mainly guerilla in type, between the Irish forces and those of Britain. A truce was signed in 1921 and a treaty concluded in December of the same year. This treaty established the Irish Free State, later called Eire. I lived, as I have said, in Dublin throughout this struggle, being seven years of age in 1916, and saw many of its chief features. My relatives were strongly in sympathy with it, hence my mind was formed to the mould of Irish nationalism. My teachers too, for the most part, had the same sympathies, and the fact that one of them attempted to counter the influence of his colleagues only made us more aware of, and zealous for, the nationalist viewpoint.

One of the chief effects of the liberation of the greater part of Ireland was that the Irish language was made a compulsory subject in our schools. But the movement for the revival of Irish as a spoken language preceded, and in great measure created, the movement in arms for freedom; and in my own school we were taught Irish as an extra subject, by enthusiasts, before it became compulsory. I was thirteen when Irish became part of the ordinary curriculum and from then on had ampler facilities for learning it than I had had for the preceding six years. During my training as a teacher much of my course of instruction was carried out through the national language; and after I had qualified as a teacher I spent many of my vacations in the Irish-speaking parts of the country; and as a result of all this study became almost bilingual. The first two books I wrote were: a translation from English of a prize novel, and a book of original short stories in Irish. The effect of my Gaelic studies on my writing in English has been very considerable. To quote no other example, my long poem on the life of St. Colmcille (*This Man was Ireland*) was based largely on a Gaelic life of the Saint, and contained many sections in Gaelic metres.

I have known from, I reckon, the age of ten, that I wanted to be a writer. This desire was confused, at about the age of twelve to fourteen, by another desire—to be a musical composer. The origin of this second ambition was that I played (or thought I played) the violin with the greatest possible enthusiasm and was led to add to the world's achievement by bringing forth some waltzes, songs, and "fantasies." These, in "one lucid interval snatched from the gloom," I burned; I decided with the greatest gravity that letters, not notes, should have the benefits of my attention, and continued on the literary path. As far as I can remember, my first verse outbreak was in the classroom when I was ten. It was, I regret to say, a satire on a fellow pupil, and, also I regret to say, endeared me to the master at the poor fellow-pupil's expense.

In desultory fashion I continued to write—stories, articles, poems. For a long time none of these had any public

success; but there were moments when I seemed to be
serving the small world of my acquaintances. For example,
I wrote some love poems, about no very definite human object and these came in useful. Not to me. To another.
"Another" had fallen in love with a very definite human
object named, I think, Kathleen, and written a poem in
which the sweet named was mentioned, and rhymed, several
times. Falling swiftly out of love with Kathleen, he went
precipitatedly into love with Eileen. Simple: he used the
poem again and replaced "Kathleen" with "Eileen." The
same process later made necessary the substitution of "Maureen" for "Eileen." Fine tactics, but alas! (or perhaps
"Hurray!") he stayed in love with Maureen, and here came
a difficulty. His afflatus had been permanently exhausted by
the one composition, and that one pleased Maureen so well
that she asked for more. The distracted lover, unable to
bear the impending loss of face, applied to me for my
poems. These I gave him and all went well. The lady
married him and even if he won her by false pretences—
well what man does not so win his wife? I should mention
here that my musical compositions were also used, by another friend, in a similiar siege, but alack! they failed.

When I was sixteen I said to myself that I was fooling
myself; and burned all my verse. But after sporadic attacks of "versing" I again became persuaded that I had a
vocation, and at about twenty-two set off in good earnest to
be a poet. Several private experiences, occuring within
the space of two or three years assisted in bringing me for-
cibly back to poetry. Of these I do not intend to speak,
having already tried to express something of them in my
poems. But I must mention that it was about this time—
when I was about twenty-three, that a young priest lit the
golden lamp of Aquinas for a group of friends and myself.
It was one of those casual encounters which are so rich in
influence. I may mention that one of the group of friends

was the Kilkenny novelist, Francis MacManus. McManus and myself read, at the suggestion of the priest, Sertil-langes' *Foundations of Thomistic Philosophy,* followed it up with Maritain's *Art and Scholasticism,* and went on to buy as many as we could of the cartload of books written by the Angelic Doctor.

For several years we read St. Thomas almost every week, and whenever we found any passage particularly skull-cracking we raced to each other's houses and tried to mend the cracks. Those long, delighted, metaphysical arguments remain in my mind as one of the thrills of my twenties. We read at the same time all the Europeans whom Frank Sheed and his wife, Maisie Ward, were bringing in, book after book, to the English-reading public—and we plunged from the translated books to others in French and Latin (with occasional efforts at the Italians). Berdyaev, Maritain, Gilson, Claudel, and so on.

I published my first book of poems, *Thronging Feet,* in 1936, and waited for the world to rock. It stayed sur-prisingly unshaken, however; though it had the kindness to give a wee tremble here and there. By the time *Thronging Feet* appeared I was at work on a second book—also of poems. Before I had completed this I had begun (in 1937) on my most ambitious piece of writing so far—the long poem on the life of St. Colmcille. But this too was inter-rupted by the necessity of writing an M.A. thesis in record time. Circumstances obliged me to write forty thousand words in five months on "The Poetic Experience according to the Philosophy of St. Thomas." (This was my M.A. thesis). I doubt if I ever worked so hard in my life—es-pecially as I was at the same time teaching school from 9:30 to 3:00 and helping to edit a magazine from 7:30 to 11:00.

I finished my thesis in the autumn of 1938 and looked again at poor St. Colmcille. But I knew this was going to be a long task, so I put it aside and began to complete the second book of short poems. This was finished and published in 1939, and I returned to the long poem. In its turn this was finished in 1941.

St. Colmcille (or Columba) was the greatest of Irish Saints and has left in the minds of the Irish a memory most intense and loving. He was the chief Evangelist of Scotland and the two countries share his legacy of faith and civilization. It had been in my mind, almost from my early schooldays, to write a book about him, and I finally did so.

The poem, which is written in varied metres, covers his entire life. Writing it was a splendid experience and a rare joy, as well as a labour and an agony. For half of 1937, and for almost the whole time between 1939 and 1941, I lived the work, carrying the growing manuscript with me wherever I was likely to get half-an-hour to add to it.

It was finished, I said, in 1941. But in the meantime the world was at war. Consequently the American edition of the poem, called *This Man was Ireland,* did not appear until 1943, and the English, called *The First Exile,* till 1944. The waiting was a long, dull trouble; but it had to be borne, and it ended. It was borne partly in the writing of new poems and a one-act poetic play. These were published in 1945 under the title, *Rime, Gentlemen, Please.* The poems are all quite short and include a great many character sketches. Many of them are humorous, though even in the humorous pieces I have tried to preserve lyricism. Humorous verse, unless it be also poetry, is of little value and the combination of poetic quality and humour is so rare that I was tempted to try what I could do in this *genre.* The play, "Lost Light," is about the Insurrection of 1916. It deals, not directly with the insurrectionists, but with the Imperialist relatives of an obscure Volunteer. It was produced in the Abbey Theatre twice, once in an Easter Week Commemoration programme and later in combination with O'Casey's "Shadow of a Gunman."

This was the second work of mine to appear on the Abbey stage. The first was a theatre version of the longest section of *This Man was Ireland*—the section called "Assembly at Druim Ceat." I played myself the part of Saint Colmcille. I should mention here that I have been a Director of the Abbey Theatre since 1940, being co-opted to fill one of the vacancies left by the death of Yeats and the resignation of Frank O'Connor.

I should like to take this opportunity of saying that I have reason to be grateful to Americans for their interest in my work. I have made friends in the States through its publication there, and I have had the honour to be made an honorary member of the Gallery of Living Catholic Authors, the Eugene Field Society, and the International Mark Twain Society.

It only remains to say that I have earned my living from 1929 to 1939 by teaching in Dublin primary schools, and from 1939 to the present by filling the post of Talks' Officer at Radio Eireann, the Irish Broadcasting Service. The title Talks' Officer is a humorous misnomer, since my programme includes talks, discussions, documentaries, poetry, and, in Irish, these plus plays. My chief achievement in this position has been the establishment on the air of the Verse-speaking movement, which Austin Clarke, one of the chief living Irish poets, and I founded.

EDITOR'S NOTE: Mr. Farren's chief publications are *Thronging Feet*, Sheed, 1936; *Fion Gan Mhoirt* (Short stories in Irish), 1938; *Time's Wall Asunder*, Sheed, 1939; *This Man was Ireland*, Sheed, 1943 (published in England as *The First Exile*, Sheed, 1944); *Rime, Gentlemen, Please*, Sheed, 1945; and (in prose) *Poetry for Pleasure*, Sheed, 1947.

REVEREND JOSEPH H. FICHTER, S. J.

FOR SIX YEARS I WAS A BRICKLAYER IN NEW JERSEY. TIMES were lush and money was loose, but in the cold winter months of the year you make an uncomfortable living that way. My local, 43 of the B.M. & P.I.U. of A., did not supply me with a sunshade in the hot summer nor fur-lined gloves in the cold winter; nor did my bosses. In 1930 I had enough of the freezing weather, so I went south permanently. I had gaped around Florida as a tourist a couple of previous winters, and liked it. This time I took a boat from New York to Savannah (which was wonderful), then rode a train straight across the south (no one ever did that twice then). In New Orleans there was a Jesuit Provincial, the late Father Salter, nephew of the Vice-President of the late Confederacy, who said he would give a Yankee a try in the Jesuit Novitiate at Grand Coteau, Louisiana.

The weather and the people seemed much nicer in the Southland, but my stay was not long because we Jesuits did

not have a philosophate in our Province at that time. So
I spent three years in philosophy and theology at St. Louis
University where I got a Master's degree in the latter subject. A year of teaching at Jesuit High School, New
Orleans, and another at Spring Hill College, Mobile, gave
me a chance to spread knowledge among bright young
Southerners (who, in spite of statistics, are not all illiterate,
you know.) Four years of theology, and ordination in 1942,
in a freezing little town west of Topeka, a year of Tertianship in another cold little town north of Hartford, intervened before I could get back to the South to teach at
Loyola University, New Orleans. After a while, the Provincial again packed me off to the North, this time to try for
a doctorate in sociology at Harvard.

That's my biography to date, and it just gives me a
chance to talk about my bibliography. When you keep learning a lot of new and interesting things about Christ and
Mary, about history with God and society without God, you
get a kind of compulsion to spread the news. You figure
that here is something a lot of other people want to know,
too; so you want to tell them. But before you are ordained
you can't preach, and when you are studying you can't
teach. So the next best thing is to write it down in magazine articles and peddle it around to the editors of *The
Catholic World, The Commonweal, America, The Sign.*
When the manuscript begins to show signs of postal fatigue
you have a choice of three things: retype it and send it to
the lesser known magazines; retype it and put it carefully
in your notes for future polishing; throw it away.

By a lucky coincidence, Michael Williams was in a care-
less literary mood when I sent him my first article in the
summer of 1934. He not only published it in *The Commonweal,* which was great honor, but sent a nice check for it.
Shortly afterwards, Father Gillis of *The Catholic World*
did the same. I then thought I owed a debt to these two

great Catholic editors, and I suppose that they and some of
the other Catholic editors of the country have sometimes
felt that I have been overdoing my gratitude in the stream
of articles I have since asked them to "consider with a view
to publication." (A lot of the rejected articles I have since
thrown away.)

Writing a book seemed another good way to broadcast the
things you figure people will want to know. And if you
don't look too closely a book seems to be a terrible job. But
if you can write a long article, you can do a chapter, and if
you write twenty or twenty-five chapters you have a book.
With the inspiration of Father Raymond Corrigan and Father William McGucken, of St. Louis University (now gone
to the heavenly source of all knowledge) I tried out the
simple procedure. The result was *Roots of Change,* published in 1939 by the D. Appleton-Century Company, a biographical appraisal of some of the "idea men" I thought
responsible for the great social, economic and political
changes of the last four centuries. The book is now out of
print; but there seems to be a lot of copies knocking around
the cheaper of the second-hand book stores, especially the
ones I proudly autographed and gave away.

Macmillan figured the market was good for another one,
so they published *Man of Spain* for me the next year. It is
a biography of the great Jesuit philosopher and theologian,
Francis Suarez. Then Herder, at decent intervals, brought
out three books, *Saint Cecil Cyprian, James Laynez,* and
Christianity. Bruce of Milwaukee adds the latest to the list,
publishing a work called *How to Find the True Religion,*
which is a textbook in apologetics for college students.

That list does not mean that all my book manuscripts
have been published. In a way, they are just like manuscripts for magazine articles because you have to find some
one who thinks they are worth publishing. My trunk is
beginning to pile up with frayed stuff that kept coming back

and is probably better left right where it is. What happens to a writer's rejected manuscripts when he dies? I wouldn't be surprised if the angel who bosses Purgatory makes you read them so you really develop that sense of shame for sins which is part of the punishment for every sinner.

The list appears to contain an unorderly hodge-podge of subjects; and if there is a thread of unity running through them it is a religious and sociological one: the theme of God's creatures learning to live in a worldly society while preparing for life in a heavenly society. There is still much to be written on that subject.

EDITOR'S NOTE: Father Fichter's published books include: *Roots of Change*, 1939, D. Appleton-Century; *Man of Spain*, 1940, Macmillan; *Saint Cecil Cyprian*, 1942, Herder; *James Laynez, Jesuit*, 1944, Herder; *Christianity*, 1946, Herder; *How to Find the True Religion*, 1947, Bruce. Not a bad bibliography for a young man of thirty-nine!

RT. REVEREND LEO
GREGORY FINK

THIS IS NOT A SECOND NOCTURN OF THE ROMAN BREVIARY! Neither is it an excerpt from the *Annals of Baronius* or the *Acta Sanctorum* of the Bolandists nor a replica of Boswell's *Life of Johnson.* In more words than I had anticipated to muster in the service of obedience to tell this story, I humbly submit the following "arcana" of my literary memoirs.

My first impression of books came to me as I sat before my good father's massive bookcase and contemplated the possibility of ascent to the top shelf where two large leather bound volumes with gold embossed titles reposed with dignity. I remember those books very well for they bore the names of *The Holy Bible* and *The Complete Works of Shakespeare.* They were carefully brought down from their high perch every Sunday afternoon, when under a canopy of blue smoke and amid the aroma of his cigar, my father

indulged in a spiritual and literary feast which was forbidden to me. The reason is apparent why those two books
became as the forbidden fruit of Paradise. My desire of
possession was allayed, however, when my dear mother
opened with the treasures of those two books by reading to
us the heroic tales of *Bible History* by Bishop Gilmour of
Cleveland, and the *Tales from Shakespeare* by Charles and
Mary Lamb. This was my first adventure in tasting the
nectar of literature.

I was blessed with the happy environment of music and
literature, for my brothers and sister under the instructions
of mother and the applause of father, never allowed a single
day to pass without the recitation of some poem or the ren-
dition of some musical composition. It made little difference
what the tenor of the day might be, either in good health or
sickness, in sorrow or in joy, we always had our daily literary and musical inspiration. The reaction was natural in
my life. I loved books and I hoped to become an author
some day. Under the impact of the psychic influence of
hero worship, I endeavored to limn upon parchment my own
concepts of men, their thoughts and their achievements. I
believed that "the pen was mightier than the sword," and
thus dreamed that my pen would pilot me safely through
the uncharted sea of life. Many things intervened to upset
my ambition and economic necessity placed me in the role
of a wage-earner in the commercial and industrial world.
Poetry and music became my recreation and not my vocation. I outlived this iconoclasm and when I entered the
Seminary of St. Charles Borromeo in Overbrook I saw the
renaissance of my literary ambition.

My professor of English repeatedly advised me not to
soar too high above the terrestrial reality of life. Once one
poetical product on the time-worn theme of "Spring" was
stigmatized as "Browningesque" and "pen-Dantique." I
was never discouraged nor deflated, but just kept on com-

posing poetry which contained many enigmatic and intro-
verted platitudes.

I was an avoracious reader in my student days and spent
much of the time in the Seminary Library, of which I was
librarian. While I do not profess to have read the original
writings of Homer, Virgil, Dante, Tasso, and Calderon,
nevertheless, I obtained translations of their masterpieces
and read them with unbounded pleasure. As a climax to
such a course of reading, I indulged in the complete works
of Milton and Shakespeare, but with an enthusiastic study
of the essays of Coleridge, Addison, and Emerson, I began
to abandon poetry for essay composition. I decided that
my ideal literary style should be a blending of the charm
and simplicity of Washington Irving and the clarity and
logic of Cardinal Newman.

Lengthy historical essays on the evolution of music and
lectures on certain grand operas were my first attempts to
write for and speak to a listening audience of theological
students and professors. I never fell into heresy or schism,
but I did evoke much criticism for my essay on Christopher
Marlowe's and Von Goethe's *Doctor Faustus,* supplemented
by Gounod's operatic interpretation of the drama. I tried
to emulate General Wallace who had never seen Palestine
and yet, like the well known Jesuit, Father O'Rourke, wrote
better about the Holy Land than those who actually visited
it. My lecture on the Holy Land was the result of much
study on the topography and history of the sacred shrines
of antiquity, but it was never delivered because my superior
told me that I was trespassing upon the work of the faculty.
The humiliation was good for me. It taught me that "prudence is the better part of valor." The craving to write
continued and virtually became my obsession. I wrote
several Hymns with music for St. Cecilia's Day and also the
melody and words for an Alma Mater Song which was sung

by the entire student body—but never published, for reasons beyond my control.

After my ordination in 1916, I was sent to the parish of old St. Alphonsus in South Philadelphia, where one of the most venerable pastors with much missionary experience became my monitor. In return for his fatherly guidance I felt that it was my duty to hand down to posterity the life of *Father Stommel: Church Builder.* My own experiences with him I described in another volume entitled *Just Ordained,* which was inspired by Canon Sheehan's *My New Curate,* and told of the first zeal of an American curate in a "dying parish." The experience of publishing, marketing and selling the first editions of these books was pleasant. I lost only twenty-five dollars in the venture to gain a place in the world's gallery of literature. My critics were tolerant and even generous. They asked for more books of the same calibre!

With a firm purpose never to write for profit but to give every honorarium received for lectures or writings to the missionary work of Mother Church, I launched forth with the ambition of stirring up the hearts of American youth with a story which would inspire the reader to "fight the good fight, to run his course and to keep his Catholic Faith." My favorite hero, St. Paul, was to be the subject of this new book. The idea dominated my very soul as I enlisted as a Chaplain in the Army in the first World War. As an Army Chaplain I found some spare time to assimilate the Acts of the Apostles and the Epistles of St. Paul. But shortly after the conclusion of the war, I returned home and was appointed curate to a very stern pastor, whose conservative administration of his parish gave me no outlet for my excess energy. Upon the advice of my confessor, I planned the proper use of my time for the period of my internment. I purchased every book available on the subject of St. Paul. The walls of my room were covered with the maps of Palestine, Asia Minor, Greece and ancient Rome. I lived the apostolic life and little realized that I was living in Bethlehem, Pennsylvania, excepting for sick calls and my routine priestly duties which were limited. I was so absorbed in my work of studying and writing the life of my hero and saint that many times I forgot the cannon-stove which naturally required coal and the removal of ashes for the proper heating of my attic room. I consoled myself with the thought that St. Paul must have been cold in the Mamertine Prison! Environment as well as heredity made me more determined to write a great book for American youth. Since I knew that my pastor knew not only the life of St. Paul but also the theology of the Apostle to the Gentiles, I took courage enough to ask him to be my first critic for the completed manuscript. The second critic I found in Monsignor McGarvey, who was a convert from the Anglican Church to Catholicism. I need not tell you I was discouraged as a result of the massacre and annihilation. No! phoenix-like my spirit reconditioned, rehabilitated and reconstructed the manuscript, and after a thorough appreciation of my critics' treatment, it was ready for publication. My motto was "Per aspera ad astra." *Paul—Hero and Saint* was ready for the printer!

It was through the kind advice of Bishop Eugene J. McGuinness and Bishop Francis C. Kelley, who were then in charge of the Catholic Church Extension Society of Chicago, that I received encouragement to present the manuscript to Father John J. Burke, C.S.P., who in addition to being head of the Chaplains' Aid Society, the editor of the *Catholic World*, and founder of the National Catholic War Council, was vitally interested in the Paulist Press of New York City. Through the acceptance of the manuscript by Father Burke and the courtesy of Joseph Menendez, manager of the Paulist Press, the first edition of *Paul—Hero and Saint* was printed, quickly sold, and followed by several other

printings which I believe will continue because the book is
both popular and inspirational for American youth.

Dr. James J. Walsh of New York City and Fordham University, whose lectures and books I always highly admired,
wrote me and assured me that "red ink was in my blood,"
and that I should not stop with St. Paul but should continue
with St. Peter, St. John and St. Luke. The result of this
encouragement was the writing and publishing of *Peter—
Commander-in-Chief*, and *John—Apostle of Peace*, while
Luke—Beloved Physician still lies upon the desk before me.
With encouragement from Dr. Walsh, I also published the
symposium of Catholic ethics of nursing, entitled *Graduate
Nurses*, for which he himself wrote an important chapter.

The work entitled *Old Jesuit Trails in Penn's Forest* I
wrote in loving memory of my good parents, since it was
from them that I learned so much concerning the pioneer
Catholics of Pennsylvania. Rev. Dr. Peter Guilday of the
Catholic University assisted me in this work but warned
me incessantly of the necessity of the proper documentation
of every historical fact which I enumerated in the book. I
respected his advice, but did not follow it, since I wished to
make the book readable for the average Catholic American.
For this defect some critics, whilst praising the originality
of the book, nevertheless hoped that in a later edition it
would be perfected. A complete and perfect history of the
Jesuit trails in Penn's forest I respectfully leave to some
future Jesuit historian.

Dear Reader, you will note that of the twenty volumes
which I have managed to write in the course of my busy
missionary, military, and pastoral life, the majority are
of an historical nature. However, I do not pose as an historian, but simply as a parish priest with a few avocations,
one of which is writing in the silence of the night from
9 P.M. until 2 A.M. My latest literary venture is a complete
history of the Sacred Heart Parish of Allentown, which is

seventy-five years of age and which in the Providence of God has been most versatile in upbuilding the Catholic Church in a dominantly non-Catholic community. I have endeavored to tell the wonderful story of this parish under the symbol of a tree which grew in Allentown, weathered the storm of rural and urban life and now speaks as a living witness of God's true Church. The title of the book is *Under the Silver Maple.*

In these words have I told you the story of my writing penchant which I sincerely hope will always be influential in advancing the greater glory of God and honor to America. May all my books inspire the Youth of America with the perpetuity of the Faith of Our Fathers!

EDITOR'S NOTE: Monsignor Fink, a Domestic Prelate and Vicar Forane, has been a Consultor of the Philadelphia Archdiocese since 1930 and rector of Sacred Heart Church, Allentown, since 1926. His principal publications include *Father Stommel: Church Builder*, Reilly, 1921; *Good Shepherds of Ireland*, Paulist Press, 1932; *John—Apostle of Peace*, Paulist Press, 1939; *Just Ordained*, Dolphin, 1933; *Martyrs of the Sacred Heart*, Dolphin, 1934; *Monsignor William Heinen*, Dolphin, 1937; *Old Jesuit Trails in Penn's Forest*, Paulist Press, 1933; *Paul— Hero and Saint*, Paulist Press, 1921; *Peter—Commander-in-Chief*, Paulist Press, 1930; *Pilgrim Tales*, Dolphin, 1935; *Trilogy to the Holy Name*, Paulist Press, 1933.

JOHN MATHIAS HAFFERT

I WAS BORN IN SEA ISLE CITY, NEW JERSEY, ON AUGUST 23, 1915, son of a newspaper publisher. At the age of fourteen I left home to become a Carmelite. Eight years later, while I was studying for the priesthood in a Carmelite seminary, a saintly laybrother there had a series of "revelations," and it was made known to him that I (wonderful, wonderful "I"!) was to make them known to the world.

Reading no more than that (and if aught else is to be said, how can more than that be mentioned in a "sketch"?), you must be exclaiming at my audacity and wondering how my books ever got into print, or also feel like sitting down and writing (as one well-meaning priest did) to the Prior General of the Carmelite Order asking how the Carmelites could encourage and employ such an heretical fellow.

Anyway, whether this saintly laybrother had a revelation or not, I believed in it. I believed in it very much. And that's my life.

He said that Our Lady of the Scapular wanted to be more known, and that for consecration to Her Immaculate Heart by the Scapular (he had never heard of Fatima, incidentally) not only would souls be brought to Christ, but peace would come to the world. He said I should make this known: To Jesus through Mary, by Scapular and Rosary.

Our mutual confessor told us to burn all writings and correspondence on the subject, at once. We did.

Then the laybrother went to a foreign mission. I was forced to discontinue my seminary studies.

Things looked as though I'd never be writing a sketch for *The Book of Catholic Authors*. I was offered a position on a secular magazine, but it was one that would have taken all my time, and I still believed in that "revelation." I thought of a chicken farm, of begging, of starting a magazine, of cutting people's lawns, of teaching school. I happened to get a very opportune chance at the latter, and proceeded to write the book, *Mary in Her Scapular Promise*. Monsignor Sheen wrote the Preface, and it became a best-seller. The last count was about 25,000 copies.

After that came the Scapular Militia, an organization to spread the Scapular Devotion, of which I ultimately became lay manager, and which was exactly what the little laybrother had predicted and ordered. It is conducted by the Carmelite Fathers. It has at present more than 26,000 members in all parts of the country. And at long last, voicing all that I had been told to voice (and trying to be a voice for Our Lady Herself in the swirl of today), we have *The Scapular*, an outspoken and very spiritually Marian magazine.

Outside of *Mary in Her Scapular Promise*, I consider my books commonplace and marvel at their popularity. I am always surprised when I meet someone who has read one. *A Letter from Lisieux* was written, as is quite obvious to the reader, just to get in "a plug" for the Scapular devo-

tion "a la Ste. Therese." And *From a Morning Prayer,*
which tells about the laybrother's revelation in all possible,
gory detail, was written to provoke interest in the Scapular
Militia. The latest, *The Peacemaker Who Went to War,* is
the life of Blessed Nuno Alvarez Pereira, a soldier who believed that the Rosary and the Scapular were the answer to
life's problems, and who got himself declared the hero of
his country (and a decree of beatification) for his not in-
considerable efforts.

As for my personal life ... well, it's just what you
wouldn't expect. I apologize for the house I live in, because
it's big. I apologize for all the silver, because it's a sign of
opulence. I wonder how I ever came to live in such a big
house, with so many possessions, when I neither have nor
have had any money, and when I really meant it those (?)
years ago when I was prostrate on a chapel floor after
promising complete poverty. I don't think you would understand it, because I'm not yet used to life myself ... to all
called "the world," I mean. But despite the war, despite the
shakiness of the peace, despite the threat of world atheism
and the use of atomic power, I'm glad to be alive today. I
would not prefer to live in any other age. I believe that
these are the days of Mary's coming, when by consecration
to Her Heart (through Rosary and Scapular, which she held
forth at Fatima), the world will finally find Christ, for
keeps.

EDITOR'S NOTE: Mr. Haffert is also in wide demand as a lecturer. His
published books include *Mary in Her Scapular Promise,* 1940; *From a
Morning Prayer,* 1943; *The Peacemaker Who Went to War,* 1945.
All are published by the Scapular Press in New York City.

JOSEPH KENTIGERN HEYDON

MY ANCESTRY IS NOT RECOVERABLE. THERE ARE HEYDONS scattered here and there down English history, like the John Heydon who went to jail for predicting Oliver Cromwell's death on the scaffold, but I cannot connect myself with any of them. It is a common name in Devon and Dorset, where it appears to be indigenous, and my knowledge of my forefathers goes on farther back than Richard Heydon of Plymouth, a Presbyterian and a God-fearing man, at the time of the Napoleonic Wars. One of his sons, Philip, used to claim as his earliest memory being taken in a rowing-boat to see the captive Napoleon when the *Bellerophon* put into Plymouth after the Battle of Waterloo.

Bad times followed the wars, and three of Richard Heydon's sons, Ebenezer, Philip and Jabez, went to seek their fortunes in Australia in the hungry 'forties. Jabez was my grandfather, and he must have been a man of sterling character for he converted himself by reading Newman's

writings, and he brought his wife—after a long struggle—
and his elder brother, Philip, into the Church. My father,
Louis Francis Heydon, was the youngest of Jabez' many
children and the only one born after his conversion.

My father was a truly great man, if it is his son who
says it. But of course I cannot do justice to him in a few
words which are supposed to be about myself. In 1881 he
married Mary Gell, whose father was also a convert and a
brother-in-law of John Ullathorne, brother of Archbishop
Ullathorne. I was their second child, born at Sydney on
January 13, 1884, and by profession I am a solicitor, as was
my father.

That reminds me of my first day in Boston, Massachusetts. I was educated at Downside, England, and at the
Massachusetts Institute of Technology. On arrival in Boston I was interviewed by the professor of English, Arlo
Bates. He asked me what my father was and I replied that
he was a solicitor. "What is that," he asked, "a commercial
traveller?" "No, a lawyer." "Oh, I suppose you mean an
attorney. Why don't you speak English!" As a professor
of English he must have known better, and I have often
wished that I had been self-possessed enough to reply:
"Well, if you want to be quite accurate, he is an attorney in
law, a solicitor in equity, and a proctor in probate. In England and Australia they are called solicitors for short, and
in America attorneys. I am not proposing to speak American just yet, and I hope I never shall." It might have won
his heart, and he might have presented me with a copy of
his book, *Patty's Perversities*. I am not joking: he had
written a book with that engaging title.

I did not take a degree at Tech. It was not necessary as
a key to any door that I particularly wanted to go through,
and I have no great regard for degrees for their own sake,
so I preferred to take the subjects I was interested in. I
was one of those boys with the knack of passing examina-

tions, and that destroys one's respect for them. I remember sitting for the Fifth Section of my law finals, Crimes and Torts. I had been through the prescribed books once, reading them alone and making notes of questions that I thought I might ask if I were the examiner; and sitting at the next table to mine in the examination hall was a solicitor's managing clerk who had had fifteen years of practical experience. I passed and he did not. Can you wonder if I do not think much of examinations and diplomas? That managing clerk knew his subject inside out, while I knew practically nothing about it and would have gladly employed him.

I had a very happy five years in Boston, for I joined Sigma Alpha Epsilon and lived four of those years in the Fraternity House, then at 263 Newbury street. One Christmas I went with one of the fellows to his home in Woonsocket, Rhode Island, and another Christmas with another fellow to Washington, D. C. But for the summer holidays I went over to England, and for my last year I brought back as my wife the girl I had loved since Downside days—the beginning of a very happy married life which is going on still.

Then to London, where I was articled to a firm of solicitors in Chancery Lane. I remember the head of the firm saying to me one day how strange it was that in winter the sun shone on his desk, while in summer it did not. I was able to explain that to him and his face was a picture of amazement.

During that time our first son was born, now an M.D. of Cambridge, and he will probably be in Boston before this appears in print, to see what America can show him in dermatology.

Then we went back to sunny Sydney, where I joined my father and carried on with him until he died, shortly before the end of the first World War.

After the war there was something of a boom in Australia and a number of new manufacturing firms sprang up, one of which I financed on debenture. It did not prosper, however, and I had to take it over to rescue my money. My scientific training came in useful then, and I put in more money instead of simply salvaging what I could from the wreck. I was lucky enough to find just the right manager, Henri Van de Velde, and we turned the corner. That was the start of Felt & Textiles of Australia, Ltd., now a large organization. I freely give all the credit to Van de Velde, who proved to be a genius. But I am convinced, too, that the undertaking had God's blessing on it.

That experience was the occasion of my first book, *Wage Slavery*, published in 1924. I had never expected to be engaged in industry and I took a trip to England to study profit-sharing and to get my ideas together generally about the claims of morality upon an employer of labour. *Wage Slavery* was the result of my deliberations.

A dozen years went by and I did not write anything more, but stuck to business, legal and otherwise. In the last twelve years, however, I have had leisure to write a few books, mainly addressed to scientifically minded boys and girls, the products of our system of secular education, who have never been taught such fundamental truths as that there is a God. I have one partly written now: *The Wonder of It;* which I hope will be my best. I do not pretend to write best-sellers; but if I can help anyone to the truth I shall be well repaid.

I want to seize this opportunity to pay my debt of gratitude to Frank J. Sheed, without whose kindly help I doubt if I should ever have had a distinctively Catholic book published. And yet, it was the merest chance that I had this friend to turn to. Sheed, like myself, was born in Sydney, and he was a young barrister while I was in active practice in the sister branch. My sister and I joined the Catholic Evidence Guild and spoke in the Domain under his leadership. It appears, therefore, that it comes down to the matter of a chance friendship that I ever got a Catholic book published.

What then of those who do not meet with such a lucky chance? I do not like the position in England. We blast about the dearth of young writers, but what can we expect? It is not true that you cannot keep a good man down. You can keep him down very easily if you do not give him a chance, especially if he is not the sort to elbow and bustle; and there is something rather incongruous in the idea of an elbowing Catholic writer. One cannot expect the thoughtful student to be a showman, and the showmanlike books we are getting are very doubtfully Catholic. It seems to me that converts have a disproportionate prominence. They mean the best in the world, of course, but they come along with the news-value of their conversion and a ready-made reputation, and the result is that the born Catholic is left out in the cold, though he may well have a better understanding of the religion that he learned on his mother's knees than the convert.

EDITOR'S NOTE: Hal P. Trevarthen is the pseudonym Mr. Heydon sometimes uses. His books published under his own name include: *Wage Slavery*, The Bodley Head, 1924; *Fascism and Providence*, Sheed, 1937; *The God of Reason*, Sheed, 1939; *Free Will and Science*, Author, 1944; *The God of Love*, Sheed, 1944; *Live and Help Live*, Author, 1944.

MARGARET ANN HUBBARD

I WAS BORN ON OCTOBER 17, 1909, ON A LARGE WHEAT FARM in North Dakota where my father had homesteaded in the early days of that country. Our home was near the little town of Souris, and perhaps twenty miles west of the Turtle Mountains and the same distance east of the Souris River. Before the herds were depleted, the buffalo used to make regular migrations from the mountains to the feeding grounds at the river, and one of their old trails can still be faintly seen across a pasture. When I was small I used to go and sit beside that landmark, trying to imagine the thundering pace of the big animals as they lumbered by in single file to make that deep, narrow crease in the earth.

I had one sister a little older than myself, and together we explored every inch of the farm. We attended the country school where my mother had taught before her marriage; but in the long winter months when the snow was piled high we were unable to reach the school, and then we had our happiest times. In the mornings my mother would give us regular lessons, and in the afternoons I taught school with my dolls or we made up wonderful programs, using the dolls as actors, and had our parents and the hired man as audience in the evening. I remember very well a certain number we had, using my favorite doll Jerry as an American doughboy posed before a wonderful background of a long brown crayon trail as conceived by my artistic sister. Together we sang "There's a long, long trail a-winding," and put our whole hearts into it.

Later, in 1924, we moved to Duluth, Minnesota, where my sister and I were graduated from Central High School and then from the Duluth State Teachers College. I was seventeen at graduation from the college, and therefore too young to teach; but the next year I obtained a position in Superior, Wisconsin, across the bay from Duluth, and I taught there for two years. I still had no idea of writing. In high school I had written wonderful themes in verse, which always earned me A because the others couldn't make rhymes. So far as making writing my career, such a thought had not entered my head.

It was at the University of Minnesota that I received my first prod in that direction. Just before graduation in 1932, an English instructor wrote at the bottom of a theme, "See me." Wondering what I had done now, I went to her office. She remarked that I had been writing some excellent themes in the subject of childhood reminiscences and that in her opinion I had a definite talent for children's writing and should go into it seriously. I was thrilled. I saw myself as an outstanding and wealthy author immediately. I went home, walking on air.

Back in Duluth, I began dramatizing fairy tales for the Children's Threatre, and when I saw *Hansel and Grethel*, the first of these, on the stage and heard people actually speaking the lines I had written, I thought I had accomplished everything in the world. In 1935 six of my plays were published by Walter H. Baker, one of these an adult play, *The Bethlehem Road*. My second adult play, *He Passed This Way*, was published by Baker in 1941.

The plays, while fascinating, seemed hardly enough for a career, and so when I found a story idea I began to mull it over. In doing research with other writers on a local history, I found a most interesting paragraph about the settlement of Pembina, North Dakota, which was just over the mountains from my childhood home. This settlement had been made at great sacrifice by a group of Scotch people, and by 1824, after many hardships, the village was prosperous and thriving. That year, however, the international boundary line was finally determined and Pembina was found to be below the line. The Hudson Bay Fur Company was not licensed to maintain posts outside of Canada, and so they withdrew their trader and consequently the main financial support of the settlers. Within a few months the village was abandoned, and a passing voyageur noted that only a few nomad Indians occupied the houses that had been built so hopefully by the pioneers.

That story seemed to me to be so pathetic and so filled with possibilities that it invited writing. I decided that I would write about one of these families; but instead of bringing them sensibly back to Winnipeg or St. Francis, I would take them up-(south) along the Red River of the North and set them down in an Indian village. There was nothing to stop me now, except that I knew nothing about Indians. To remedy that, I went to the Leech Lake Chippewa Reservation in Minnesota and spent a summer among the Indians. It was a marvelous experience. In my talks with the Indian women, through an interpreter, I gleaned more material than I could use in one book. The Indian lore in the resulting book, *Little Whirlwind*, is all authentic and comes from original sources.

The next winter I spent in Texas, gathering material for *Seraphina Todd*. I have always found it best—and most delightful—to go to the part of the country about which I write, because in seeing a locale and its people one gains impressions that could not possibly be read in books. This leads my friends to remark that being a writer is certainly an easy way of making a living. I admit I love it, but the easy-ness is another matter. Writing is a hard grind, much of it plain routine, but with enough bright spots to make up for whatever dull business it requires.

I wrote *The Hickory Limb* from a remembered visit to the Smoky Mountains; and later *Lone Boy,* for which I did my research in the friendly city of Helena, Montana. When the war came along it put an end to my travelling. Feeling that merely writing was not enough to be doing at such a time, I took a course in radio communication and worked as a radio operator for twenty-eight months, finishing with that job in October of 1945. I did very little writing during that time, for I found that after working eight hours a day I had no enthusiasm for the typewriter. Writing definitely demands a leisurely existence in my case.

Early in 1946 I was awarded the first of the fiction fellowships offered by the Bruce Publishing Company of Milwaukee, Wisconsin, for a manuscript of a novel based on the life of Hans Christian Andersen. This is entitled *Flight of the Swan.* I never worked on anything so absorbing. In the eleven years of its evolution from play to novel, I never grew tired of it. In this time, of course, I did much other writing; but each time I came back to Hans he seemed like an old friend to welcome me. I had always loved his stories. From his fairytales I drew a picture of the man, and using this with the incidents he himself relates in his autobiography, I wrote my novel.

People often ask me how I started to write, and therefore, how should they begin? My answer is simple. I wrote what came into my head. Every writer must do the same. As early as possible, find the field for which you are best suited and then stick with it. A very wise man once said that there is no genius in the world like the genius of energy and industry. I agree with him. Combine energy with talent for any creative work—that is the recipe for success in one's chosen field.

EDITOR'S NOTE: Miss Hubbard's practice of residing in the locale about which she is writing explains her present residence in Louisiana. Her published books include dramatizations for children of *Puss in Boots, Hanzel and Grethel, Pinocchio,* and *Little Black Sambo,* all issued by Baker, in 1935; the plays for adults, *The Bethlehem Road,* Baker, 1935, and *He Passed This Way,* Baker, 1941. Macmillan published her *Seraphina Todd,* in 1941, *The Hickory Limb,* in 1942, and *Lone Boy,* 1943; Bruce her *Flight of the Swan,* in 1946; and Johnson of Richmond her *High in the Hollow,* in 1947. Miss Hubbard is a member of Pen and Brush, New York City, and of the Gallery of Living Catholic Authors.

SHELIA KAYE-SMITH
(Mrs. Theodore Penrose Fry)

I WAS BORN IN HASTINGS, A SUSSEX COAST TOWN OF SOME 70,000 inhabitants, where my father practiced as a physician. He had come there from the country, and his heart, I think, was still among the fields and farms rather than in the somewhat prim streets of a Victorian seaside resort. Certainly the heart of his daughter was never in the streets. From my earliest childhood I hankered after the countryside some five miles outside the town, for Platnix Farm where my sister and I used to be sent to be happy and safe while our parents travelled in Europe. I lost no opportunity and used every available means of transport—bicycle, horse, my own legs—to take myself out there as often as possible; and it was not long before the stories with which I entertained myself came to be set among the fields and lanes where they are still set, even when the entertainment is not for me alone.

I was educated at the Hastings and St. Leonard's College, where my favourite subjects were literature and history. I was fairly bright, but not studious and my elders soon gave up making me sit for public examinations. I had always been interested in religion, and at School this took a definitely High Church turn. My father was a member of the Church of England, while my mother had been brought up as a Scottish Presbyterian, so my religious grounding was rather vague as to doctrine, though the atmosphere of my home was always devout. At school I received some very clear instruction on High Church lines, and ideas which had hitherto been vague now became clear and inspiring. It was not till many years later, however, that I definitely associated myself with the Anglo-Catholic movement in the Church of England.

While at school I was busy writing for my own delectation only. I wrote in penny exercise books stories of, I suppose, some 10,000 words in length, all highly romantic and nearly all set in the country near my home. I had now definitely made up my mind that I would be an author and immediately on leaving school I started my first full length novel, *The Tramping Methodist*. It was not originally intended for publication, but by the time I had finished it I had come to feel in need of a wider audience than my single self or even than my family. I was totally ignorant of the procedure to be followed to secure this end, for I lived so entirely remote from literary circles that I had until then met only one author—a struggling writer of short stories who could do little beyond give me a little good advice on my prolixity, contempt of probability, and excessive use of adjectives.

It was in the pages of some journal that I picked up the information that the Society of Authors criticized and advised on the work of unpractical writers. I joined the Society as an associate, since I was not eligible for membership, having published nothing, and in great fear sent them my manuscript for advice. I received it back in due course with a most encouraging report and some very useful suggestions for its improvement. When I had carried these out I sent it off again—this time to a literary agent, having been recommended to one by the Society.

Here, however, an unexpected difficulty arose. The agent wrote to say that he could not undertake to read the manuscript, still less send it around to publishers, unless it were typewritten. I had made a fair and faultless copy in my best handwriting, with the margins beautifully ruled in red ink, and this new demand filled me with consternation, for almost literally I had no money. Enquiries at a local typewriter office showed me that I should have to find three pounds, ten shillings, to have my manuscript copied. All I had was a shilling a week pocket money, and though I had always been a disgrace to my arithmetic class at school I knew enough to calculate that my income would be mortgaged for at least eighteen months if I could obtain the money from no other source.

In desperation I decided to earn it by the sale of what scanty accomplishments I possessed outside authorship. For a month I dusted and swept and earned ten shillings at the end of it, for three months I taught elementary subjects in a school, and received two pounds twelve and six as the reward of my labours. I was still short by seven and six of the required sum, but as I had (not surprisingly) been sacked by the mistress of the school and was no longer required by the housewife, my parents came to the rescue and paid up the rest. I have been earning money now for over thirty years, but I am sure that I have never worked so hard as I did for those first three and a half pounds.

The money so hard earned, however, was well spent, for the book found a publisher with only a little difficulty, and since then my literary life has been smooth sailing, with-

out those storms which have shaken or even sunk so many,
especially those starting as young as I did. Since that day
I have written more than twenty novels, but none has given
me the same thrill as that first book—so young and so crude
that when I last attempted to read it (to take my mind off
an air-raid) I found myself wanting to collect every copy
in print and burn them. Yet the first copy I received had
been such an object of pride and joy that I remember I slept
with it under my pillow.

Those first years of authorship were exciting enough to
absorb most of my ardours and interests. It was not till I
was older that I turned to those more usual to girls in their
twenties. I began to enjoy dances and parties, clothes and
company, but when I met my husband, his background was
not social but religious.

I was now a convinced Anglo-Catholic and he was one of
the assistant clergy of the church I attended. Our marriage
created a certain amount of discussion in High Church
circles, for many Anglo-Catholic clergy followed the ideal
of a celibate life. In actual fact, several leaders of the
movement were married—as were its founders, Dr. Pusey,
Dr. Keble, and Dr. J. M. Neale—but I was told that these
were old-fashioned, or had committed themselves in the
days of their youth, before they had realized their call in its
fullness. I personally had long been convinced that the
celibacy of the Anglo-Catholic clergy was a matter of personal vocation and could not possibly be held in the church
of England as a binding rule. However, feeling ran high
enough to make it necessary for my husband to move to another parish, and the first five years of our married life
were spent in London.

Here, as a clergyman's wife, I had many opportunities of
seeing the Anglo-Catholic movement from inside, and in a
short time had lost most of my illusions. I still, however,
regarded the thought of seceding to Rome as a "tempta-

tion," and even when this attitude had been modified by my conviction of the Catholic Church's superior holiness and the Anglican Church's schism, I still felt I could not take a step which might wreck my husband's clerical life. I was not yet convinced of an imperious call, but I was sufficiently shaken to decide that if I saw tendencies toward a change on his side I would open the subject.

This is what actually happened, and we both found that we had been following independently the same train of thought. The problem was how the thing should be done. This we found easier to solve than many others in our situation. For one thing we were financially independent, for another my husband's vicar was proposing to retire, so that he would have anyway to look for a new appointment. At the same time, by another of those "coincidences" in which a Catholic may see the working of Divine Providence, we had the offer of a small estate in Sussex, some ten miles from my old home and in the very heart of the country I had loved from childhood.

We had first seen Little Douce Grove as Anglicans, and when we became Catholics we wondered how we should manage to practice our new religion, as the nearest Catholic church was nine miles away. Here again Providence intervened in the shape of a Diocesan traveling mission which supported two priests touring the countryside with everything necessary for the celebration of Mass, which they said in stables, barns, inn parlours, private houses, anywhere where they could find a congregation. We offered a room over our garage, and Mass was said in the district for the first time for many hundred years.

Immediately isolated Catholics began to spring up like mushrooms in the fields, some who had married "outside the Church" were reconciled to it, those who had not seen a priest for years returned to the Sacraments, and many children were baptized. Soon our congregation overflowed its upper room, and we were able to build a church—a tiny church indeed, but big enough for so remote a district, and lately a cemetery has been added, the only Catholic cemetery within many miles.

Little Douce Grove is still our home, though a little war-torn after five years in Bomb Alley, as this part of England was called during the war. Mercifully the church is un-damaged, and I like to think that it has been a help and comfort to many Catholic soldiers camped round here in preparation for D Day. Sometimes even the car-park out-side has been full of them, hearing Mass through the open doors when the inside was crowded.

My own work during the war has been mainly to keep the place going during my husband's absence on work with the National Fire Service. I have also done a certain amount of writing for propaganda purposes; while before the fall of France brought the threat of invasion to our corner of Eng-land this house was a refuge for three London families under the Government's evacuation scheme. Now that the war is over I hope to get back to my writing again.

EDITOR'S NOTE: The more recent novels by Sheila Kaye-Smith are *Ember Lane*, Harper, 1940; *The Secret Son*, Harper, 1942; and *Tam-bourine, Trumpet and Drum*, Harper, 1943. And her late non-fiction includes *Kitchen Fugue*, Harper, 1945, and (in collaboration with G. B. Stern) *Speaking of Jane Austen*, Harper, 1944. Her auto-biography, *Three Ways Home*, was published by Harper in 1937.

BLANCHE MARY KELLY

LIKE MOST OTHER PEOPLE, I WAS BORN, AND ALTHOUGH IT was a long time ago (1881 to be exact), I heard so much about it that it sometimes seemed as though I could remember the event. I was the oldest of seven children, and we all grew up in an atmosphere of music and books, books becoming in my case a matter of paramount interest, even in childhood.

My mother, having greatly loved the Sacred Heart Convent in Albany which she had attended, filled me with a desire to go there too, so I never had any dread of going to school. And besides, for me school held the fascinating promise of more books, more understanding of the whole wonderful realm of books. I can only say that when I went to Kenwood, where I received all the formal education I have ever received, those expectations were fully realized, and I began to hope that some day I might have a hand in the making of books.

That expectation, too, has been realized. After graduating from Kenwood I spent several years in rather intensive although "free-lance" study, following my own bent and by some sort of intuition learning things that were to stand me in good stead when I eventually came to New York intent upon finding a job. Careers for women were then in their infancy, but I seemed to have found mine when I became a member of the editorial staff of the *Catholic Encyclopedia*, where I found myself doing things that I would have done any-way, using the things I had hitherto learned and learning new things, including an intensive knowledge of editorial and publishing procedure.

After the completion of the Index volume of the *Encyclopedia* under my direction, I was awarded the degree of Doctor of Letters by the College of Mount Saint Vincent, on the basis of that work and various writings that had been published over a period of years. I was not previously known personally to the administration of the College, but a few years after that I was asked to join the faculty in order to introduce into the curriculum a course in journalistic and critical writing.

This has turned out to be my real career—teaching; for I have been here nearly twenty-five years. I have taught at one time or other most of the English courses. I am now Chairman of the Department, and find my work not only interesting but thrilling. I am now an institution.

Before I came to the Mount I had published a small volume of poems, *The Valley of Vision,* containing only a few of those I have written, although I have written fewer than I might if my critical sense had not long since told me I would never be a major poet, and a life of Our Lady, *Mary the Mother,* one of a series of devotional lives projected by the Encyclopedia Press. Since then I have published *The Well of English,* an interpretation of English literature from the Catholic standpoint, and *The Sudden Rose,* a study of the unity of art.

In addition to my teaching, I now contribute a weekly critical article under the general title "Adventures Among Books," which is sponsored by the Cardinal Hayes Literature Committee, in New York, and syndicated to the Catholic press by the National Catholic Welfare Council News Service, in Washington, D. C.

EDITOR'S NOTE: Dr. Kelly's published books include: *The Valley of Vision,* Encyclopedia Press, 1916; *Mary the Mother,* id., 1919; *The Well of English,* Harper, 1936; *The Sudden Rose,* Sheed, 1939; *The Eternal Purpose,* Harper, 1945; and several pamphlets.

RAYMOND E. F. LARRSON

AT A RETROSPECTIVE GLANCE, A FACT LESS SIGNIFICANT TO me by all the facts subsequent to it for over thirty years than one fact by which it becomes of increased significance, both in the present and pertinent to the past, and for the future, I was born in Wisconsin, in a small, somewhat illustrious town, Green Bay, in 1901. The town itself historians do not often forget, at least for one extraordinary fact, that it is on land discovered by an agent from Quebec, from which he had been sent west to discover a northwest passage to the Orient: indeed, in spite of inconclusive evidence, many more popular historians relate that when Jean Nicolet, the agent, set foot on Wisconsin soil, arrayed in the robe of a mandarin, firing two pistols, he indeed believed the land China, the savages whom he frightened by his pistols veritably Chinese. But the history of the town is not mine, the facts concerning it none concerning me; the fact of my birth there insignificant of itself, and insignificant to me

until a far later fact almost all the facts concerned with my
birth and my subsequent days there:—that later fact that,
—apart from the place of my birth, apart from almost all
association with it, in forgetfulness of it, in consummation
of my being, a being that put apart from itself associations,
even dear associates,—in 1932, I was more significantly
born, entering the Church. The years since then are those
of my youth: what went before now has to me a personal
and transcendant significance, one it had not. My youth
since by becoming a Catholic has become my age, my age
an infancy and youth, my youth an age from which I wholly
sprang, departing it,—I think, with amusement, somewhat
as Zeus gave Athene birth.

The essential facts of my life, both before my Conversion
and since, seem to me, at times, spare, at others, of a com-
plexity and significance I am astonished by, a significance of
strangeness, almost of myth, yet they are not to be reduced
to summary, requiring more examination and detailed analysis and exposition than such brief note as this. But let
this suffice:

As a prelude to becoming a Catholic,—though prelude to
such a transformation of my days and being I never could
have anticipated that it was, or that it could be,—I went,
one day in 1926, to a pier in Brooklyn to see two friends
off on a pleasure cruize to the West Indies. Departing them,
having left at her address in Fifth Avenue a companion, I
set out afoot, abandoning my taxi, and went on up the
Avenue, intending to find a friend, Jane Heap, whom I had
promised, vaguely, to visit at *The Little Review,* of which
she was one of the editors. When I had found her, and was
about to depart her, in bidding me good-bye she spoke as
one bidding me adieu for a long time, and when I exclaimed
at her tone I was astonished to discover that she that night
sailed for France, a fact I had forgotten. I lamented I was
not departing with her. Immediately, she gave me chal-

lenge: that I *do*. But though she made it sound a ridiculously easy thing to do, to depart for France in a few hours' time, it was obvious to me I could not, piqued as I was: was I not almost penniless? But such an argument satisfied not Jane Heap. *Of course*, if I really wanted to, she maintained firmly I doubtless could, for surely (it appeared clearly enough to her) there were of my friends ones who, so to speak, were in wait for chance to afford me exactly such departure! But though I was unconvinced, roused however delighted by what seemed her fantasy, I left her, and hurriedly, when she had exacted of me agreement I sail with her that night provided I could. Strangely enough, by means of another friend as intermediary, I arrived that night at the Cunard pier prepared to sail—prevented from sailing only by the fact the gangplank had been taken up just before I arrived at the boatside.—To Jane on board, I pledged myself to follow her on the next boat.

And so I did.

In France, vicissitude, fantasy, drama might be said to have taken some interest in my life: it became at once fantastic in detail, gay, and, more than ever, one taught by sorrow its lesson, retrospectively. For a time, I lived in some luxury, sufficient to be unimpressed by the Ritz: for other times, the expenditure of a *franc* was a matter of moment; at others, the arrival of a cheque from *The Dial*, to which in those days I most frequently sold poems, was occasion for extravagance of gesture, and wine in the cup without dregs, wherein had been *cafe noir* and unsweetened sorrows.

During those days, I wrote, but wrote little: poems for *The Dial*, others for *Transition, The London Mercury;* a single published story, one for *Transition*. Of Paris, I saw much, even well-nigh all; of Europe, little. I went to stay with a friend in London, found there a city without discontent, a city of excellence of conversation it is good even to remember occurred—with a strangely unassorted list of people: Wyndham Lewis, Leonard Woolf, T. S. Eliot, Alfred Hitchcock, a young and experimental director then; Frederick Ashton, in the first lights of extraordinary press-notices; Osbert Sitwell, Viola Garvin, Alfred Dobson. Returned to Paris, I got to know a revulsion of feeling against it and Montparnasse bars, a dissatisfaction difficult even then to define, impossible of dissipation, one I recall once resulted in my saying to miscellaneous friends around a table at the *Dome* I should not be amazed if I became, one day, impalpably and uncertainly afar, a Catholic. But not until ten years later, and return to America by force of circumstance, did I.

The force of circumstance was of a complex nature: I started with a friend to London, to remain, perhaps forever. I got no farther than across the channel: whence, I was forced to return. My *visa* had expired, and I could not enter England again. Indeed, I was arrested, returned to France. In France, that night, I was arrested again: my *visa* for residence in France, too, had expired. Thereupon, I remained for a fortnight or so in Dieppe, then, because money was too long in reaching me from America, and I was forced to depart, I went to Bruxelles. But before I departed Dieppe, I had begun to write with greater ease, with greater meaning to me than ever before.

In Bruxelles, in Bruges later, the ease of my writing continued: fragments, movements in a whole, a poem of such length as I could not set, written as they occurred, uncollected, unarranged in sequence. Indeed, not until I departed on ship from Antwerp, and had been for some days at sea, did I begin, in conscience, to assemble the poems I had written. Their sequence achieved a coherence of design that pleased me. When I landed in New York, *O City, Cities!* was finished. Soon after, it was accepted, presently pub-

lished. So my first book came to be.—For years after, there
was not another.

In 1932, accompanied by the beginnings of mystical wisdom, sufferings as I had not before known, (sufferings
which seem now mildness indeed, compared to what followed), I entered the Church. Thus began my life: what
went before seems, now and again, almost a stage of pre-
natal being.

The subsequent events are, plainly put, as these notes demand, not exceptional. Yet, when I regard what has be-
fallen in so few years, I am astonished at the nature and
significance of experience I cannot even indicate here, briefly, as I must write. Suffice it I entered the Church, I returned to Wisconsin, I went to California because I could
not scrupulously say a friend nay and accompany him not.
There, I wrote, there I was assigned to the Writers' Project,
worked for a time under the ludicrous title of Editor of Culture, wrote criticism of Paintings for Lincoln Steffens'
Pacific Weekly. When I departed California, it was to edit
a weekly newspaper in a small Florida resort, Clearwater.
Thereafter, I spent months in Georgia, in Jacksonville, and
in Georgia again, on a cousin's plantation. When I had left
Georgia and the turpentine pines behind, and returned to
New York, I had with me a second book of poems. But it
was not published at once: one publisher, then another,
praised it, could not sell it. Presently, Coward-McCann had
published it. It was *Weep and Prepare*.

One day I found in a place I remember no more a prayer
of Saint Gertrude's. I made a copy of it, and when I came
upon others, copies of them. In such fashion, I began a collection of the prayers of the Saints for my own delight.—
But the collection grew to such extant, as time elapsed, that
it seemed expedient to do else with it than keep it for my
delight. I set to work to enlarge it, and when I had spent
weeks and months at research, *Saints at Prayer* was ready

for the press,—so voluminously the publishers took much
from it before it appeared in print. The research incidental
to its preparation was an almost constant discovery of
riches : I have not yet come to their end. Two books of tales
followed, tales and anecdotes and biographies the Saints
wrote, books which will to be published in due course.

What writing else I have done remains, by force of circumstance, in various stages of completion. Of it, and of
work I now accomplish, there will be several books. But
when they will be, I am not certain. Presently, presently—
Though the circumstances of the time is not one of re-
joicing, one *does* rejoice. One rejoices and awaits another
time, reading as though it were tomorrow's newspaper *The
Apocalypse* of Saint John. One rejoices and regards the
despairing city, the toppling cities : behold, there seems almost not one habitable, not one one wishes always to be.
One has seen too plainly another, the City of Promise. At
the toppling of walls one grieves not : the toppling seems the
building walls more firmly of another.—The dusts blind not
one's eyes. The litter of the times one can disengage even
one's ears from hearing increasing afar. Time seems to
have time for their falling.—One awaits the time when they
shall have fallen, and *The City of Promise* shall be plain.—
So much only now for these days.

These few facts are not even a complete graph. They say
little, very little. The life is in else than facts concerning it.
Beholding itself plainly, it is to itself even then a mystery.
That mystery loses not luster in the dusts afar. Rather do
the dusts increase that mystery in joy.

Even in these days, it is a fact greater than any other,
any other than that one is of Christ. One *is*.

EDITOR'S NOTE: Mr. Larsson's published books include *O City, Cities*,
Harcourt, 1929; *Wherefore Peace*, 1932, and *A Sheaf*, 1933, both
"poems in pamphlet," issued by Modern Editions; *Weep and Prepare*,

Coward-McCann, 1940; and *Saints at Prayer,* Coward-McCann, 1942. In 1937 he collaborated with August Derleth in editing the anthology *Poetry Out of Wisconsin.*   Mr. Larsson has in preparation a book of poems to be entitled *Sonatinos,* and a collection of tales by the saints which will be published as *Wreath of Wonders.*

REVEREND CUTHBERT
CHARLES LATTEY, S.J.

I HAVE BEEN INVITED TO CONTRIBUTE AN AUTOBIOGRAPHICAL chapter to *The Book of Catholic Authors,* and in spite of a preliminary shudder, I have had but little hesitation in accepting the invitation. I have found the United States so generous in appreciation of my work that I should be sorry to seem in any way churlish in return. This is all the more the case by reason of the tremendous development of biblical studies in the States, in which loyalty to the clear lead of the Holy See has clearly played no small part. The result has brought me much consolation, and it is an additional inducement for me to write that the invitation to do so must find its explanation to some extent in the growing interest in matters biblical, which I should desire to do all I can to encourage. I am happy to have had some relations with the scholars and their work in the States, as witnessed, for example, by some contributions to that excellent periodical, *The Catholic Biblical Quarterly.* I also realize that this great advance across the Atlantic must have, and to some extent has already had, considerable repercussions over here. To a large extent it is true to say that for the average Englishman religion means the Bible, and anything that can be done in the way of explaining and defending it in English tends to save what Christianity is left in the country, and to check the drift into nothing at all. For the sake of Catholics also, the work is important, as helping them to understand and appreciate the word of God, both for their own profit and for that of others, whether within or without the fold.

I have not thought it out of place to dilate a little upon this subject at the outset of my paper, because it gives the key to my own labours, such as they have been, and to even my own spiritual advance. For within the course of life set me by Holy Mother the Church and (within that again) by my own religious order, I have (I think) found most help in the spiritual life from the writings of St. Paul, who helps us so much to understand all that Christ should mean to us, and develops for Christians already well instructed what is to be found in all essentials in the four gospels, and especially in the writings of St. John. I should wish to add that I have found nothing but encouragement in my life from the Holy See and from my Order. In regard of the principles involved, it may be enough to point to the *Providentissimus Deus*, the great biblical encyclical of Pope Leo XIII, which is a kind of *Magna Carta* of biblical studies, and has been followed up by other papal encyclicals pressing its instructions home. In practice (to mention only this) two Cardinals Secretary of State had written to commend and encourage the *Westminster Version of the Sacred Scriptures*: Cardinal Merry del Val at its inception, and Cardinal Maglione at the completion of the large edition of the New Testament. The superiors of the Order in their turn have given me ample time and opportunity to pursue

these studies, and particularly on their own initiative sent
me on a tour to Palestine and other places of biblical interest which has proved invaluable.

I profess myself a Londoner and a Victorian by birth and
conviction. I was born on 12 May, 1877, in the Royal
Borough of Kensington: royal by reason of Kensington
Palace, which (I believe) is no longer used by royalty. In
those days Kensington was the most Catholic part of London, and perhaps still is; E. V. Lucas in one of his books
imagines a lady of the maiden aunt type giving an amusing
warning of the danger of allowing a Protestant young lady
to live there. We were indeed a large pack of children, re-
lated or acquainted, and all Catholics; three sisters of the
Cumming clan, all married, represented for my own circle
the centre and nucleus of the group. My father was also of
Scottish origin, though his family had passed two or three
generations in Ireland, without picking up the faith; he was
a London doctor with a good practice, and I owe much to
him, though he died before I reached my teens. He was a
good man, and I trust the prayers of a lifetime have helped
him to the vision of God; I remember Bishop Ward, the
brother of Wilfrid, strongly agreeing that the Lord can
foresee our prayers and hear them beforehand, and that the
Church acts on this belief in several places in her Masses for
the dead. The faith came to me from my mother's side, going back to an Italian great-grandfather. When her parents
were married, it was still tolerated that the boys should follow the father's religion and the girls the mother's, so that
her brother was by rights (so to speak) a Presbyterian;
but by the time she married herself, all the children (thank
God) had to be Catholics. A mixed marriage, I venture to
think, is a very difficult affair when the mother is a Catholic
from what it is when she is a non-Catholic; two of my own
cousins, daughters of my mother's sister and of a Protestant, are nuns, and have spent most of their religious life as

superiors, the one among the Dominican tertiaries, the other among the sisters of Nazareth.

I was the youngest of five, with four years separating me from the next youngest; and dearly as my mother and I loved one another, my parents had all the older children to cope with, so that in my earliest years I was left largely with a dear old French nurse from Normandy, who had been long in the family and was a devout Catholic. Hence I came to speak French practically at the same time as English; French was the language upstairs, and English downstairs. This has been very valuable to me in every way, for from the point of view of religion there has seemed to me a kind of perpetual Franco-Prussian war going on, with the best books of Catholic defense and exposition in French, and the most dangerous attacks in German. After my entry into the Society, I found the houses of our exiled French fathers a great source of profit. Upon the spiritual side I found much help from a stay of a few months in the novitiate of our Paris province, then at Canterbury; and the joint theologate of our Paris and Lyons Provinces at Ore Place, Hastings, contained some very competent professors of European reputation, such as my dear friend Père Condamin, an expert in Hebrew and the Old Testament. The French have a strong tradition of solid sanctity from which we have much to learn, and indeed the Church in England, when all is put together, owes an immense debt to French Catholicism, in which debt I gladly acknowledge my own personal share. To say this is not, of course, to question a no less enormous debt to Catholic Ireland.

To have been at school at Beaumont College, within view of Windsor Castle, was naturally to conceive a Victorian prejudice at an early stage. The property was at first used as the novitiate of the English province of the Jesuits, moved thither from Stonyhurst in 1856; but in 1861 the novitiate was moved to Manresa House, Roehampton, near

London, and Beaumont became a school, retaining the dedication to St. Stanislaus. Queen Victoria was gracious to it
almost from the first; for the most part she was not un-
friendly to those who were frankly Catholics, but disliked
the "Puseyites," as they were then often called (the modern
"Anglo-Catholics"), regarding them as enemies within the
camp. The rector was never presented at court, so that the
Queen never entered our grounds, but thrice she drove to
the open space before the college gates to receive loyal addresses and bouquets, once while I was at school there, once
before, and once afterwards. She always had a gracious
smile, too, for the Beaumont boys if she met a group of
them in Windsor Forest, which is just across the road from
the school grounds.

The zenith of my school career (if not indeed of my
career as a whole!) seems to me to have been the first year
of the preparatory school to Beaumont upon the hills behind
it, the finest preparatory school, as I think it may still claim
to be, of any in the country, designed with the utmost care
down to the last inkpot by Bentley, who won thereby the
contract for Westminster Cathedral. The chapel, with its
oak stalls, is more especially a thing of beauty. Cardinal
Vaughan invited competition for the cathedral, but Bentley
thought it beneath his dignity to compete; whereupon the
Cardinal, who had his eye upon him the whole time, invited
him to indicate some specimen of his work, and St. John's
Preparatory School did the rest. Top boy in the school, captain of cricket and football, in charge of some electric lights
and of discipline in a gallery, and so forth,—I don't think
that I have ever succeeded in feeling so important as I did
then, and I still make a kind of surreptitious claim to have
been a founder of the school.

But there is more in my Victorian convictions than that.
What I remember is a feeling of tremendous security, which
has almost completely departed. In our sea-girt isle, with

a strong fleet and a prosperous trade, we had singularly
little to fear. The country was still predominantly Christian, and so was Europe in general, and no one dreamed of
such aggression—and such dire weapons of aggression—as
we know today. The condition of the working classes certainly left much to be desired, but the country was too rich
and too Christian to let their condition become quite desperate, and the dawn of better things was already breaking.
It was a question whether socialist or communist agitation,
with discontent almost for its avowed object, has made
them happier. Adult suffrage has now arrived; but democracy, such as it is, seldom shines in matters of foreign
policy, which under more skillful and stable guidance might
well have avoided these appalling wars. However, I must
not plunge into politics.

Let me conclude with a tribute to Oxford, some spires of
which can just be seen from the roof of this college, situated
as it is upon the outskirts of the Cotswolds. To that, too, I
am conscious of a great debt, chiefly in the way of intellectual training, and of help in later studies, but also in a
more general way, comprising also much in the way of
personal relations. The debt embraces some great Oxford
names, such as Pelham, Bywater, Sanday; but most of all
Dr. H. J. White, formerly Dean of Christ Church (*i.e.* head
of the college, Cardinal Wolsey's foundation), whose great
work on the Vulgate was a common interest that led to a
friendship which is a cherished memory. The Society of
Jesus has met with much kindness at Oxford, one example
of which concerned me. When Father Clarke, the founder
of Campion Hall, died suddenly, there was no Jesuit father
qualified by four years of graduate residence to carry on
the hall; but the then Vice-Chancellor, Dr. Fowler, President of Corpus Christi College, took it upon himself to ap-
point Father O'Fallon Pope, S.J., an American by origin,
temporary master of the hall, and to matriculate myself and

three others.   The question was raised whether we were not acting *ultra vires;* no mischief was intended, but it was thought well to arrange, as theologians would say, a *sanatio in radice.*   Father Charles Plater and another of the four, alas, are dead; but I myself and another father, I strongly suspect, are the only living persons to have been matriculated as members of the University of Oxford by special statute.

EDITOR'S NOTE: With Father Joseph Keating, S.J., Father Lattey edited the *Westminster Version of the Sacred Scriptures.*   His other publications include *Back to Christ,* Paulist Press, 1919; *First Notions of Holy Writ,* Longmans, 1923; *Paul,* Bruce, 1939; *Readings in First Corinthians,* Herder, 1928; *Thy Love and Thy Grace,* Herder, 1924; and *Back to the Bible,* Kenedy, 1945.   He organized the Summer School of Catholic Studies, at Cambridge, and edited a number of its annual collections of studies.

ARNOLD LUNN

I WAS BORN ON APRIL EIGHTEENTH, 1888, IN INDIA; FOR MY
father, the late Sir Henry Lunn, was at that time a medical
missionary. My mother is Irish. I was educated at Harrow and Oxford, where I edited the *Isis*, the undergraduate
paper. In 1909 I had a severe mountaineering accident,
with the result that I was not accepted for military service
in the first European war.

In 1913 I married Mabel Northcote, whose brother, the
Earl of Iddlesleigh is a convert to the Church. I have three
children, of whom the eldest, Peter, served as a gunner
throughout the siege of Malta, and the second was one of
the lucky ones who returned from Dunkirk. Peter followed
me into the Church, as did my daughter.

Shortly after leaving Oxford I wrote *Harrovians*, which
was based on a careful diary which I kept at school, and
which was the first realistic school story. In that remote
age, the English Public Schools were still a secret subject,

and the book, which became a best seller, got me into a good deal of trouble.

After the first World War I became involved in the organization of British ski-ing. I invented the "Slalom," one of the most popular forms of competitive ski-ing.

Meanwhile I had begun to study the Church. In 1924 I wrote *Roman Converts*, an attempt to solve a problem which had puzzled me. I could not understand how men of outstanding intelligence could possible accept the Roman claims.

In 1933 I was received into the Church by the Rev. (now Rt. Rev. Msgr.) Ronald A. Knox, with whom I had previously exchanged controversial letters which were published under the title of *Difficulties*. The book is now quite unobtainable. The story of my conversion I told in *Now I See*, which has been translated into German and Italian.

It is, perhaps, a little unusual for the same author to have books on theology and sport translated into foreign languages. My contributions to Apologetics have been translated into German, Italian and Spanish, and my writings about mountaineering and ski-ing into German, French, Italian, Spanish, Swedish, and Japanese.

From 1936 to 1938 I was assistant professor of Apologetics at the University of Notre Dame, where I was extremely happy.

Among the best things of my life have been the friendships which I owe to my contacts with American Catholics and American skiers.

EDITOR'S NOTE: Mr. Lunn's more recent books include: *Whither Europe*, Sheed, 1940; *Come What May: an Autobiography*, Little, 1941; *And the Floods Came*, Eyre, 1942; *The Good Gorilla*, Hollis, 1944; *The Third Day*, Newman, 1945.

REVEREND DAVID P. McASTOCKER, S.J.

A LATIN WRITER ONCE OBSERVED THAT AUTOBIOGRAPHIES could readily be reduced to three facts: the person's birth, life, and death.

Of the last, there is no obituary to chronicle as yet, although there is a witticism that some people are actually dead years before their burial in mother earth.

About my birth, I had, naturally, no personal knowledge of this blessed event. It occurred on August fifth, 1884, in the royal city of Guelph, Ontario. My mother, Bridget Heffernan, was the youngest member of her family and the only one actually born in Canada. There is an ancient phrase which tells us that "Strength comes from the North." A still more ancient delineation of a valiant woman is in the Book of Proverbs. My mother (God rest her noble soul!) fitted Holy Scripture's description perfectly. She accomplished what today would be considered an impossibili-

ty. She decently reared eight children on the kingly income
of fifty dollars a month.

My father was of Irish lineage too. He hailed from
County Antrim and, according to the testimony of my
younger brother (also a Jesuit priest), our relatives have
lived from generation to generation in a sequestered village
outside Belfast. To speak of me as of "Scotch-Irish origin,"
as the Bruce boys do, makes my Jesuit brother fighting mad.

Now appears the family skelton.

Some twenty-odd years ago a dear friend visited Scotland.
He discovered a genuine McAstocker clan. And while he
did not bluntly tell me they were horse thieves, he did assert that they were horse traders. He went further, re-
marking that, instead of speaking there of a Shetland pony,
they talk of a "McAstocker."

I readily perceive objections in the words, Scotch-Irish.
These nations have not different racial roots. They both
possess the same Celtic strain. In this instance animosity
springs from history. It seems that a man by the name of
Oliver Cromwell settled groups of Scottish Presbyterians
in northern Ireland for the avowed purpose of weening
Catholics from their Church. The plan did not succeed.
Nor do I believe that any ancestors of mine were concerned
with it. There is a monument in Randalltown to a brave
young McAstocker who was killed while fighting the Black-
and-Tans before Ireland won her independence.

I incline to agree, therefore, with the publishers about my
Scotch-Irish origin. To begin, one of the few vivid impressions of childhood occurred when I first saw a colored lad
trotting a race horse back and forth in front of the store
for my father to admire. Though I have witnessed few, a
horse race has always thrilled me to the very heart. Moreover, I am rather partial to Publicans, horse thieves, and
sinners in general.

Last, but not least, is the fact that a Celt is one who dwells in the open, one who has no desire to be fenced in.

While Divine Providence has so ordained that over thirty years of my life have been spent for the greater part indoors, it appears to me that a semi-invalid gets closer to the workings of nature than one in vigorous health. The writings of Robert Louis Stevenson seem to prove this assertion, and I can personally affirm that disabled men and women in various sanatoria and rest homes have a more intimate knowledge of the little common subterfuges used by little common wild animals to avoid capture than the ordinary healthy person has.

However, let us be frank—brutally frank—in speaking about illness, especially when it is protracted long beyond the usual period. From a natural viewpoint there is no idealism or romanticism in such an existence. Quite the contrary. It spells monotonous days filled with lassitude of body and, at times, depression of spirit. It means wakeful, feverish nights when one wonders if dawn will ever appear. Worst of all, a chronic invalid usually becomes superstitious about his ailment. He considers himself as separated from the rest of normal individuals—a pariah to be shunned lest he infect healthy people. A sense of injustice and futility frequently overpowers him at this point because the very precautions he takes to combat contagion make friends and visitors more and more apprehensive.

Notwithstanding such phobias, a chronic invalid has plenty of time to reason things out for himself. He probably has little or no religious background and, in the first months of his illness especially, he is in a vindictive frame of mind. Why, he asks himself, as I treated so unfairly? Why am I put indefinitely on the sidelines?

But there are many leisure hours in sanatoria, and reason conquers at last. Like the Good Thief beside His Master on Calvary, the invalid realizes that his own mistakes and sins have brought him to this sorry plight. He now experiences a new orientation. His face is toward the East, toward light and gladness. Will he ascend higher? Will he accept God and His Divine Commandments? Some do; some do not.

It is, then, the supernatural atmosphere which gives to unremitting crosses and trials both joy and stability. The elevator of life goes up and down but few recall that it is while down that the elevator takes new beings aboard and aids them in their journey upward. The selfsame lesson is inculcated by nature. Downward the rain falls and, as a consequence, upward the grain grows. Downward the Son came, down to the depths. He was an outcast, a leper, and a pariah, in order that we who are, in a restricted sense, outcasts, lepers and pariahs, may feel that we are very dear to Him and have an added reason for trusting in His infinite mercy.

About my writings, there is little to recount. In the first volume I ever wrote under a nom de plume there is an idea expressed which I have earnestly tried to follow. Longfellow's "Excelsior" expresses it in a word. Here is the paragraph:

"I think it rather amuses him to be made a fuss over: but to be canonized—that is different. For in proportion as he is worthy he naturally feels far otherwise. And the sense of so vast a discrepancy between what he considers his havings and his deservings, produces a strangely saddening effect; yet ends by making him determined to shorten the distance between what he is and what he thinks he ought to be. This is the finest trait in his character. One may expect great things of a person not too well contented with himself."

This spoke my first hero. Nor have I knowingly deviated from this standard of always striving to go a step beyond that last effort. Catholic prose and poetry will continue to progress in proportion as we turn our sights unceasingly on higher, fairer literary horizons. There is one prominent secular weekly that increases the offering fifty dollars or more when an author's second manuscript is accepted. This method is a concrete stimulant to the very principle I have enunciated.

The American Catholic literary scene has been greatly enriched in recent years by promising young poets. Many of these are priests and nuns who, besides a hard day's work in classroom or laboratory, court the fickle muse when regular assignments have been completed. In former years such a way of acting was not considered a prudent course to follow. Students whose names frequently appeared in print could be given an unusually difficult examination. In those days I suppose it could honestly be stated that I was not exactly prudent. At all events—during class hour, mind you!—I noticed for the first time a red light in a building across the yard. It was the temporary chapel for an overflow of students billetted in makeshift quarters. Forgotten entirely were the professor's words. I was in another world entirely and, in a few minutes, I had written

MY FRIEND ACROSS THE WAY

From my little study window
    I can see a lamp's faint ray.
'Tis the ever-faithful Watcher
    Of my Friend across the way.
Through the day I oft look over
"All for Thee" is what I say,
And I fancy it's a comfort
To my Friend across the way.

When the sky is bright and cloudless
    And my heart is also gay,
In my joys I'll not forget You,
    Comrade mine, across the way.

> If the day be dark and dreary,
>   Drifting 'round me mists of gray,
> Then I whisper "Don't desert me,
>   Dearest Lord, across the way."
>
> Let the years be hard and toilsome,
>   Still my life is one bright May,
> For my burdens all are carried
>   By my Friend across the way.
> When I leave my study window
> At the close of Life's short day
> Through the gates of death I'll take Him,
> Take my Friend across the way.

When these lines were submitted to the editor of a popular Catholic monthly, he replied: "If you have a carload like this, please send them to me."

Years later, when dining with the late Frank Spearman who wrote so many fine Western novels, I said to him and his beloved wife: "Frank, I would give anything to have been the author of *Whispering Smith.*"

Graciously Frank Spearman replied: "And I would give anything to have written 'My Friend Across the Way' ".

The future of Catholic literature in America is neither bright nor gloomy. Despite complaints from some quarters, it is my humble opinion that Catholics read more proportionately than any other group. Of course, this reading habit should be incessantly stressed lest we lose the ground that we have gained.

Some twenty years ago three priests turned the tide of American public opinion against the anti-clericals of Mexico. Bishop Kelley, formerly editor of *Extension,* was one. The second was Father Gillis, the Paulist, editor of *The Catholic World.* The third came to me in California a broken man. Because of illness he had been relieved as

editor of *America*. Said this Father Tierney to me one
day: "To win the battle in America, the Church needs three
dailies. Let us have one in New York, one in Chicago, and
a third in San Francisco or Los Angeles."

Let us not say such things are impossible. *The Christian
Science Monitor* puts us to shame in this respect.

EDITOR'S NOTE: Father McAstocker, who was ordained by Cardinal
Gibbons in 1913, later founded and served as first rector of Bellarmine
College, in Tacoma. His published books include *The Carpenter*,
Bruce, 1934; *The Consoler*, Bruce, 1938; *Flash Lights*, Bruce, 1929;
Himself, Bruce, 1933; *Herself*, Bruce, 1934; *My Ain Laddies*, Strat-
ford, 1922; *The Little Virtues*, Bruce, 1940; *Speaking of Angels*,
Bruce, 1946.

SISTER MARIELLA,
O.S.B.

THE ST. CROIX RIVER, ITS WILD WOODED CLIFFS ON THE WIS-
consin side and its creeknetted shores on the Minnesota side
—these constituted a priceless playground incidentally purchased for his children when Joseph Gable moved his family
to Marine-on-St. Croix, Minnesota, in 1901. In the heart of
the small, picturesque village, then called Marine Mills, Mr.
Gable bought a four-story flour and feed mill, a ten room
house, and fourteen acres of land. His estate included two
trout ponds, a noisy trout stream that tumbled in waterfalls
through a ravine back of the home, and sloping terrain,
which Mr. Gable soon covered with orchards, berry patches,
truck gardens and flower beds. It is a tribute to his abili-
ties, integrity, and lovable character that he, a Catholic of
German descent, was elected for many years to the offices of
mayor and president of the school board by the town folk,
who were predominantly Swedish Lutheran, and who in all
other matters maintained a closed circle.

The Gables brought two children to Marine, Joseph four, and Mary, who was born at St. Croix Falls, Wisconsin, December 15, 1899. Three years later, John was born, and this boy became the closest companion and playmate of his older sister. Together they swam in the river, built dams across creeks, waded in the icy water, and spent the winters skating, skiing, sliding. But more important than these, they loved exploring the inexhaustibly exciting countryside. There might be a newly-discovered patch of dog-tooth violets on the Wisconsin cliffs, a luna moth pursued a whole summer afternoon along the river banks, partridge berries under pine needles, a new cave behind tumbled rocks. Soon they discovered the need of names for all they saw, and they struggled with bird, flower, and butterfly guides, taking great pride in establishing the identity of all they saw. They converted a room in their home into a "museum," which, besides containing carefully labeled birds' eggs, moths, and nests, simply crawled with vermin. The inevitable day of housecleaning brought tears and heartbreak.

With so many vigorous interests out of doors, Mary did not read many books, but she brought more than ordinary emotional response to those that she did read. *Tom Sawyer* had to be taken in very small sections, because her fear for Tom's fate, when he was lost in the cave, was so great that she could not breathe without pain. Sometimes a book could not be relinquished—even under pressure. It was her mother's opinion, however, that a girl could not set a table satisfactorily by carrying the silverware in the left hand while she held a book in the right, and wept copiously.

When Mary was eleven, she wrote her first poem in order to quell her mother's indecision in choosing a suitable reading for John, who was to perform in a program in the town hall. The poem began,

> I am a big white snow-man
> Just come from the cold North pole—

In spite of the flatness of its doggerel, it did give an opportunity for effective costuming and dramatization. The family was satisfied; the town folk liked it.

By the time Mary was fifteen she had become a good cook, a seamstress capable of making her own dresses, a very poor pianist after seven years of unwilling practice, and had finished the ninth grade in the local public school. Then she was sent to St. Benedict's Academy, St. Joseph, Minnesota. Until she went to St. Benedict's she had been able to go to Mass only rarely by making inconvenient trips to neighboring cities—Stillwater or St. Paul. The liturgy of daily Mass at the academy, the spirit of the Sisters of St. Benedict, and friendships with girls of her own tastes and faith, these opened a new world for her.

A month after her graduation from the academy in her seventeenth year she entered the novitiate of the Convent of St. Benedict, at St. Joseph, and took the name Sister Mariella, O.S.B.

To one so young, so high-spirited, and so accustomed to the free run of woods, hills, and streams, the discipline of the novitiate was difficult. At the end of her canonical year she made triennial vows and was assigned to Bismarck, North Dakota, to assist in opening St. Mary's High School under most rugged pioneer conditions. She herself taught all the subjects in first and second year high school, including two years of Latin and of English, algebra, geometry, ancient and medieval history, typewriting and shorthand. In 1920 she pronounced perpetual vows.

After a year at Melrose, Minnesota, she remained at the College of St. Benedict, assisting with teaching and prefecting in the academy while she earned her degree of Bachelor of Arts, which she received in 1925.

In spite of hard work and full days, she found time to write poetry, some of which she sent to *America*. Father

Francis Talbot, S.J., wrote to her, "One of the greatest joys of an editor's life is that of making a new discovery, especially if the discovery be a poet before unknown to him. I feel I have discovered you as a real, authentic poet."

Commonweal, America, and *Spirit* published her poems, which were later collected in the volume, *Blind Man's Stick.* Her poem "To a Carrara Madonna" was set to music by Charles Repper in arrangements for both solo and choral presentation.

In 1928, Sister Mariella took her Master of Arts degree at the University of Minnesota and spent the following year in New York City studying at Columbia University. It was decided, however, that she should finish her graduate work at Cornell University where she could use the great Fiske collection of Dante books and study the *Divine Comedy* under Lane Cooper. She was elected to Phi Beta Kappa, and received her Ph.D. in 1934.

Upon her return to the College of St. Benedict, she was appointed chairman of the department of English, a position which she has held ever since. She considers one of the most important services of the English department a course in *The Divine Comedy* in translation, which is offered annually unguarded by forbidding prerequisites, thus enabling every student in the college to become acquainted with the greatest Catholic poet. Her essay "Guidance for Student Poets" demonstrates in what way Dante is, for young writers, the safest and most competent guide. It is Sister Mariella's strong conviction that should a very gifted student appear, who might ultimately become a Catholic writer, the college could render no greater service to her development than to have her sit at Dante's feet—long and lovingly.

She has, for the past twenty years, been moderator of *St. Benedict's Quarterly,* and gives more than ordinary attention to the development of student writers. She believes that the success of her students in the annual *Atlantic Monthly* contest is attributable to what they call their "forty-hours' devotion"—a meticulous revision through draft after draft of their work.

In 1937, Sister Mariella wrote a pageant, "So Let Your Light Shine," which has since that date been presented annually at the College of St. Benedict. The purpose of this pageant is to initiate the freshmen into the life of a Benedictine college by acquainting them with the fourteen centuries of Benedictine tradition and culture. The culminating point in the pageant is the passing of fourteen torches to the freshmen, which they receive from the great Benedictines of the past—Gregory the Great, Augustine of England, Bede, Anselm, and many others. Against a background of living scenery, and accompanied by a choir of a hundred choral readers, the story of the past is told in interpretative dancing.

One of Sister Mariella's special interests is Catholic fiction and its problems. Recognizing fiction as the least mature and effective of the forms developed by the Catholic literary revival in England and America, and knowing also that a great Catholic fiction could exercise a profound influence, she has repeatedly explored some of its problems. She has, moreover, edited two volumes of short stories of special interest to Catholics: *They Are People,* is a collection of stories about nuns, monks and priests, by contemporary writers of the first rank. *Our Father's House* brings together stories which illustrate the Catholic concept of personality, or which are significant for Catholic local color, or for some teaching of the Church. This volume is prefaced by a thorough investigation of the relationship between the idea of personality in the Thomistic sense and the accurate determination of Catholic fiction. Another essay exploring the problems of the Catholic fiction writer has been included by Vincent J. Flynn in *Prose Readings,* a textbook

for college freshmen.   Sister Mariella reviews fiction for
The Commonweal.

Sister Mariella admits that houses are necessary for
shelter in Minnesota.   But she sheds them for the sweet out-
doors as often and as completely as possible.   In winter she
skates or walks down lanes where snow-laden evergreens
are a source of never-ending delight.   In spring, summer,
and fall she takes her work outside, but she is up and away
to all corners of the great convent farm lest she miss some
aspect of teeming life: the orchard bursting into bloom, a
litter of young pigs, pink as rose petals, young ducklings
cavorting in their pool, hot-beds sprouting radishes and
lettuce.   She can smell water a mile away and goes toward
it like a compass needle to its pole.   Books, she feels, are
all right to read and to write, but they are much less good
than the open book of the radiant world, and their only
justification is that, like the butterfly nets she used as a
child, they attempt to catch and imprison forever some of
God's splendor in the flying moments.

EDITOR'S NOTE: Bruce Humphries published Sister Mariella's first collection of poems, *Blind Man's Stick,* in 1938; Sheed & Ward issued
her short story anthologies, *They Are People,* in 1942, and *Our Father's House,* in 1945.   Sister also collaborated in *Prose Readings,*
Scribner, 1942, and *The Press in the World Today,* Marquette University Press, 1941.   She contributes in prose and verse to the leading
literary and professional periodicals.

BRUCE MARSHALL

BRUCE MARSHALL WAS BORN IN EDINBURGH ON JUNE 24, 1899. His father was a stock broker. His mother, who was the disciplinarian of the family, died when he was nine, just two months before he won his first school prize. His father sent him at once to boarding school, at which he was at first unhappy, and from which he ran away twice.

At school the boy's literary tendencies first revealed themselves in the *Junior Journal,* for which he wrote a hair-raising short story. It was not, however, until he went to Saint Andrew's University that Marshall began to visualize himself as a writer, when, as an Anglo-Catholic of eighteen, he wrote short stories with a religious basis.

Converted to Catholicism on January 1, 1918, Marshall went as a cadet to the army, in which he was commissioned as a second lieutenant on June 25, 1918. While in the trenches he wrote his first novel, *A Priest of Mars,* sending home regularly five pages to a friend in England.

Wounded, and taken prisoner by the Germans on November 5, 1918, Marshall subsequently lost his right leg.

Determined to be a writer, he nevertheless decided that it would be a matter of years before he would be able to earn his living with the pen. Accordingly, he finished his university course, and took in addition the diploma of chartered accountant.

In 1924, his first published novel, *This Sorry Scheme,* won a prize award in Britain, and was also published in the United States. Practicing as an accountant in Paris from 1926 to 1940, it was not, however, until 1931, that Marshall first began to make his name with the appearance of *Father Malachy's Miracle.* But even after that there followed a lean period while he sought to find both himself and his public.

In 1928, Marshall married Mary Pearson Clark, a Scots girl whom he met in Paris. They have one daughter, Sheila, aged sixteen, at present with the nuns of the Sacred Heart in Hove.

Forced to leave Paris in June, 1940, Marshall again joined the British Army, beginning again as a Second Lieutenant in the Royal Army Pay Corps, and finishing as a Lieutenant Colonel in the Displaced Persons Division of the British Element of the Allied Commission for Austria.

Once again, as during the first war, Marshall wrote while he soldiered, and it was during this recent period of military service that he began really to make his name as a writer. *The World, the Flesh and Father Smith,* which is his best book so far, was written on Saturday and Sunday afternoons between January and June, 1943, while Marshall was serving under a particularly irascible commanding officer in the Royal Army Pay Corps.

His next book, which is about the adventures of a British army colonel billeted with Austrian nuns in Vienna, is being filmed by Metro-Goldwyn-Mayer. It is entitled *The Red Danube.*

EDITOR'S NOTE: Mr. Marshall air mailed this sketch from Paris in May, 1947. He is scheduled for an American lecture tour during the 1947-1948 season, under the management of W. Colston Leigh, Inc., New York City. Mr. Marshall's twelve or more novels include *This Sorry Scheme*, 1924, Harcourt (awarded the Harrap Prize, 1924); *Father Malachy's Miracle*, 1931, Doubleday; *The World, the Flesh and Father Smith*, 1945, Houghton; *Yellow Tapers for Paris*, 1946, Houghton.

BROTHER DAVID MARTIN, C.S.C.

PEOPLE WHO SAY THERE IS NOTHING IN A NAME HAVE NEVER experienced the difficulties that come to those who, like myself, never seem able to settle on a single name and keep it. I was baptized Edward Sylvester Martin, and being the first-born, I had an importance that never would have come to me had I been one of the later additions to the Martin household. My father's relatives, finding Edward too formal, called me Eddie, a shortening to which my mother was allergic. Henceforth my name was Sylvester Edward, soon shortened to Syl. And while this new cognomen made no hit with its bearer, there was very little he could do about it. Relief came when I started to school, where I was immediately nicknamed Red, a name which bore some small relation to the color of my hair and which was more acceptable to my boyhood companions who were unable to get the name Sylvester out of their systems.

Upon entering Religion, I found that neither Red nor Sylvester were acceptable but was offered David as a substitute. This I grasped with eagerness as one of the first fruits of the hundred-fold that was promised in this new life. At last I could settle for a name that I really liked! But my satisfaction was short-lived, or at least was not long-lived enough, for since that time obedience has dictated that the Brothers resume their original surnames in order to lessen the confusion resulting from the many duplications of names in educational and other records. All this will help to explain why some writing of mine has appeared under the name Brother David, while other writing has the by-line Brother David Martin. When on occasion the legal name is required—but then, let us rather speak of our amendment. Library catalogers who are obliged to clarify the names of much-married women authors have always had my sympathy but those who must do the same for Religious Brothers and Sisters have also my share of commiseration.

I was born in Chicago's West Side on March 8, 1901, with the aforementioned results. My next big adventure was starting to kindergarten, which I attended for two days and then wailed myself home. Later, at five and one-half, I went to a neighboring German Sisters' School, where I said my prayers in German and read reams of German script without understanding a single word of it. When I was eight the family moved to Palos Park, Illinois, about twenty miles from Chicago. There I attended a one-room school that served a countryside as unurban as the setting for a George Eliot novel. It was around this one-room school, which was so close to home that we could leave when the bell rang and still fall into the proper place in the line, that some of my happiest recollections revolve, and some of the most amusing. Since there was but one room, there was of necessity but one teacher. But what teachers they were!

There were two of them during my sojourn there—a Miss
Murphy and later a Miss Files. They not only taught the
required subjects to eight grades of boys and girls but they
also put on plays and other entertainment as well. And if
that was not enough, they started off the day and ended it
with a three-mile walk over rough country roads.

What slightly complicated matters during Miss Murphy's
career with us was an avalanche of about eight Bohemian
children, ranging in ages from six to sixteen, who had recently arrived from Europe and had moved into the neighborhood. (The walking neighborhood of that pre-schoolbus
period had a radius of about four or five miles.) Since the
newcomers could not speak a word of English, it was up to
Miss Murphy to teach it to them. This she did by lining
them all up in front of the class and then telling them to
"hop" to "skip" or to "jump" after she had first performed
these feats herself! Inside of a month they could all hop,
skip and jump with the best of us. Teachers were giants
in those days, even Miss Files, who would have needed help
to tip the scales at ninety pounds.

It was Miss Files (or was it Miss Murphy?) who planted
the first seed of ambition in me for writing, by praising a
composition that I had written as a class duty. I have no
recollection as to the subject of this opus and never saw it
afterward. But whatever it was, the incipient ambition
died aborning, even though the recollection remained. In
fact, all scholarly pursuits bored me soon afterward; bored
me to such an extent that I left school when I was about
sixteen for the beckoning fields of pecuniary employment.
The humdrum life of a stay-at-home wage earner with the
Santa Fe railroad, however, soon paled upon my restless
nature, and before I was eighteen I had taken up my abode
on the mesa lands of New Mexico. But the distant range
of the San Mateo mountains whetted my appetite to see

more of this enchanting world and before a year had passed I was on the borders of Old Mexico, in El Paso, still working for the patient Santa Fe.

By this time the wanderlust really filled my waking hours and before long I had severed my connection with the Santa Fe (doubtless to our mutual relief) and found myself in California in the City of the Angeles. This mecca and culmination-of-things-to-be-hoped-for to thousands of weather-weary and glamour-conscious midwesterners held my youthful interest only long enough for me to get a good square look at the broad Pacific. That mis-named and savage deep can be as temperamental and skittish and unpacific as a thunderous mountain storm appearing in a quiet evening sky. Looking at the ocean and seeing the Unknown from the vantage point of the harbor quelled any doubts that I might have had and recharged the ever-present tingling sensation in my feet. And since what one looks for hard enough is generally found, I soon found myself aboard the oil tanker, "Frank H. Buck," bound for Portland, Oregon.

We had scarcely left the breakwater behind when the "Pacific" ocean showed her true colors and made me heartily wish that I had never left the solid ground of Illinois. But two years later I was still a "sea-faring man" taking a short respite in the "home" port of San Francisco, after visiting a large portion of the Western Hemisphere.

It was while in this California city that I received word that my father was dying at home in Chicago. I hurried back and although I found my patient sitting up in his hospital bed, in two weeks he was dead. This event shocked me into a realization of the emptiness of the world and of the futility of its charms and ambitions, and after orientating myself to this new concept of life, I found myself knock·ng at the doors of the Brothers of the Congregation of the Holy Cross.

The first of these doors was the Brothers' Postulate at Watertown, Wisconsin, where the Superior fried a dish of bacon and eggs for me on my arrival and I met the rest of the Brothers and Postulants after they had returned from a picnic. "Well," said I to myself, "if this is giving up all things, I think that I will be able to manage it."

But life was not all a picnic with bacon and eggs *au Superieur* but I soon became accustomed to it and after seven months of study and enough work to kill insomnia, I left with eighteen others for the Novitiate at Notre Dame, Indiana. Mother met us as we came through Chicago and, not taken in by our holy opinion of ourselves, remarked that we looked like a convention of undertakers.

In the Novitiate we began the real work of becoming Religious. The habit was worn, we had an intensive training in the spiritual life, and on Sundays, rain or shine, went on a picnic of buns and hot dogs. Soon the year was completed and we took temporary (three year) vows, and were sent to Dujarie Hall, Notre Dame, the House of Studies. In this house we again took up books but after less than a year I found that books still bored me. My Superiors then sent me as a Prefect to the Minims, a boarding school maintained at that time at Notre Dame for younger boys. Father Sorin had affectionately called them his Princes, but after I had been with them six months I referred to them as my Princes of Darkness.

After allowing the boys six months of my wisdom, I was sent to the then budding University of Portland as librarian and it was there that I recaptured that love of books, the seed of which had been planted by Miss Files (or was it Miss Murphy?).

My undergraduate college work was completed there and later, a year was spent obtaining a professional library degree at the University of Washington. Upon my return,

I began work on a Master's degree from both the Universities of Oregon and Portland and obtained it from the latter in 1940.

EDITOR'S NOTE: Brother David, who is still librarian at the University of Portland, is the author of *American Catholic Convert Authors*, 1944, Romig, as well as editor of and collaborator in *Catholic Library Practice*, 1947, University of Portland Press. He was a member of the editorial staff of the *Catholic Book List* from 1942 to 1945 and has been editor of the *University of Portland Bookman* since 1941. He is a member of the executive board of the Catholic Library Association.

REVEREND C. C. MARTINDALE, S. J.

ONE MAY WELL FEEL ONESELF LESS AND LESS AT HOME IN A world from which all privacy is vanishing; but if the following lines may be regarded as an expression of gratitude, I shall dislike them less.

I am, then, grateful first for the 'evangelical' element in my home up-bringing, responsible for a sense of the divine presence and power, of sin, of the charm of the gospel narrative, and of the majestic or tender diction of the *Authorized Version*. I was not conscious of specifically Christian dogma, and very soon began to dislike the unreal 'tone,' as it seemed to me, of institutional Anglicanism and the mannerisms of the clergy.

But even before I went to Harrow, the poems of Vergil suggested to me the notion of some universal spiritual empire; and, at school, fragments of Plato and Aristotle hinted at the existence of 'truth' as such, independent of class, epoch, or nationality. But this did not interfere with that phase of pessimist disbelief through which all young men were then expected to pass.

When, by the grace of God and the intercession of Our Lady of Lourdes and Saint Aloysius Gonzaga, I had been received into the Church, I ventured to ask for and was granted admission into the Society of Jesus.

Being ill, I went for most of my novitiate to the south of France. As a boy I had always been made to talk French or German till my dinner, so I felt at home in that *historically* Catholic atmosphere and in an ancient house, drenching my body and soul in the sun and intoxicating beauty of Provence. Two years of scholastic 'philosophy' followed, rigid but invaluable preparation for four of classical literature and philosophy at Oxford. The former should rescue you from sentimentalism, subjectivism, vague thinking or intellectual escapism: the latter humanises; and nothing in the world will ever compensate for our progressive loss of classical culture. At the same time, my sense of history as a continuous flow of living reality awoke, together with a new appreciation of the invasion of the supernatural life of Grace.

This considerable tumult demanded expression, and during these and following years I began to write some clumsy little stories à *thèse* (though when writing I was unconscious of any 'thesis' ...) which ultimately became *In God's Nursery* and *The Waters of Twilight*. God was always 'nursing' the immature, even pagan, soul: spiritual waters ceaselessly made their way through the twilights of humanity.

Both as to background, and in experience of men and women, I was much helped first by becoming ill at Oxford and being sent to Italy where I had not been since childhood: I returned thither afterwards, and to Holland and France, in pursuit of manuscripts of the Latin poet Ausonius, and thus met for the first time Monsignor Ratti,

later Pope Pius XI, and, privately in Rome, the holy Pope
Pius X.

After my ordination in 1911 I was again very ill and was
taken by friends for a long motor-tour through North
Africa and home by Italy, the dear land of Austria, South
Germany and the Rhine.

All years are formative; but these, I suppose, were
specially so. They contained much of which I say nothing.

Before my theology, I had had three years of teaching
and now had two more which brought us into the war of
1914-1918: I was sent to Oxford and Father Plater pitched
me headlong into 'war-work,' which meant looking after a
number of hospitals, air-stations, a couple of German
prisoners' camps, and the giving of fortnightly retreats to
wounded soldiers or 'cadets,' most of them ex-N.C.O's, very
tough—in fact, a high percentage was Australian or New
Zealander and friendship with these has been one of the
most intimately and enduringly precious things in my life.
Indeed, those years, when it was natural to work thirty-six
hours a day, were, in the midst of so much tragedy, almost
intolerably happy: you perceived the terrific potentialities
of the soul, and, you may say, touched as with your fingers
alike humanity and God acting directly upon it. Enough
lessoning for a lifetime of humility and faith not to be
learnt in schoolrooms or the comfortable world!

It was evident that after the war all universities would
be crammed: it seemed necessary to create, to restore, well
beforehand, Catholic organisations to welcome Catholic students. These were very soon federated within this island,
and I was appointed 'president' of this federation. But it
was equally clear that Catholic students (and ex-students)
everywhere should be in contact, to foster the 'Catholic
mind' in a world ever more brutally or sentimentally pagan-
ised. Impossible to describe here the creation and at first
rather agitated development of the 'secretariate' of groups

in various lands now officially known as 'Pax Romana.' (I
thank God that the second great war, far from destroying
such work at home or abroad, has witnessed its astonishing
development. No Catholic of good will dare stand aloof
from any other.) This put me in touch with many persons
and groups in other visit-able lands, especially Austria and
Germany (for whom our Federation made a really vast collection of clothes and money), and Poland and Jugo-Slavia,
so that I can now assess much better the renewed martyrdom of these lands. Also I began to wish for more Catholic
literature intended less for the devout or the specialist expert than for intelligent young men and women of 'university standard.'

But in 1928 I was invited to the International Eucharistic
Congress to be held in Sydney. I thus began to learn how
uniquely lovable and responsive is the race of Seamen.
Many other voyages were to intensify this new knowledge:
could any hour become happier than that of Mass for the
stokers and others, mostly at four A.M. and maybe on deck,
when all without exception had been shriven and all received their Lord? Well, there were radiantly happy months
on land too—in New Zealand and then Australia, which I
tried to sing of in *The Risen Sun*. Unluckily in New Zealand we had a bad motor accident the full effects of which
were not fully diagnosed, odd as it may seem, till long afterwards, in Denmark.

However, in 1930 I was sent to seek the sun in South
Africa, and experienced yet again the incredible kindness of
a new world—and learnt also to esteem and indeed love that
native race to which we owe so serious a service and so
grave a reparation. And Nature itself displayed vast new
treasures of beauty. *African Angelus*, largely out of date
now, yet contains some grateful permanent impressions of
South Africa. This visit made up to me for missing the
Carthage Congress—I was by now on the permanent com-

mittee of such Congresses—but Dublin in its turn made more than compensation.

Then came a cruise to Greece and Dalmatia, followed at once by the Eucharistic Congress in Buenos Aires; across the Argentine by special train and over the Andes and all up the Pacific coast by Pan-American Airways and again from Panama to New Zealand and Australia for the national Congress at Melbourne (recorded in *Athens, Argentine and Australia*) : and the Congress in Manila (enabling me to make a fourth visit to Ceylon), and finally a fourth visit from Rome to Budapest for the last Congress before the world fell to pieces. Between that Congress and the actual outbreak of war I was mostly in hospital: but was thought fit to accept an invitation for ten days' lecturing in Denmark in April, 1939. I arrived on the sixth; the Germans on the ninth; and the ten days became five and a half years.

Evidently this has been the picture of a patchwork quilt, with many of the patches ill-stitched or more or less deliberately omitted. Still, I discern a sort of pattern, which I need not describe here. I see, at any rate, that certain elements have made decisive differences—the first War: retreats to soldiers and miners: the Sea: Australia and New Zealand: my sojourn, all too brief, among the African natives: the Eucharistic Congresses: the appalling tragedy of the last six years: and, more continuously, the study of the lives of the Saints. We live in a world which is not exactly chaos, for definite theories—at their most intense, almost forms of humanistic mysticism—have crystallised within it: Nationalism (confined to not one nation only) : Nazi Racialism; Russian 'Communism' in the strict sense. In each of these has been seen, or is seen, an Arrogance Enthroned; Man, who should be so good, turning when self-established in the Holy Place, into worse than brute. The frightful Parodies of the Apocalypse display themselves—the Dragon fights with Michael: Wild Beasts caricature the Lamb: the World-Wanton, the Bride of Christ. To see this clearly, horrible though it be, is a grace, and matter for gratitude. It seems incomprehensible that it should not be glaringly visible to all. A grace indeed, if the world itself just by endeavoring to be God-less proves to us the Necessity of God, the reality of the soul and of sin: the need of Redemption. And a surpassing grace if by Faith we know of the Incarnation, and of how it pursues itself in all manner of Communions and in particular the Eucharist, and of how all men of whatever race are now to be brothers all over again, in Christ, and are called to be Saints. The Sea, the barren sea of chaos and division, is no more, but is itself 'made new' and becomes that crystal Sea which rings the Throne of God and on which the feet of the Sanctified may stand.

EDITOR'S NOTE: Father Martindale is now stationed at the Jesuit Church on Mount street, in London. His more recent books include *Poplar Leaves and Seaweed*, poems published only in England, by Sheed, in 1940; *Towards Loving the Psalms* (issued in England under the title *The Sweet Singer of Israel*), Sheed, 1940; and his Holy Week talks over the B.B.C., *Creative Love*, Sheed, 1946.

SISTER MARY
ELEANOR, S.H.C.J.

(Eleanor Slater)

BORN IN OAK PARK, ILLINOIS, FEBRUARY 18, 1903, THE FIRST home I remember is a square frame house in Rochester, New York. It was a house that was really a home—with an older brother in it who was always making elaborate mechanical contraptions out of cardboard (he is now a physicist), a mother who was always ready to join in any make-believe, and a professorial father who would take time off from correcting papers or writing books to make wonderful doll-houses or magical tops that would spin rainbow-colored papers into whirling discs of white. There was a college campus to play in, with sphinxes that one could sit on in front of the library, and a fascinating geological museum with models of strange prehistoric animals in it—a dinosaur, a megatherium, whose names we delighted to roll on our tongues almost as soon as we could talk. There was a backyard with trees for climbing, raspberry bushes, orioles and yellow warblers, and there were wonderful walks to take. It was not a Catholic home, but it was one where God was loved and honored, a home where it was natural to write poems for one another for birthdays or Christmas. One such poem, written by the professorial father for his seven-year-old daughter's birthday, began:

> Seven times seven times fifty-two
> Is more of a sum than I can do,

and it ended, characteristically:

> There's only one perfect rhyme for seven
> And that is the rhyme of the kingdom of heaven.

It was a childhood, too, that had its high and far experiences—sights of the snowcapped peaks of the Rockies, of English castles and cathedrals, of Scottish highlands and Dutch villages. It was also a childhood of books,—Mark Twain's *Joan of Arc*, Dickens and Scott almost as far back as memory goes, Blake's *Songs of Innocence*, Wordsworth's "Daffodils" and Shelley's "Cloud." At fourteen, there was a semester in a boarding school in El Paso, Texas, with its vivid Spanish atmosphere; at sixteen, a boarding school in New England; then college at the University of Rochester— that place of earliest memories. It was a queer, interrupted college-course, broken in the middle by two years in bed,— but that is not a bad apprenticeship, with time to read, write, and think. Poems accumulated in a black leather notebook, and appeared the year after college in a slender volume, *Quest*, Volume XXII of the Series of Younger Poets sponsored by the Yale University Press. Volumes in that series are still issued—two a year. To be eligible, one must be an American under thirty, and the book must be one's first.

After college, the general question of vocation expressed itself in a special form: Which were more important to work with, books or people? Did one have to choose, or could one give oneself to both? The *books* led to graduate study in English at Radcliffe and teaching in the English department at the University of Rochester. *People* led to a variety of adventures in social service—on the Mexican border, in the Tennessee mountains, in the Boston slums. Sometimes the people turned into books, as when the Boston children found place in a monograph, published by the Society for Research in Child Health and Development, or when the passing of a well-known and well-loved figure—Bishop Charles Henry Brent of the Episcopal Church, Chaplain General of the A.E.F. in World War I, suggested the writing of a biographical study (published in 1931).

Religion was becoming more and more important; yet not religion as one found it in the Protestant churches I knew. The Saints were growing real through books and travel. What kind of Church did Christ leave behind Him? Was it an outward Church based on the authority of a visible hierarchy, or an inward Church based on the authority of the Holy Ghost in the individual soul? I looked about. The Catholic Church was the best exponent I could find of the former, the Quakers of the latter. I could not see logic in anything in between. The Catholic Church seemed very strange and frightening; the Quakers were doing such splendid things for the poor and the oppressed; I gravitated toward them; I joined them. Yet I knew that if ever the Catholic Church should come to seem to me the right church, I should have to retrace my steps and join it. This time came, but not till after I had served for a year and a half as a member of the staff co-ordinating all Quaker relief activities. I resigned this work to become a Catholic, and providentially there was an opening in the English department at Rosemont College, Rosemont, Pennsylvania, maintained by the Sisters of the Holy Child Jesus. I was baptized in the college chapel in the fall of 1940 by Father Joseph McSorley, C.S.P., and took up my duties as a member of the faculty. But I knew that it was only for a year—that I was being called to something more. The following year I entered the novitiate of the Society as a postulant, made my first vows in 1944, and am once more on the Rosemont faculty. Just before entering the novitiate, another volume of verse was published, *Why Hold the Hound.* There have also been poems and articles in various periodicals.

Anyone who has received the gift of faith owes thanks to many apostles, known and hidden. I am glad here to give thanks to old Mexican gardeners and serving-maids, to Irish children in two-room tenements, to the friend who first took me to a Catholic church, to the nuns who befriended me and the priest who instructed me, as well as to a whole company of saints and those who have written about them. Apostles *incognito* they are, and I am grateful to every one.

VERY REVEREND MICHAEL J. MILLER, O.S.M.

IN MY YOUTH I NEVER THOUGHT OF BECOMING A WRITER. I did not think I was good enough, although I always got high marks in English. I was more given to mathematics and science and later I took to philosophy with great avidity.

Even in my grammar school days I could not get interested in cheap novels. All the boys in our neighborhood were reading "Dime Novels." I tried to read them, but could not get interested in them. *Red Tiger's Trail* was the name of one of them, which my friends prevailed upon me to read. They said that it was the best of all and to read it through which I did with great effort and sheer determination. But that was the last and the only one I ever read. I did not have a taste for cheap literature with its incoherent plot and flimsy thinking. Father Finn's books were then my favorites.

Later the classics appealed to me strongly. My English course extended throughout my years of study even to the priesthood. In the later years it extended itself mostly to oratory. Oratory? We studied all kinds of oratory, all kinds of books on oratory. Cardinal Gibbons' and Cardinal Manning's chapters on oratory were of the greatest help to me. I got more out of just one chapter of their books than from some entire books on oratory. In composition, Shakespeare and Washington Irving proved of great assistance. I wrote sentences and paragraphs from all the authors. Lytton's *Last Days of Pompeii, Fabiola, Ben Hur* had a strong appeal for me. I read over and over again in the original tongue such authors as Shakespeare, Goethe, Dante, Fenelon, Horace, Cicero, Demosthenes and others. My leaning was to become a speaker rather than a writer, as you can readily see.

Detroit is my home town. It is my home town, because it is the place where I spent the best days of my youth. My folk still live in Detroit, and it is the place where I spend most of my vacations. To me it is the best city in the nation, for it is my home town. It was there I received my early training and education, graduating from St. Joseph's Commercial College with highest honors. It was a thrill, indeed, to receive a gold watch as the prize for excellence from the hands of Bishop Foley and my diploma from the then mayor of Detroit, Mayor Maybury.

I was not a very studious boy, and yet I did study my lessons from day to day. I made it a point never to get behind in a single study, not even for one day. Each day I reviewed in short the lessons of the few previous days, if only by glancing back through the book to see if I knew what I had gone over. This getting of daily lessons and even cursory review of preceding lessons, made all very easy for me.

I would not study immediately after school; but going directly home, I would put my books on my desk and would run out and play out of doors. I say immediately, but sometimes there was an errand to run for my mother and I would do that first, and then run out and play.

We had quite a spirited neighborhood in our part of Detroit. We were wide-awake kids and took everything in season. We spun tops and flew kites. In the marble season my pockets bulged with marbles, for we played marbles "for keeps," which was a mild form of gambling where skill paid dividends—not loaded dice! No rackets!

In the baseball season I carried a ball and glove (a catcher's mitt) around with me ready to play without the slightest provocation. All I needed was another boy or two for the joy of throwing and catching a ball. I was a catcher, and even as young as eleven and twelve I might become a "ringer" for another team at a dollar a game. That was big money in those days.

Soccer and shinny had their place in the Fall and later, ice hockey. Of course we threw snowballs and built forts and snowmen. But I am supposed to tell you how I became a writer. I am supposed to tell facts of my life.

I am just now finding that very hard to do. When you write about yourself, you are walking on very thin ice. You know that at any time you might fall right through and get all wet; or, somebody may come along and trip you up and you fall through with a crash. Well I must try anyhow, however precarious may be the venture.

I have already said I did not study very hard and that is true. I study easy; I might say very easy. What you can do best you do easily. You just get interested and curious to know.

One hour was the limit for my homework. One hour. That was from five o'clock to six. I made it a point to get

home at five o'clock. I said I made it a point. But it was
generally a quarter after five or even half past five before I
could break away from my playmates and games and get
back home.

Immediately upon arrival, I would get out my books and
start work. First I would look the lesson over and then
start writing. We had supper at six o'clock every evening.
I said six o'clock; but before a large family of ten could
all get into their places, before they could all be called in
and ready for supper, it was generally a quarter after six.
Then after supper I was free for the evening.

I belonged to the Junior Athletic Club at St. Joseph's at
the age of fourteen and fifteen of which I was elected president, mostly because I was the best fighter and champion
pool player. I was not tough or a bully. Anything but that.

I was called Saint Miller, half in derision, perhaps, half
in admiration. The sisters told the children I saw my
guardian angel like St. Aloysius. But, of course, I did not,
as I had to admit to my little sisters at home when they
persistently probed me about it. For didn't Sister Hilde-
garde and Sister Ernestine tell the children in their respec-
tive classes that they had no doubt that I saw my guardian
angel?

My mother used to dress me up very neat and tidy in a
brown suit, a tan tie and a brown derby with a deep brown
feather in it. This proved quite a temptation for the boys
I chanced to meet on the street, especially the bullies.

I may have been a pious boy and all of that and a good
student with the good Brothers who taught me, but nobody could call me a sissy with impunity. Being a well
trained boxer (as I told you) I could well take care of the
bully and felt no scruple of conscience at being called a
sissy.

But there I go telling you how I became a fighter, not a
writer. At that time I thought little of becoming a writer.

I was just a strong, healthy boy who played hard, but did not study hard. With the mind you do not do things hard. It is the body that does things hard, by laborious exercise. The mind does things easily and smoothly. It is with curiosity and co-ordination of thoughts that the mind does its task. Work becomes a pleasure when you work with will and thought and love.

When I studied for the priesthood with the Servite Fathers, I kept up the same easy habit of acquiring knowledge and with it virtue. I continued to study easily and co-ordinately and to review my studies at least ten minutes a day.

The result was I had plenty of spare time and I endeavored to make the most of all I studied and to take notes on principal subjects. I found time to pick out special passages from authors. I studied the classics in Latin, Greek, English, French, German and Italian. Besides, I wrote sermons from philosophic and scientific studies, but especially from theology. Altogether I wrote five books of sermons when I was a student. I mean note books.

I shall never forget the thrill I got in my first year of ordination, when I was chosen to give the Lenten sermons in the Milwaukee Cathedral, while I was teaching at the seminary. Since then I have been speaking averaging at least a couple of hundred times the year.

As head of the Missions for many years, actually engaging in quite continuous mission work and lecturing, I gained an easy flow of thought and language. I must not overlook my continuous work in instructing converts for the facility of ready and orderly thoughts and for facile and ready expression.

All these things served me in good stead as a writer because of the easy and logical flow of thought it presented. The many contacts I made gave me a practical psychology of life with abundant stories and comparisons. I had a very fine scientific course as well as a very complete curriculum in philosophy.

The purpose of my writings has been to explain life by science and philosophy, as well as theology; using, besides, the broad common sense of the teachings of experience.

Though I had written a number of articles and poems for magazines and periodicals, as also at present I am the columnist of *The Servite*, yet until 1934 I had not written a book. From that time in quite rapid succession has appeared: *What Is Wrong; The Broadcast From Heaven; Jesus, the Mediator; Love; Knowledge; Thought; Poems; The Power and Wisdom of the Cross; A God-Given Mother.*

I had always steered shy of writing books and had to be coaxed into writing them. I had preferred to speak; I had made it my career.

Now, however, I enjoy the complimentary letters I have received, the book reviews, and especially the conversions to the true Faith which God in His goodness has made my books the instrument of.

I must confess that I was quite thrilled when I got a letter from London, England, stating that I had been chosen for their forthcoming volume, *The Principal Poets of the World.*

It gave me no little pleasure, too, to be made an Honorary Member of the Eugene Field Society. I am proud of the certificate of Honorary Membership they have sent me.

May I here take this opportunity of thanking those concerned for including me among our Catholic writers. For this I shall always be grateful.

I must say that writing was never a primary factor in my life which has been almost entirely spent as an executive. It has become more of a hobby, a pastime. My familiarity with the mental world and experience in the many contacts of actual life has given me an increasing urge of expressing my thoughts and soul emotions in sympathy with other minds and hearts. Above all, I have striven to gladden the path of life and to make its ways more understandable by pursuing the true, the good and the beautiful.

EDITOR'S NOTE: The Servite Press, 3131 Jackson Blvd., Chicago, published the following of Father Miller's books: *Jesus the Mediator, What is Wrong?, A God-given Mother, Poems, Knowledge, The Power and Wisdom of the Cross,* and *Thoughts.*

CLARENCE P. MILLIGAN

I WAS BORN IN DETROIT, MICHIGAN, ON JULY 17, 1889, AND was educated by the Jesuits at Detroit College (now the University of Detroit), graduating with the degree of B.A., and later becoming an M.A. I acquired my law degree at the Detroit College of Law. I was a reporter on the staff of *The Detroit News* for three years while studying law, and did a turn at almost all "beats" but the political. After acquiring my law degree I engaged in general practice at Detroit until 1938, when I retired to California to devote myself to writing.

Since coming to California I have written three books. The first, *Death Valley and Scotty*, is an historical and geological account of Death Valley, California, and its principal character, Walter Scott. The second, a novel entitled *Angel with a Spoon*. The third, another novel, *The Wonderland of John Devlin,* with characters and scenes laid in and around Detroit and Windsor.

In Detroit I contributed to *The News, The Free Press, Detroit Saturday Night,* and *The Michigan Catholic.* And now in California I write a newspaper column entitled "Rimes and Reasons," and contribute verse and articles to such magazines and newspapers as *The Catholic Mirror, Los Angeles Examiner, San Diego Union, Poetry* (Chicago), *American, San Francisco Examiner,* and *Los Angeles Saturday Night.*

I am married and have two daughters, both of whom are now married, and we all make our home in Southern California.

WILLIS DWIGHT NUTTING

WITH THE EXCEPTION OF ONE GRANDMOTHER, WHO WAS THE daughter of German and Swiss immigrant parents, my forebears were old line Americans from before the Revolution. Most of the men were educators or ministers or both; but one, Thomas Hunt, was a military man, who had the honor of helping General Hull surrender Detroit to the British in the War of 1812. (By the way, there is a Leib Street in Detroit. That Leib was my great-great-grandfather.)

My father was Charles C. Nutting, professor of zoology at the State University of Iowa, and my mother was Eloise Willis Nutting, of Iowa City, Iowa.

I was born on March 10, 1900. My youth was that of the average middle western small town boy. My parents desired to make a cosmopolitan out of me, and we traveled considerably, but out of cussedness I was determined to remain a provincial middle westerner, and I have succeeded pretty well. Very early I developed a consuming love for the land in our middle west and for our people on it. Iowa City is still for me the center of the world.

When a freshman at the University of Iowa, and eighteen years of age, I accompanied my father on a zoological expedition to the British West Indies. There I came in contact with the Anglican Church. The very real religion of the English clergy and their black people gave a rude jolt to the rather conventional Presbyterianism which I had absorbed from our Sunday school at home; and, on my return to Iowa City, I joined the Episcopal Church and determined to study for the ministry. The Reverend Paul Boynton James, rector of my home parish, gave me my first insight into the meaning of the Church. He was of the "Anglo-Catholic" school of thought, and that school became mine. I really believed that the Anglican Church, after converting its own members to the true Faith, would sweep the country and force the Holy See to recognize it as a part of the true Catholic Church.

In 1920 I was fortunate enough to win a Rhodes Scholarship, and after graduating at Iowa, I went to Oxford in the fall of 1921 to study Theology. Keble College, Oxford, endowed to perpetuate the Oxford Movement, was my home for three happy years. That I was exposed to the best educational system in the world I have no doubt. That I did not profit by it to the full I regret. But there is nothing like it anywhere in the world. In the winter of 1923-1924, after taking my B.A. in Theology, I wrote a B.Litt. thesis on the Modern Greek Orthodox Church. This necessitated a five months sojourn in Greece, where I was unexpectedly thrown into work with the Greek refugees from Turkey.

Returning to Oxford in the summer of 1924, I was ordained to the Anglican ministry by the Bishop of Oxford. I went immediately out to the diocese of Antigua, British West Indies (the place where religion had first hit me). I had worked in the Cathedral parish there only six weeks when exposure in a hurricane sent me to the hospital with a bad case of pleurisy and threatened tuberculosis. As soon as I was well enough to travel I was bundled off home with the order never to return to the tropics again if I wished to stay alive.

Since I was a semi-invalid, I got a place as a chaplain to a private family in the mountains of Colorado. Health returned, and I took a parish in a little mountain town. We had a most interesting institution there. The Episcopal Church was almost everything: school, library, hospital, relief center, and even a seminary. But in trying to prepare some boys for the ministry, I finally came to the conclusion that I could no longer stay in the ministry myself. In trying to teach the "Anglican position," my grounds for confidence in that position crumbled, and in April, 1930, I resigned my position. I went back to Iowa City to live with my mother, my father having died three years before, and on July 12, 1930, I was received into the Catholic Church.

This meant starting all over again. No easy job at thirty years of age. A very short sojourn at the Beda College in Rome satisfied me and everyone else that the priesthood was not my calling, and I returned home once more. This was in the depths of the depression when there were no jobs. I went out to California and worked on a big ranch near Marysville for eight months as a companion to the "Grapes of Wrath" Okies. You really scrape the bottom in that kind of job and place.

An opportunity for a graduate scholarship at my home University opened up, and so in the fall of 1931, I went back again to do a Doctorate in Philosophy. I was told by everyone that the study would lead nowhere, for since I was a Catholic I could not teach philosophy in a secular school, and since it was secular philosophy that I was studying I could not teach it in a Catholic school. But I wanted to study

Modern Philosophy to see what was the matter with it, so I did, and I think I found out. But the study has never resulted in a job. I got my Ph.D. in July, 1933, writing my thesis on the philosophy of a German Catholic, Joseph Geyser.

The Sisters of Saint Francis at the College of Saint Teresa, Winona, Minnesota, were kind enough to give me a job teaching, of all things, Greek and German! I started in the fall of 1933, and that first year of teaching was taken up largely in keeping one lesson ahead of the students. I switched to History the next year.

On August 1, 1934, I married Eileen Barry, of Denver, whom I had known in my Colorado days. Her parents both came from County Cork, so I am Irish by marriage, at least.

In the fall of 1936, we came to Notre Dame, where I got a place in the History Department, and here we are.

In 1939, Sheed and Ward published a small book of mine entitled *How Firm a Foundation,* a work on Apologetics. This was the one tangible result of my doctoral studies.

My family now (May, 1947) consists, besides my wife and myself, of Teresa (aged nine), Charles (aged eight), Theodore (aged four), and my wife's mother, Mary Frances Barry. We live on a "Homestead" of two acres about a mile and a half from the University, where we produce as much of our own food as we can.

My chief interest is in my family, its religion, and its integration into the larger community of parish and neighborhood. To this end I am interested in the liturgical revival, in family education, in small communities, in economic independence, and in the traditions of rural America.

I am a member of the Catholic Rural Life Conference and chairman of the executive committee of the Decentralist Conference, which has just had a meeting in Oklahoma City. My love for the middle west and for the traditions of provincial America grows all the time, and I look forward to the day when the rural American will understand the Catholic Faith, and when the Catholic Church will understand him.

To set forth my longing for the revitalizing of the traditions of rural America I wrote a book, *The Reclamation of Independence*, which has just been published by Berliner and Lanigan, two Notre Dame boys who have set up a printing and publishing business in a small town in the Sierras.

EDITOR'S NOTE: Dr. Nutting is the author of *How Firm a Foundation*, 1939, Sheed & Ward; *The Reclamation of Independence*, 1947, Berliner & Lanigan, Nevada City, Calif.

JOHN J. O'CONNOR

WILL YOU WRITE AN ARTICLE? A BOOK? A FEW EDITORIALS IN a hurry?

I am a very lazy person. But I am also a very easy-going, obliging fellow. Thus it happens that I make all sorts of promises to editors and publishers, which they expect me to keep. My life, as a consequence, seems to be a perpetual race against a deadline. I would like to be lazy, but I really haven't time for it!

In looking back over the past few years, I seem to resemble the tumbler of Notre Dame (or was he a juggler?) who went through his act before the great Paris cathedral built in honor of Our Lady, because he didn't know what else to do. A writer hasn't any choice in the matter. A writer must write. In that way he gives honor and glory to God, Who gave him the ability to write in the first place, and he also makes his individual contribution to the thinking of countless people not only in the United States but in

all parts of the world. If a writer can lead people a little
closer to God and can help other writers and workers in
building a new Christian civilization, he can feel sure that
he is taking part in one of the noblest crusades to which any
human being might dedicate his efforts in the short space of
time he is upon this earth.

The career of most writers usually falls into three
periods. During the first and most difficult period, when he
is a young student in high school or college, he does a lot of
experimental writing that apparently gets him nowhere.
During the second period, he begins to have some of his
work published, while continuing to study the difficult art of
writing. During the third period, he has begun to master
the art of writing, to achieve considerable fluency in putting
his thoughts down on paper, and to have his work win an in-
creasingly favorable acceptance among editors and publishers. At long last the writer is launched in the full
stream of life and finds more to write about than he has
time to write it.

So far as I can remember, I did no writing in high school.
During my college days at Georgetown, I did a lot of
writing. All of it was bad, and I succeeded only in building up a mountainous pile of rejection slips from editors
all over the country. One of these editors, indeed, sent me a
friendly note asking me not to send him any more manuscripts until I had read at least one issue of his magazine
from cover to cover. During this period I subscribed to
every mail-order course in writing that came my way. I
cannot say that none of them did me any good. It would
be more accurate to say that they kept alive my interest in
writing and kept me pounding my portable typewriter during my leisure hours. This was a good thing because the
only way to learn how to write is to write, to keep on
writing, to persevere in writing though the heavens fall.

After my graduation, I became a history instructor at

Georgetown and thus had ample time for study and writing. This is an ideal combination for many reasons. Preparation for class-room work and the actual work in the class-room are not nearly so time-consuming nor energy-consuming as eight full hours spent in a busy office or factory. There is always time left over from teaching for free-lance writing. Again, there is an intellectual atmosphere in a college or university which is very helpful to a writer. It is possible to talk things over with some of the older members of the faculty, to test out your ideas, and to learn from their wisdom and experience.

Usually some of the other faculty members are doing part-time writing, and it is very stimulating and encouraging to join an informal authors' club on the campus. Under these favorable circumstances a rejection slip does not quite seem like a death sentence. The other faculty members have received their full share of rejection slips and have schooled themselves to regard them as merely spurs to better literary production. This is a very valuable lesson. Finally, teaching always means a monthly pay-check and hence a fledgling writer can support himself during the early difficult years.

Many of the happiest days of my life were spent at Georgetown. The president of the university, W. Coleman Nevils, S.J., was writing a one-volume history of the grand old institution; the vice-president, Edmund A. Walsh, S.J., was writing a series of books on Russia; Theodore Maynard was gathering material for a biography of De Soto; other faculty members were writing either for professional or popular magazines.

I was carrying a full teaching schedule of twelve or fifteen hours a week, doing post-graduate work in law and history at night, speaking in the public parks of Washington as a member of the Catholic Evidence Guild, publishing a small travel book on the Old Country which I called *Twenty-Five in Ireland*, serving as Washington correspon-

dent for the Religious News Service, wooing Eleanor Louise
Crowley—and writing a number of articles which were
actually published and for which, all things considered, I
was paid handsomely. By the time I left Georgetown I had
completed the second period in my training for authorship.

In 1936 I accepted a position on the faculty of Teachers'
College and the Graduate School of St. John's University,
Brooklyn, New York. As my working hours were in the
late afternoon and evening, I found it possible to do some
writing and to take on the part-time job of Catholic editor
of the Religious News Service, a news syndicate sponsored
by the National Conference of Christians and Jews. Within a year, as a result of having read one of my articles,
Michael Williams asked me to succeed George Shuster as
managing editor of *The Commonweal*. My new position not
only brought me in touch with the leading Catholic writers
of the day, but compelled me, regardless of my feelings at
the moment, to do a considerable amount of editorial
writing every week. A free-lance writer can do an article
when he feels like it, or when he has something important
to say. An editor, on the contrary, must grind out copy
every week in the year, regardless of the state of his nerves
or his stomach, and regardless of the fact that he may not
be brimming with scintillating ideas. Work on a weekly
magazine is a wonderful discipline for any writer. It is
really a pity that there are so few Catholic publications on
which a young Catholic writer can find employment at a
worth-while salary. When *The Commonweal* was sold, I
stayed in Brooklyn and devoted all my time to teaching and
free-lance writing.

But not for long. My promotion to chairman of the history department occurred at about the same time that a
need arose for a college sociology text. I had been teaching
the subject for some time in the undergraduate college and
had written extensively on it. I therefore teamed up with

Walter L. Willigan to produce a new text. It took us about a year to gather the material and illustrations, and to do the actual writing. *Sociology* was published in 1940. Our book was dedicated to the conviction that Catholic educators should focus attention upon a teaching objective that differs in essence from any purpose served by non-sectarian instruction. We asserted that an introductory work in sociology should be directed toward imparting a truly Catholic conception of the individual's role in social processes. To this end we tried to integrate sound Catholic doctrine and sound factual data into a coherent whole. The book had such a good sale—it is now in its second edition—that the publisher gave us a contract for a more advanced college text in the same field.

Social Order, a much larger work of approximately seven hundred pages, was published in 1941. This was the first college textbook to analyze the social and economic principles proclaimed to the world by Pope Pius XI and interpretated for the United States by the archbishops and bishops of the National Catholic Welfare Conference. As in the earlier volume, we attempted to combine the fundamental tenets of the Church and the most recent and reliable sociological data.

As soon as I had finished my part of the work on *Social Order,* Ross Hoffman asked me to contribute a volume to a new series of books to be called the Christendom Series. The series was intended to provide informative reading for both Catholic and non-Catholic readers; for study clubs in the parochial units of the Confraternity of Christian Doctrine; for study groups in Newman Clubs; and as collateral texts in colleges, normal schools, and senior high and preparatory schools. Working under the immediate direction of Herbert C. F. Bell, I went to work with a will and did a great deal of research in English history, with particular attention to the remarkable growth and development of

Catholic life in the British Isles from penal times to the
death of Cardinal Manning. My small volume, *The Catholic
Revival in England,* was published in 1942.

Meanwhile, I had become deeply interested in interracial
work, principally because of the pioneering work of Father
John La Farge, S.J., and George K. Hunton, and in due
course of time was elected to the Board of Directors of the
Catholic Interracial Council in New York. This was followed by election as Councillor of the United States Catholic
Historical Society, and my appointment as the first editor
of a Catholic news service published by the Center of In-
fo mation Pro Deo in New York City.

By this time, however, the United States was at war with
the Axis powers and I was called back to Washington, my
home town, to serve on the public relations staff of Lt. Gen.
Levin H. Campbell, Jr., Chief of Ordnance, U. S. Army.
During the hectic war years, Ordnance was a forty billion
dollar corporation, and General Campbell directed the design, production, storage, packaging, shipment and main-
tenance of more than 2,000 major pieces of fighting equipment and 700,000 different kinds of spare parts to keep this
equipment, ranging from bicycles to forty-ton tanks, in top
combat condition. During my years in The Pentagon I did
all kinds of writing, but I was so tired when I got home in
the evening that I was practically forced to give up my
Catholic writing altogether. I somehow managed to do a
few articles, editorials, columns and book reviews, but my
spare-time production was at a low ebb.

With the end of the war, shortly after V-J day, I accepted
appointment as managing editor of a new magazine called
Logistics, published by the Army Ordnance Association.
This is a technical publication, dealing largely with the
problems of military supply. I did not return to teaching
at St. John's University in Brooklyn because we had found
it necessary to buy a house in Washington, two of my chil-

dren were in school, and it was difficult to find adequate living quarters either in New York City or Brooklyn.

At the present time, I am an editor by day and a lecturer in logic in the School of Foreign Service at Georgetown by night. I have resumed my work with the Catholic Evidence Guild and have become secretary of the local Catholic Interracial Council. Quite recently I was elected to membership in the Gallery of Living Catholic Authors. I am a member of the editorial staff of *The Magnificat*, a contributing editor of *The Commonweal*, a member of the book review staffs of *America* and *Books on Trial*, a columnist for *The Interracial Review*, and am collaborator on two textbooks, one in history and one in sociology, which are scheduled for publication in 1947 and 1948.

I am the father of five husky children, have a number of lecture assignments, and am still trying to find time to publish more than one full-length article a month.

Journalism is a grand career. The monetary rewards are not large, it is true, but more than ever before, a Catholic writer today can speak to a global audience and exert a real influence in restoring our war-cracked civilization to Christ. What more could anyone want?

EDITOR'S NOTE: Dr. O'Connor's books include *Twenty-Five in Ireland*, Brent Knold Press, 1932; *The Catholic Revival in England*, Macmillan,, 1942; and as co-author, *Sociology*, Longmans, 1940, *Social Order*, Longmans, 1941, *World Order*, McMullen, 1947, *Basic Sociology*, Heath, 1946.

VERY REVEREND VICTOR FRANCIS O'DANIEL, O.P.

BORN FEBRUARY 15, 1868, IN A PART OF WASHINGTON COUNTY Kentucky, which, in straightening the lines between the two counties, was thrown into that of Marion in 1869, Father O'Daniel was baptized at St. Rose's, Washington County, March 17, 1868. He was the fifth child of Richard Jefferson O'Daniel and his second wife, Nancy Hamilton. Jeff O'Daniel were usually most prompt in having newly born children baptized, but the weather was so cold and the roads were so bad when little Victor was born, that a month passed before the saving waters flowed over his brow.

Victor O'Daniel received his early education mainly in the parochial school at nearby Cecilville, although he had earlier been taught by private instructors and had attended the public rural school. Believing that he had a vocation to the priesthood, he applied for admission into the Dominican Order, was accepted ,and received the habit at St. Rose's,

Sunday, March 21, 1886, from Father Constantine Louis
Egan, subprior *in capite.*

Vocations to the priesthood were scarce in the days when
Victor O'Daniel entered the Order. At that time superiors
found it necessary to accept candidates to the Order before
they had completed their study of the humanities. Thus it
was necessary to train the young men in languages and the
classics during and after their novitiate, despite the fact
that Canon Law frowned upon the practice. And the training of these young men presented a problem. Priests were
all too scarce, and the superiors found it all but impossible
to spare men who could devote themselves to teaching the
novices. So very often this task had to be relegated in part
to more advanced novices. This was even more against the
Church's idea concerning novice training, although it was
not explicitly forbidden by the law then as it is today.

Young Brother Francis O'Daniel was one of the advanced
novices chosen by his superiors as a teacher. Victor (or
Brother Francis, which was his religious name) O'Daniel
had been endowed by his Creator with a brilliant mind and
his rapid advance as a student caused his superiors to feel
justified in casting him very early in the role of professor.

The double labor of student and teacher was difficult. Yet,
in spite of the difficulty, young Brother Francis found time
to indulge his aptitude for historical study and research for
which he had been so well adapted by nature and education.
Nature had given him the keen mind and unquenchable
thirst for historical truth that goes to make great historians, and being the offspring of an old English Catholic
family he imbibed a love for Catholic tradition and history,
one might almost say, with his mother's milk. So from the
very beginning Father O'Daniel saved all that he could get
his hand upon concerning the history of the American Dominicans. Any document he could find concerning the Dominicans or a Dominican he salvaged and kept as a sacred

trust. The fact that American Dominicans today have an archives is a mute but eloquent testimony to this statement. Such an archives exists today only because Father O'Donnell "gathered up the crumbs lest they be lost."

Father O'Daniel's love of history was soon recognized by his brethren and all looked to him to save the history of the Province, but it was many years before he could devote himself to this work with the intensity that the work demanded. His duties as a professor and preacher long deterred him from true and lasting union with his first love. His adoring moments with the muse Clio were moments stolen from his assigned work. For many years the ardous labor of historical research was Father O'Daniel's recreation. And it was well that it was, for thereby the history of the Dominican Order in the United States was preserved.

On June 16, 1891, having completed his courses in philosophy and theology at St. Joseph's Priory, Perry County, Ohio, Victor Francis O'Daniel was ordained to the priesthood in St. Joseph's Cathedral, Columbus, Ohio, by Bishop John Ambrose Watterson, of Columbus.

In 1893, Father O'Daniel was selected by his superiors to study at the Dominican House of Studies, in Louvain, Belgium, to deepen and broaden the scope of his theological learning. It had been the plan of the superiors to send Father O'Daniel to Louvain three years earlier, but he had pleaded with them to be allowed to remain in this country because of his mother's illness, an illness which the young Dominican thought would lead (as it did) to her death. At Louvain the youthful Father O'Daniel was no more content to confine himself to the study of theology than he had been in the United States. Here, too, he found historical research to occupy his restless mind. He delved into the historical soil of the continent to trace the roots from which St. Joseph's Province, the American Dominican Province, had sprung. Upon leaving Louvain in early June, 1895, Father

O'Daniel went to Rome for about two weeks. There he was shown the General Archives of the Order, and while he did not have time to make a study of them at that time, he saw that a study was necessary and resolved to return for that purpose as soon as he could. From Rome he proceeded to England and Ireland, and in both countries gathered as much historical material as his short stay allowed.

At the Provincial Chapter of St. Joseph's Province, held in October, 1895, Father O'Daniel received the first official recognition of his historical study when he was appointed historian of the Province in association with Father John Raymond Volz. The act making this appointment reads:

"It will be their duty to collect documents relative to the life and works of the fathers in the United States, so that the history of the Province may be written at an opportune time."

The intention of the capitular fathers was no doubt laudable, but their appointees were not excused from their regular work, nor was any financial aid offered them. Father O'Daniel was an overburdened professor of philosophy and theology. Where would he find time to make the researches that were so necessary? He taught in the Province of St. Joseph until 1901, when he was sent to Benicia, California, to teach in the House of Studies of the Dominicans there. While this assignment removed him farther than ever away from the documentary sources which were his heart's desire, he was fortunate in that he came into contact with such men as Fathers James Benedict McGovern, James Antoninus Rooney and James Louis O'Neil, erstwhile members of St. Joseph's Province. These old men proved to be mines of historical information.

At the end of April, 1906, Father O'Daniel journeyed to Rome to take the *ad gradus* examination, an examination given by the General to all who are presented by their Provinces as candidates for the Dominican Mastership of Sacred Theology, the highest degree the Order can bestow.

While in Rome, he found time to make an exhaustive study of the General's Archives, and on his way home he did more research work in England and Ireland.

Upon his return to the United States, he was assigned to the teaching staff of the Dominican House of Studies, Washington, D. C. He taught at this institution until 1909 when he received the degree of Master of Sacred Theology. He asked for and received at that time permission to take a sabbatical leave. The year granted him he spent in the several European archives wherein the history of his Province could be found. He returned from his "vacation" to assume once again the now distasteful position of professor. But in 1913 he was permitted to resign his chair of theology and devote himself entirely to historical research and to the building of an archives for the Province.

It was at this time that Father O'Daniel started the writing career that was to place him in the first rank among church historians in the United States. The first articles which he wrote for historical reviews appeared under the pseudonym "D.F.V." This attracted the attention of scholars in the field. It was by means of them that he made the acquaintance of Father Peter Guilday, a professor of church history at the Catholic University. This friendship, founded upon mutual scholarly interest, was to endure a lifetime. Recognizing the need for an organ for Catholic historical scholarship, Father O'Daniel and Father Guilday founded in 1915, *The Catholic Historical Review,* of which Dr. Guilday became the editor and Father O'Daniel, associate. Their busy pens kept the *Review* supplied with articles and it was within its pages that most of the articles in church history written by the new famous Dominican historian appeared.

Once started upon his career as an historiographer, Father O'Daniel consecrated himself more and more to this life he loved. In 1916, he produced his first book, *The Order*

of Friars Preachers, a work on the general history of the
Order. In 1917, *The Very Reverend Charles Hyacinth Mc-
Kenna, O.P.,* a biography of the great Dominican preacher
and apostle of the Holy Name, came off the press. This
was followed by *Bishop Edward Dominic Fenwick of Cincinnati,* one of the great works to come from the pen of an
American historian, in 1920. *The Dominican Lay Brother*
appeared in 1921. Other books from his seemingly tireless
pen came in quick succession: *An American Apostle,* 1923;
Bishop Richard Pius Miles, 1926; *The First Disciples of St.
Dominic,* 1929; *Dominicans in Early Florida,* 1930; *A Light
of the Church in Kentucky,* 1932; *Snatches of O'Daniel,
Hamilton, and Allied Genealogy,* 1933. Then, after a long
lapse given over to preparation for it came *The Dominican
Province of St. Joseph,* 1942. Father O'Daniel, although
now in ailing health, is still working, this time as collaborator, on a new work, a pictorial history of the Dominican
Province of St. Joseph.

EDITOR'S NOTE: Father O'Daniel received the honorary degree of Doctor of Literature, from Mount St. Mary's College, Maryland, in 1924,
and was made an honorary corresponding member of the Institut
Historique et Heraldique de France, in 1938.

REVEREND WILFRID PARSONS, S. J.

FATHER WILFRID PARSONS, S.J., WAS BORN IN PHILADELPHIA, March 17, 1887, of a family which, starting in New England, made its way before the Revolution, to South Jersey and then to the Quaker City. His father's father, however, was a Methodist and became a Catholic at the age of seventy-two, some ten years before his death. His father's mother was a Catholic, and on her mother's side, had a grandfather who was a pillar of the parish of the Jesuit Church of Old St. Joseph's in Philadelphia around 1770. His mother's father, whose name was Avery, came from England, but her mother, Susanna Welch, came from Ireland. His mother is still (1945) living, aged eighty-five. So much for heredity.

Incidentally, Father Parsons got his first name from his maternal uncle, who was Father Wilfrid Avery, a Passionist, who is buried in Louisville, Kentucky, and when his elder sister Elsie became a Sister of Notre Dame de Namur

she also took the name, and is Sister Wilfrid du Sacre
Coeur, S.N.D. She was one of the first Sisters to get a Ph.
D. in Classics at the Catholic University, where Father
Parsons now is a professor of political science. Sister Wil-
frid also teaches political science at Emmanuel College, in
Boston, besides Latin. She was Dean at Trinity College,
Washington, for about ten years.

He started his education in kindergarten at the age of
four and a half, spent a year at public school, then went to
parish school in the Gesu parish, became an altar boy at the
Gesu, went to St. Joseph's High School, and entered St.
Joseph's College at the age of fifteen. Father Parson's
mother, who had been a school-teacher in the public schools,
"heard his lessons" every night, and even scanned his Latin
themes (Greek was beyond her), and did the same for his
five brothers and sisters. She also took discreet care of his
reading, and the result was that before he was well sixteen
he had read all of Walter Scott, most of Charles Lamb, and
all of Shakespeare, and various others into which he dipped
with not much comprehension, like Ruskin, De Quincey, and
Thackeray. Nobody was ever able to get him to read
Dickens, and he remembers violent controversies with his
youthful contemporaries over the relative merits of Scott
and Dickens. I suppose that accounts for his still being an
incurable romantic. But he still remains convinced that
the one and only prescription for a writer is to read.

Wilfrid Parsons (then known as J. Wilfrid Parsons—his
mother had a great devotion to St. Joseph, and never quite
forgave him for dropping the "J" later), entered the Jesuit
Novitiate at St. Andrew-on-Hudson, Poughkeepsie, New
York, on August 14, 1903, at the age of sixteen. He spent
two years as a novice, took his first permanent vows on
August 15, 1905, spent two years in the Juniorate studying
the Latin and Greek and English classics, and in October
1907, left for the Jesuit House of Studies at Louvain, Bel-

gium, at the age of twenty, to study philosophy for three years. There he also learned to speak French, and to read Spanish and Italian, and got a smattering of Flemish (Dutch) and German.

During that period an event came about that was destined to have an influence on his future. Father John J. Wynne, S.J., who was at the time editor of *The Messenger*, and of the *Catholic Encyclopedia*, came through Louvain in 1909, with the news that he was about to start a new weekly called *America*. He was looking for writers and regular correspondents. He signed up Wilfrid Parsons as Belgian correspondent, and the young journalist's first dispatch appeared in the second issue of the young weekly, in April, 1909. From then on, he had at least one or two articles in the paper every few weeks for the remainder of his stay in Belgium until June, 1910.

There followed what was then the usual five-year service as high school and college teacher in the humanities at Boston, New York, and Worcester. During these years (1910-1915), he kept his hand in by contributing at least one or two articles a year to *America*, and he also reviewed books for it. His interests during these years were purely literary. In 1915, he started his theology at Woodstock College, Maryland, and was there until 1919, having been ordained priest May 18, 1918. Shortly after this latter date, his whole class, twenty-two in all, volunteered for service as military chaplains; but only one, now dead, was accepted. During these four years, he also published one or two articles a year in the periodicals.

Theology finished, he was informed that his future lay as a professor of theology. Having received his S.T.D. at Woodstock, he was sent to Rome for further study for two years, and at the end received the higher degree of *Magister Aggregatus*. During these two years his only writing was that of his dissertation on the Mystical Body in the Fathers, and that was in Latin. He then for one year had his "tertianship," which is the third year of Novitiate which Jesuits must take after their studies are finished, and in September, 1922, began to teach the treatise *De Ecclesia* at Woodstock for one term.

The second term of that year was intended to be passed in study, but in February, 1923, a violent controversy broke out in New York over the Divinity of Christ, due to the heretical sermons of an Episcopalian minister, Dr. Percy Stickney Grant. Father Parsons was called to New York to write a series of articles in *America* against Dr. Grant. When, in July of that year, Father Richard H. Tierney, S.J., then Editor-in-chief of *America*, was called to Rome to attend a General Congregation of the Society, Father Parsons stayed at the general offices of the magazine as Acting Editor-in-chief and remained there until June of the following year. In September, he was back at Woodstock teaching History of Dogma, but when Father Tierney had a serious breakdown in September, 1925, he was again called to New York and put in charge of the magazine. He was to remain in that position for eleven years, which, as H. L. Mencken wrote him when he retired, is one year longer than any editor ought to remain.

The writing interests of Father Parsons quickly changed from the humanities and theology to public affairs, though religious questions remained uppermost with him. He wrote much about such events as the evolution trial at Dayton, Tennessee, the doings of the Ku Klux Klan, and the religious controversies at the time of Al Smith's campaign, the persecution in Mexico, the settlement of the Roman Question in 1929, and similar questions where the interests of the Church were involved. The Roman Question was the occasion of his first book, *The Pope and Italy*, a small volume of 134 pages. Two extended trips to the capitals of Europe, in 1925 and 1928, gave him a first-hand acquaintance with personalities and situations abroad, and supplied him with an abiding interest in international affairs.

The coming of the Depression of the 'thirties turned his attention to the subject of economics and especially to the interaction of government and business, and the advent of the New Deal intensified his interest in that direction. Most of his writing during his last five years at *America* was in that field, but early in 1936 he wrote a book on Mexico, *Mexican Martyrdom*. He had been told by a Mexican priest, now Bishop Miranda of Tulancingo: "I despair of your eternal salvation if you do not put into a book all you know about Mexico." Under that threat, he had no choice but to write it. Carbon copies of many documents in the archives of the Apostolic Delegate to Mexico, Archbishop Ruiz, were put at his disposal for this purpose.

In May, 1936, Father Parsons was finally relieved of his duties as Editor-in-chief and was sent by his superiors to Georgetown University, to teach political science in the graduate school there, then undergoing reorganization. Shortly after arriving there, he started to write a book which he had long contemplated, to contain the thoughts which he had entertained on government for some time. This book finally appeared in 1939, under the title of *Which Way, Democracy?*

Meanwhile, he was appointed director of libraries at Georgetown and immediately became interested in the large number of old and valuable books in the Riggs Memorial Library. In an old attic he discovered very many treasures, and began the formation of separate collections. He was especially intrigued by the old Catholic books published in America. The only bibliography we had of these previously was that of Finotti, *Bibliographia Catholica Americana*, written in 1872. Finotti, however, had listed less than three hundred books published before 1820. With the help of many librarians around the country, this number was enlarged to six hundred and ninety. Under strong urging, Father Parsons carried the bibliography on to 1830, with the result that four hundred and ninety six other titles were discovered for the added ten years. This hobby of Father Parsons' resulted in the publication, also in 1939, of his *Early Catholic Americana,* which lists eleven hundred and eighty seven titles of Catholic books published in the United States before 1831.

In 1939, Father Parsons was asked to undertake courses in political science at the Catholic University, in addition to his other duties, which now included that of Dean of the Graduate School at Georgetown. His superiors did not see their way at the time, however, to release him for that work, but in October, 1940, he joined the Catholic University faculty as a full-time professor of political science. He moved over to Brookland, and founded Carroll House, the house of studies of the Jesuits studying at the Catholic University, of which he has been superior since that time.

During the nine years since he left the editorship of *America,* he has found time to contribute articles, of both a scientific and popular nature, to *America, Thought, The Sign, The Catholic World, Columbia, The Review of Politics, Theological Studies, The Biblical Quarterly, The Catholic Sociological Review, The New Scholasticism, The Modern Schoolman, The Messenger of the Sacred Heart,* and other periodicals. He also contributes since 1943 a weekly column of comment to *America* under the title of "Washington Front." Besides that, he gives frequent lectures on his specialties, and has lately become chaplain of the Washington Inter-racial Council, which he helped to found.

Father Parsons, since going to Georgetown, has taught a course in the Development of Christian Political Thought, and for this he has made copious translations from the Fathers and Medieval writers, and with the help of these he is slowly preparing a large-scale work which will trace political thought in the Church from the Gospels to the present day. He is also working on a popular book which will bring up to date the thought set forth in *Which Way, Democracy?*

EDITOR'S NOTE: Father Parsons published books include: *The Pope and Italy*, America Press, 1929; *Mexican Martyrdom*, Macmillan, 1936; *Which Way, Democracy?*, Macmillan, 1939; *Early Catholic Americana*, id., 1939; also several pamphlets, including his Catholic Hour radio addresses.

RICHARD PATTEE

BORN IN PRESCOTT, ARIZONA, APRIL 17, 1906, OF FRENCH AND Irish descent. Raised in southern Arizona, on the Mexican border, and educated in the public schools of that area. University education received at the University of Arizona, Tucson. A.B. degree received in 1926. Attended the Catholic University of America after that to secure the degree of Master of Arts in 1927. Undergraduate work in the field of history and economics. Graduate work in political science and history. In 1927 became instructor in political science at the University of Puerto Rico in the West Indies and remained at this post for two years. In 1929, prompted by a keen desire to see the inside of South America and not merely the external facade of the capital cities that most travelers think is the real thing, I spent more than a year wandering about the interior of the continent, most of the time in Bolivia, Brazil, and Paraguay. I spent nearly eight months in eastern Bolivia, in the jungles and swamps, for

no earthly reason except an insatiable curiosity to see what
it looked like. I had no ulterior motive; no scientific end,
and no support other than my own. This journey included
a long trek through the Amazon and Madeira country of
Brazil.

During this same period of time, I visited Venezuela, the
West Indies, and gradually extended my travel experience
to include most of the Latin American world. In 1928, I
visited Europe for the first time, spending most of the
period in Portugal and Spain, and attending in the former
country the University of Coimbra for the purpose of acquiring a knowledge of the Portuguese language.

I returned to Puerto Rico in 1931 and taught for another
year before embarking once more for Europe to spend a
period of study at the University of Louvain, in Belgium.
This period afforded an opportunity to visit more of
western and southern Europe—from Scandinavia to Italy
and the Iberian peninsula. I did the usual student stunts:
rucksack junkets all over Germany, Austria, Switzerland,
etc. This culminated in another period of service at the
University of Puerto Rico, from 1933 to 1936. This time as
assistant professor of history. Marriage in 1934 did not
place any serious damper on travel proclivities. I spent the
summer of 1936 in Mexico as lecturer before the Seminar on
Latin America, directed by Hubert Herring. Later on
visited Cuba, and then to Peru and Ecuador for research on
a volume, later to be published in the Spanish language
under the title of *Gabriel Garcia Moreno y el Ecuador de su
tiempo*. During this period of time I contributed regularly
to a considerable number of Hispanic American journals,
largely in the more or less academic fields of history or political science.

In 1938, I entered the service of the Department of State
of the United States, Division of the American Republics.

From this I passed to the newly created Division of Cultural Relations and remained there, as Assistant Chief, among other things, until the summer of 1943. The activities consisted of the launching of the cultural relations program and the whole exchange undertakings that grew rapidly from 1938 onward. Academic activities of one kind or another absorbed a certain amount of time, even during this period of government service. I taught at the Spanish School of Middlebury College in Vermont in 1939, 1942 and 1943; lectured at the Laval University summer school in 1942 and 1943, and was lecturer in Hispanic American civilization at the Catholic University of America from 1940 to 1943. This time too was occupied with numerous lectures in colleges, universities, forums, and like groups. In collaboration with Mr. Arturo Morales Carrion, of the University of Puerto Rico, I published a two-volume work on the nineteenth century in Europe, in the Spanish language, entitled *Historia de Europa en el siglo XIX.* Also a smallish volume on the Negro in Brazil, translated from the Portuguese of the distinguished Brazilian anthropologist, Arthur Ramos.

I left the service of the Department of State in 1943 and became a sort of traveling observer and writer for the National Catholic Welfare Conference of the United States. This included a year's residence in Mexico, where I also served as visiting professor in the Faculty of Philosophy and Letters of the National University of Mexico. A second year was devoted to the Caribbean and northern South America. The product of this period was a considerable amount of writing for journals, newspapers and magazines in the United States, Canada, Mexico, South America, and England.

I published several brochures, such as *The Catholic Revival in Mexico,* and *Catholic Life in the West Indies,* under the auspices of the Catholic Association for International Peace. Also a volume in French, issued as a result of a series of ten lectures in Haiti under the auspices of the Ministry of Public Instruction, called *Essai sur l'evolution historique de l'Amerique espagnole*. In Mexico in 1944 was published my large volume on Catholicism in the United States, entitled *El Catolicismo en los Estados Unidos*. This same work appeared in a Spanish edition in Madrid in 1946. Heath issued my textbook for college and university students of Spanish in the United States—also in the Spanish language—*Introduccion a la civilizacion hispanoamericana*.

I was press representative of the National Catholic Welfare Conference News Service at the United Nations meeting in San Francisco and have written abundantly for Catholic papers in this country and abroad and especially for this press service. I also served at San Francisco as consultant to the United States delegation on behalf of the National Catholic Welfare Conference.

I am now serving as consultant in international affairs to the General Secretary of the N.C.W.C. in Washington. Also lecture extensively having delivered some one hundred lectures during 1946 in the United States and Canada. Toured Cuba during the summer of 1945 for the purpose of speaking all over the island on Catholic social doctrine. Was one of the organizers in 1942 of the first Inter-American Catholic Social Action Congress, and co-president of the second Congress held in Habana, Cuba, with delegates from twenty-six countries.

I have three sons. Have no formal political affiliation. Belong to the Knights of Columbus and the Cosmos Club, Washington, D. C., and have served as President of the American Catholic Historical Association.

Hobbies consist of detective stories and Pullman cars, for the latter of which I have a special predilection.

Write and speak normally in English, French or Spanish, although most of my writing has been done in the Spanish language which I have used the greater part of my life. Have done almost all my university teaching in that language and prefer it as an instrument for public speaking or writing.

CHARLES JOSEPH GHISLAIN PIETTE

(Father Maximin, O.F.M.)

"Some are born great, some achieve greatness, and some have greatness thrust upon them."

I WAS NEITHER BORN GREAT NOR WAS GREATNESS THRUST upon me. Through my own achievement, by patient and hard work, I made my way to success.

I was born on a farm in Longueville, a village of the Province of Brabant, in the Walloon part of it, eighteen miles southeast of Brussels, on October 8, 1885. My father died when I, the second youngest of a family of seven, was but four years and a half old. The heroic determination of my bereaved mother to see her children supplied with a well-rounded education at any cost to her personal welfare, left an indelible impression on my youthful mind.

After attending the public primary school of my native village (1891-1898), I enrolled at St. Anthony's College, Lokeren, in eastern Flanders, in 1899. Here I studied the

classics of Greek and Latin antiquity, together with French,
Flemish, English and German. This was splendid cultural
foundation for my future studies including Hebrew, Ara-
bian, Syriac, Italian, and Spanish.

In 1904, I joined the Franciscan Novitiate at Thielt.
After seven years (1905-1912) dedicated to philosophical
and theological studies, my superiors sent me to the Faculty
of Sacred Theology at the Catholic University of Louvain.
These higher studies were interrupted by the World War of
1914-1918.

On the morrow of my graduation as Bachelor of Sacred
Theology, in July 1914, I was called by the Belgian Army
to serve, first as a Red Cross stretcher-bearer, then as a
Chaplain, during the battle of Liege. Stationed at the St.
Lawrence Military Hospital on August 6, 1914, two days
later I went with an ambulance truck to rescue soldiers from
the battle field, near the fort of Fleron. The German officers
there requested me to transport five of their prominent men
to the St. Elizabeth Hospital, Maria Hilf in Aachen, guaran-
teeing me military protection to and from the hospital.
Three times that day I crossed the firing line and was an
eyewitness of the destruction of three villages along the
highway: Battice, Herve, and Cheratte. In the evening of
the same day, on the way back, at Herve, despite my military protection, I was arrested with my driver, and once
more had to cross the firing line. About eight o'clock that
evening I found myself facing a German firing squad within
the barracks at Aachen. Why they did not kill me and my
driver, nobody knows. The next day both of us were sent
to the concentration camp of Munster Lager in Hanover.
During that captivity I was transferred to Otterbergen,
near Hildesheim, then to Zelle-Schloss and to Soltau. Finally, in December, 1914, I was returned to occupied Belgium
where I began a preaching campaign to help restore morale
among my compatriots. Liege, Namur, Brussels, and many

country towns assembled crowds to hear these sermons.
Even the Gestapo spies took some interest and I was sum-
moned before the jury of the war Tribunal. After three
sessions of more than three hours each I defended my sermons so well that the Judge had to dismiss all the accusa-
tions as baseless. But even though the prosecution ended
in a dead-lock, a complete acquittal by the Gestapo was impossible. Therefore I had to pay for my success with a new
captivity in the fortress of Gross-Strelitz in Upper Silesia.
After two months of hardships, I succeeded in October,
1916, in returning to Belgium where I resumed my preaching campaign.

In 1917, my Superiors appointed me Director of the Academic Circle of St. Capistran in Brussels. This organization, holding public lectures twice a week on all modern
questions, be they philosophical or social, scientific or artistic, under my leadership became the most prominent of its
kind in the country. As many as seventy-two similiar
groups were created and affiliated with the Circle of St.
Capistran in the "Federation of Circles and Lectures."

In 1918, I founded a publishing society called La Lecture
au Foyer, or Fireside Reading. It published more than a
hundred and fifty books and pamphlets, besides the monthly magazine *Revue des Conferences et Conferenciers*, or
Review of Lectures and Lecturers.

The activity of these two organizations was slowed down
by the World War of 1939-1945; but they resumed their
life in high gear after the liberation of Belgium.

After the first World War I returned to my theological
studies at the University of Louvain. In 1920, I graduated
as a Doctor with the highest distinction. Five years later I
received the supreme degree of Doctor and Master of Theology. My thesis, based on thirteen years of research was
John Wesley in the Evolution of Protestantism. The first
two editions were in French. The first edition was awarded

first prize in the competition between the four universities of Belgium, in 1926. The second was crowned by the French Academy, Prize Marcel Guerin, in 1927. The English editions, due to collaboration with Rev. J. B. Howard, of Bakersfield, California, did not begin to appear until 1937. They have been reprinted several times, and a new edition is now in preparation.

During 1927-1929 I attended Harvard University and became a Master of Arts while working with Professor George Foot Moore.

Beside many articles and pamphlets I wrote the following books: *L'Union des Eglises. Ses raisons et ses obstacles* (Montreal and Brussels, 1929) ; translated into English as *The Union of the Churches: Arguments for and against* (Brussels and Denver, 1934). As a reminder of my first stay in the United States I wrote *Dix jours au volant sur les routes de Florida* (Brussels, 1934), an as yet untranslated record of "Ten Days Driving in Florida."

While a professor of theology and of history in Brussels, I came back to the United States for my vacations every summer from 1936 to 1939, inclusive. I came to continue my researches in the evolution of religion in North America, a subject upon which I began in 1925 and which I continued at Harvard.

My last trip over was made on the ill-fated Normandie in May, 1939. The global war caught me in the United States and kept me here. Unable to rejoin the Belgian Army, I served as an auxiliary chaplain in the U. S. Marine Corps. I became an American citizen in 1945.

Most of the documentation assembled since 1925 on the religious evolution of North America being kept in Brussels, I found it impossible to finish the manuscript of "Methodism in the Religious Evolution of North America." During these researches I also collected a wealth of documentation on the old Spanish missions in Mexico and the southwest.

Deeply impressed by the outstanding personality of Fray Junipero Serra, during the last five years I assembled 262 original manuscripts on this great apostle of Upper California. As a result I have ready for press "The Letters of Fray Junipero Serra, the Founder of California and His Franciscan Missions." The text will be published in Spanish-English and in Spanish-French, with a critical introduction and notes.

In 1944, the Most Reverend Delegate General of the Franciscans for North and Central America, Father Mathias Faust, invited me to become a resident Associate Member of the Academy of American Franciscan History, inaugurated at Washington, D.C., on April 18, 1944.

EDITOR'S NOTE: Sheed & Ward published the English edition of Father Piette's major work, *John Wesley in the Evolution of Protestantism*, in 1937.

CHRISTIAN REID
(1846 - 1920)
by Sister Lucy Marie, O.P.

TRUTH IS MIGHTY AND SHALL PREVAIL. GOLDEN WORDS! AND for Frances Fisher Tiernan, known to the literary world as Christian Reid, they were golden words emblazoned on the pure gold Laetare Medal awarded her for her outstanding services to American literature. The honor was conferred at Belmont Abbey, North Carolina, May 31, 1909. The late Father James A. Burns, C.S.C., then president of Holy Cross College, Washington, D. C., representing Notre Dame, said in an address delivered on the occasion:

"Your services to American literature have made your name a familiar and loved one in thousands of households. You have interpreted the highest ideals of life and conduct ... It is to express its appreciation of your efforts in behalf of wholesome reading, and especially your influence upon the youth of our country, that the University of Notre Dame confers on you the Laetare Medal for the year of Our Lord nineteen hundred and nine, and prays that you may be spared many years to shed light and strength on the paths of your people."

Since this memorable presentation thirty-eight years have elapsed, a reasonable time after which to pass some sort of judgment on such high praise, for the gentle southern lady whose life was so hidden, yet whose name and works were so well known.

Death ended her labors some twenty-seven years ago; too brief a span to apply the test of time to what she has written, yet long enough to permit a check on her appeal to the present generation. Just what chances does she have with the youth of today? How do they react to this precise, prudent, polished southerner? Do they find her too idealistic, her philosophy out-of-date, her fiction plots stale, her characters too good to be true?

A religious high school teacher recently pondered these very questions. Christian Reid had once been required contemporary reading for her classes. Lately, however, she had been neglected through the requirements of more recent fiction. The teacher resolved to make amends, and incidentally to get first hand answers to her questions.

The library yielded several volumes, well-worn and mended. These she assigned to as many students for oral report in ten days. The results were gratifying, even surprising. Despite class discussions, and the fact that the cat was out of the bag as far as plots were concerned, others asked to read the volumes.

Frances Christine Fisher was born in Salisbury, North Carolina, in 1846, with an ancestory distinguished for a spirit of public service, love of religion, generosity, tolerance and culture. They were statesmen, scholars, and warriors. In 1868 she left the religion of her parents, who were Episcopalians, and embraced the Catholic faith. In 1887 she married James Marquis Tiernan of Baltimore. The union was happy, but short, for her husband died in 1898 after a long and complicated illness.

The next thirty years of her life were filled to capacity

with writing, teaching, promoting church and civil activities. In her sixty-sixth year, with nearly forty novels to her credit, one might expect her to rest a little from her labors. But the ruination of her silver-lead mines in Mexico brought her face to face with the problem of providing for herself, her invalid sister, her brother's children, and her aged aunt. This she did with her pen, despite her own physical infirmities. She did it cheerfully and earnestly up to her latest breath. In 1920 she was caught in the influenza epidemic, and then by pneumonia, from which she died on March 24th. She was buried from the Sacred Heart church, and laid to rest in Chestnut Hill cemetery, Salisbury.

Mrs. Tiernan's interest in good reading and her desire to promote it quickened her activity in Salisbury. There, through her influence, several circles and clubs were formed, she directing and inspiring the members, training them to enjoy the best and to select the kind of books that would combine entertainment with an ever widening horizon of thought.

The benevolent hand of Christian Reid has endowed American literature with more than forty novels, plus numerous poems, a drama, and hundreds of short contributions to magazines and periodicals. Broadly speaking, her novels fall into five groups: her early works, including her *Southern Plantation* and *Small Town Series;* stories with European background, the result of her trip abroad; stories of Mexican setting; travel, and adventure stories; and didactic novels.

Her first novel, *Valerie Aylmer,* 1870, met with more than expected success, and encouraged her to produce the Plantation Series—*Morton House, Mable Lee, A Daughter of Bohemia, Hearts and Hands,* and *Bonny Kate.* All of these deserve high merit. *Morton House* was especially praised by Orestes A. Brownson, a man certainly never given to overpraise anyone, least of all a woman writer. Of it

Maurice Francis Egan wrote fifty years after its publication: "The memory of this book remains with me as a vision of delight... It is a good book for youths of both sexes, and for the old, the story like all of Christian Reid's novels, takes them back to the dreams of youth."

The Small Town group presents two interesting and well-written novels. *A Question of Honor*, and *After Many Days;* also a travel sketch, *The Land and the Sky*, which made Ashville and the western section of North Carolina famous throughout the country.

A Question of Honor is a society novel of post Civil War time. For plot, theme, and character delineation it is comparable to Jane Austin's *Pride and Prejudice*, although the solution, which is too long coming, taxes the patience of the reader. Protestant critics praised it for its purifying and elevating tone, and for its clear portrayal of the teaching of the Church on the sacredness of the marriage engagement, and the heinousness of suspicion and tale bearing. *After Many Days*, a tale of thwarted ambition, also possesses fine qualities of description, suspense, and skill, but the reader is scarcely prepared for the unreality that colors the conclusion.

In *Land and Sky* Christian Reid deviated from the plan of a small town novel and wrote the daily happenings of a party of travelers through Ashville and a section of North Carolina. It was her love of the country that drew from her pen majestic descriptions of towering mountains, glowing sunrises and sunsets, and amusing and interesting reactions of the travelers to their experiences. So great was the appeal of the book that the Southern Railway Company adopted its title as a slogan. The reward was increased patronage.

Feeling the need of wider experience and new material, Frances Fisher arranged a trip abroad in 1879-1880. For a decade following her return from the Old World her pen found drink in the fountains of Paris, Rome, and Venice, in such novels as *Heart of Steel, Weighed in the Balance, Armine, A Comedy of Elopment,* and several others.

The *Heart of Steel* is Irene Lascar, whose proud and unforgiving life points to the truth that the hating soul does more harm to herself than to the object of her hate. *Weighed in the Balance* was intended for an allegorical novel, but early in the story the allegory is buried in the events that transpire. This story and also *A Woman of Fortune* develop plots around the evil and good of money. With Christian Reid money was never a first end; she regretted that it had even to be considered. She decried the materialism of the day and the rampart passion of accumulating wealth for wealth's sake.

For a swift running love story of this period *A Comedy of Elopement* is recommended. Her great achievement is *Armine,* a novel proving logically and thoroughly the fallacy of communism. The story is a splendid tribute to the author's intelligence, and is marked by sincere, earnest feeling and excellent character delineations.

Her marriage in 1887 to James Marquis Tiernan, already noted, opened the door to new surroundings and experiences. Mr. Tiernan, a mineralogist, saw in the Mexican silver-lead mines a lucrative investment, and arranged to open and operate five of them. This necessitated the Tiernans' residing in Mexico.

The scenery, the people, their customs and costumes fascinated Mrs. Tiernan, and before long she had embarked on literary ventures with a Mexican background. Of this group are *Carmela,* a romance of unrequited love; *The Picture of Las Cruces,* which deals with the effect of environment upon association; and its sequel, *Lady of Las Cruces,* a melodramatic mystery; another master travel sketch, *The Land of the Sun;* and *A Daughter of the Sierra,* now conceded to be not only the best novel of this group, but one of her very best.

A trip with Mr. Tiernan to the West Indies deeply impressed her and gave birth in 1896 to *A Man of the Family*, and in 1898 to *The Chase of an Heiress*, both stories of Santo Domingo.

Yvonne Prevost is the "man of the family" who incognito seeks a family treasure buried in the French section of the island. Intrigue and melodramatic adventure march the plot along swiftly and breathlessly. Splendid descriptions of the island and its people, and especially the picture of the adult population dancing and swaying in the moonlight, won the interest of a vast reading public and rated the book a best seller in 1897. The merit of *The Chase of an Heiress* lies not so much in the fast moving plot as in the descriptions of the war ravaged Spanish section of Santo Domingo.

In 1908 *Princess Nadine*, her last adventure story appeared. It is a fast moving thriller of high society life, Nadine being the daughter of a Russian prince and the grandchild of a California miner. The plot teaches a lesson of loyalty to principle, and reveals the duplicity and dishonor which often lurk in affairs of state. This novel was translated into Italian.

Because Christian Reid was zealous and generous, because she knew the important role literature plays in the development of character, she was a teacher as well as an entertainer. Young people are often more strongly impressed by books than by sermons. This influence the author sought to exert through several especially designed didactic novels.

The first of this group, *A Little Maid of Arcady* (1893), shows that worldliness is not the parent of happiness; *Vera's Charge* paints the futility of trying to escape unhappiness and remorse in dissipation and excitement; *A Far Away Princess* has an anti-divorce theme; *The War-*

grave Trust is a well-planned, interesting romance in which sound principles of honorable business are pitted against selfish commercialism; *The Secret Bequest,* her last novel, portrays the struggle of a strong man against the love of a beautiful woman and a rich inheritance.

But her masterpiece is *The Light of the Vision* (1911). It is a story for the serious-minded man and woman, a story which points clearly that the Christian way is the way of sacrifice. It is a tremendous, gripping tale, simple, sound, lofty, but human. The soul at the brink of death is George Raynor, a brutish, devilish, good-for-nothing; the victim in this case is his divorced wife, Madeline, who, having since her divorce embraced Catholicity and learned the value of the coin of sacrifice, remarries George, now a helpless invalid, and by holy, patient care and prayer and suffering, saves him from self-destruction and brings him to a holy end.

Christian Reid was a Victorian and a romanticist. Her gentle nature, her inheritance of culture and refinement, her sheltered life, and her lofty ideals made her so. Debasing language, violent scenes, and crude actions had no place on her pages. She had scruples about putting "damn" and "damnable" in the conversation of George Raynor, but she could think of no other way in which he would express himself.

Her characters are drawn from the refined cultured class, the class she knew best, and they are thoroughly American. Her women characters exceed her men in numbers and excel them in delineation.

Her plots are interesting, her style clear; it is never involved, but at times lacks color. She is exceptionally skillful in creating suspense, and her descriptive power is equal to the best in American literature. Grace and beauty of expression mark her refined and fluent diction. Humor is not one of her assets, but its absence is more than compensated for by vivacious sprightliness that characterizes all she writes, and by a refined and happy wit that marks the conversation of her characters.

When the Reverend Daniel E. Hudson became the editor of the *Ave Maria* in 1874, he made an effort to obtain the services of the best American writers. Christian Reid was among the early and regular contributors. She was very modest about her accomplishments, almost too modest. It was Father Hudson more than others who gave her encouragement, noted with pleasure the praiseworthy reviews, and advised and sustained her against adverse criticism. She was ever grateful to him for this kindly interest, as several letters on record testify.

Christian Reid wrote for the joy of writing and for the good she would thus be able to do. She set for herself the highest standards and was constant in trying to reach them. Her best literary creations are the embodiment of what she would wish to do or be under similar circumstances. Beautiful and noble as are some of her brain children, her own life surpasses them all in beauty and nobility. If she fall short of permanence or a marked degree of popularity, the fault will not be so much hers as her readers', because they will not be far-seeing enough to appreciate her outlook on life.

EDITOR'S NOTE: The Ave Maria Press, Notre Dame, Indiana, publishes the still available titles of Christian Reid. Sister Mary Magdalene, writing under her secular name, Kate Harbes Becker, published a *Biography of Christian Reid*, in 1941. This book, a reliable and sympathetic full-length study of the author and her works, is available from Sister at Sacred Heart Junior College, Belmont, North Carolina.

JOSEPH J. REILLY

MOST OF US ARE CONSCIOUS OF OBLIGATIONS TO A FEW PEOPLE whom we can never adequately repay. Sometimes this sense of debt is realized early and grows steadily with the years. This is the case with Joseph J. Reilly, who was born in Springfield, Massachusetts, and educated in the public schools. His parents were Irish born and came to America as children. Their belief in prudence, honor, industry and the Faith they had inherited, together with their understanding of the value of education, was imparted to their children.

To be their son was his first stroke of good fortune. A second was a Classical course in one of the half-dozen best high schools in New England. His third was his older brother whose fine mind, passion for learning, and legal training at Harvard Law School equipped him to be a rare mentor for his worshipful younger brother who followed him to Holy Cross College in 1900 and in due time became, like him, editor of the college monthly, *The Purple*.

On going to Fordham University in the autumn of 1904 as an instructor in English and in History he discovered that the transition from an undergraduate somebody to a teaching nobody, though a considerable anti-climax, was a challenging introduction to a profession whose joys were not always apparent at first sight. A year of law (after teaching hours) at the newly established Fordham Law School, while it had a fascination of its own, convinced him that the satisfactions he found in teaching were incomparably greater than those discoverable in law. He thereupon enrolled in the Graduate School of Columbia University, devoting his non-teaching time to English and Comparative Literature and receiving his M.A. degree in 1909. At Columbia he studied under a second great teacher, Brander Matthews, receiving from him and from such men as W. P. Trent and William Lawrence an incentive to further graduate study.

Two years before taking his degree at Columbia he resigned from Fordham to accept an instructorship in English at the College of the City of New York, whose President, John H. Finley, poet and man of letters, was an inspirational influence, especially to the younger members of the staff.

Three years at City College, coupled with continued work in English at Columbia, left little leisure for writing but provided him with opportunities for enrichment of mind and spirit for which he has never ceased to be grateful. Out of them came the resolve to realize two dreams: to spend at least a year at Yale, and ultimately, if his finances allowed, to secure his Ph.D. there. The magnets that drew him to New Haven were five Yale immortals whose work he knew and admired and under whom, in the event, he studied: H. A. Beers, G. H. Nettleton, A. S. Cook, Wilbur L. Cross, and the late William Lyon Phelps.

President Finley warmly seconded his ambition and secured him a year's leave of absence. In the autumn of 1910 he entered the Yale Graduate School for what proved to be a kind of *annus mirabilis*. With so many intellectual stars on his horizon to point the way and nothing to divert him from complete dedication to study and research, Dame Fortune smiled once again, bringing him, among other things, the abiding friendship of Wilbur Cross, the great scholar, and of "Billy" Phelps, the greatest teacher he ever knew. In Wordsworth's *Prelude* he found the phrase that said everything: "Bliss was it in that dawn to be alive."

The award of a University Fellowship (1911-1912), followed by an extension of his leave of absence from the College of the City of New York, made possible another year in New Haven and the writing of his dissertation (a study of James Russell Lowell as a critic) under the sponsorship of Professor Albert S. Cook. He received his Ph.D. in June, 1912, and, reluctantly declining an instructorship at Yale and yielding (with some misgiving) to the spirit of adventure and the lure of a highly attractive salary, he accepted the post of Chief Examiner for the Massachusetts Civil Service Commission.

Nine years in this position under the same roof with the Governor and the Legislature proved to be a rich experience, for it brought him into contact with leaders in professional and business life throughout the State whom he induced to serve as Special Examiners, gave him opportunities to study human nature from many new angles, and revealed some at least of the mysteries which are popularly supposed to envelope the mind of politicians at work. He found them unfailingly friendly and co-operative once they were convinced that no special favors were possible for anyone whether in or out of politics.

In the interest of economy and efficiency he effected many procedural changes, and awakened a fresh state-wide interest in the opportunities provided for public service through competitive examinations. His work brought him recognition beyond the borders of his own state: he was elected Vice President of the Association of Civil Service Commissions of the U. S. and Canada in 1919-20 and President in 1920-21.

During his residence in Boston he published *Lowell as a Critic,* gave courses of lectures at the Catholic Summer School of America and, on the invitation of Cardinal Hayes, at St. Joseph's Summer School, Sullivan County, New York, contributed to *America, The Commonweal, The Catholic World,* and various educational journals, and carried on a study of Newman first begun at Columbia and continued at Yale.

Meantime, although his Civil Service position was in a real and broad sense educational, he came to feel for himself the truth of Professor Phelps' saying that it is possible to "love to teach as a strong man loves to run a race." The road back lay through the Superintendency of Schools in Ware, Mass., where he spent five years, 1921-1926, modernizing the system, building a junior high school, establishing a fund to help defray the college expenses of worthy students, making a campaign (with a success which surprised him) among the foreign born to continue their children on into high school, giving University Extension courses on the short story by lecture and radio, completing those studies on Newman which were published as *Newman as a Man of Letters,* and, in many ways most important of all, marrying, in 1922. He has one child, Joseph J., Jr., born in 1931.

He and his wife spent the summer of 1925 in Europe, realizing a long-cherished dream and finding particular delight in the art treasures of Paris, Venice, Rome, and Florence and in the haunts of the great English poets.

His work at Ware brought him several offers in larger educational fields, among them the Presidency of the State Teachers College at Westfield, Mass. He accepted instead an Associate Professorship of English at Hunter College, New York City, in 1926. He was promoted to a Professorship in January, 1927, and in addition appointed Librarian of the college in 1928, positions he still holds.

He has found his new life in New York immensely stimulating. He has managed to edit two more books, write two more volumes of essays, teach a course in English Romantic Poetry and one in Nineteenth Century Prose, give lectures, Commencement addresses, and radio talks, and foster the growth of the Hunter Library from 31,000 to 160,000 volumes.

His interest in Newman has led to numerous lectures in the East and Middle West, among them Newman Club audiences at Yale, Harvard, Smith, Columbia, Massachusetts Institute of Technology, and New York University. He is an active supporter of the Newman Club movement, to whose founder, a former President of Hunter College, Dr. James M. Kieran, he dedicated his *Fine Gold of Newman.*

In the summer of 1945 he was invited by the Newman Association of Great Britain to represent the colleges and universities of the United States at the Newman Centenary Conference held under the sponsorship of the Archbishop of Westminster (August 18-25). Scholars from many countries met to pay tribute to Cardinal Newman and to study his life and work and the application of his ideas to problems of today. Dr. Reilly read a paper on "Newman's Place in English Literature."

Plans are under way to translate his *Fine Gold of Newman* into Portuguese, an indication, it is to be hoped, of a developing South American interest in the great Oratorian.

When he reflects on how much more he ought to do to achieve his aims he falls into something like despair but finds consolation in the words of "Billy" Phelps' idol, Browning:

A man's reach should exceed his grasp,
or what's a heaven for?

When he feels depressed over human short-comings (chiefly his own) he remembers "Billy's" sense of humor and unquenchable optimism and is reclaimed.

EDITOR'S NOTE: Dr. Reilly's published books include: *Lowell as a Critic*, Putnam, 1915; *Newman as a Man of Letters*, Macmillan, 1925; *Dear Prue's Husband and Other People*, Macmillan, 1932; *Of Books and Men*, Messner, 1942.   He also edited *Masters of Nineteenth Century Prose*, Ginn, 1930, and *The Fine Gold of Newman*, Macmillan, 1931.   In collaboration with Katherine Crofton, he edited the collection of editorials by Father James M. Gillis, C.S.P., entitled *This Our Day*, Paulist Press, 1933.

ALBERT PAUL SCHIMBERG

TWO THINGS, IT SEEMS TO ME, GAVE RISE TO MY BOYHOOD dream of becoming a writer.

Mine was a reading family. One of my early memories is of my parents and brothers and sisters listening to what was read aloud in the light of a kerosene lamp. There weren't many books in the home of a workingman in those days, but what we had we cherished. Later, the number of books grew larger, and there were more magazines, too. I read avidly all I could lay my hands on: poetry, adventure and travel stories, biographies, novels if they were properly robust, not overly sentimental; and the dime novels which cost a nickel, not a dime, and were by no means the youth-destroying literary poison which some people said they were.

When I went to St. Joseph's School in my native town, Appleton, Wisconsin, the whole forenoon was devoted to studies in the German language. At first I rebelled against studying German, but in time I got along quite well and enjoyed it. I have long since been grateful that I was compelled to study *die schone deutsche Sprache,* and regret that I did not also acquire thus easily, as children do, a command of the French language. My maternal grandmother tried to teach me French, but she died before we had got very much further than *une, deux, trois.* I am not defending the practice of giving little Americans their religious instructions exclusively in any foreign language, but as a cultural asset the acquisition of languages in addition to that of one's own country is something for which to be grateful.

At school I hated arithmetic, grammar, penmanship; liked reading (in German almost as much as in English), history, geography, and most of all "compositions," the little literary exercises demanded of pupils in the upper grades. These compositions, which so many of my schoolmates disliked and found difficult, were comparatively easy for me and I delighted in them. My teachers, at St. Joseph's and later at Sacred Heart school, also in Appleton, seemed pleased with my efforts and, of course, this encouraged me immensely. They meant well, I am sure, but I am afraid they are to blame for helping me indulge the preposterous dream, the fantastic ambition. They and my whole family's interest in books; an interest which in my case meant also an intense interest in those who wrote books.

After the ninth grade, which included a few high school subjects, I had to leave school. By that time I had begun to write, sometimes on a borrowed typewriter, and had sent off a number of manuscripts. I imagined that the editors were waiting impatiently for my contributions and would send me sizeable checks by return mail. Of course, nothing of the sort happened. A few of the manuscripts were accepted, always by editors who had no honorarium budgets at their command. But at least I got the thrill of seeing in

print something I had written, and is there in all the world
another such thrill for a boy with his head full of a dream?

One of the first magazines to print anything I wrote was
Our Young People, a flourishing juvenile magazine published in Milwaukee. The late Charles O'Malley accepted
for *The New World* of Chicago a translation of Adalbert
Stifter's *Heidedorf*, and sent me an encouraging letter
which I have kept. However, I had to make a living, so I
worked in a photographer's studio for two years and two
years in a furniture factory, and then became a cub reporter
on *The Crescent,* a daily newspaper in Appleton. After two
years in Washington as secretary to a Representative from
Wisconsin, I returned to Appleton and to newspaper work
there and in Kaukauna, Wisconsin. Then in the fall of 1919
I enrolled at Marquette University in Milwaukee for the
long-deferred, constantly-desired college education. I shall
never forget all that was done for me by Father John
Danihy, S.J., and Father Joseph Reiner, S.J.—God rest
their souls!—and other members of the faculty, and the
general stimulating atmosphere of the university. For me,
the most valuable and enjoyable courses at Marquette were
those in philosophy, history, English literature, and sociology.

Before going to Marquette, I had managed to get a number of manuscripts accepted and while at the university was
able to meet some of my expenses by selling articles, essays,
verse. *The Magnificat* accepted a number of manuscripts,
and I shall always be grateful for the generous encouragement given me by the editor, Sister M. Ignatia. A day of
days was the one on which *America* accepted the first of
several contributions. I succeeded, too, in breaking into
The Catholic World, Columbia, Extension, and other Catholic and secular magazines. In 1922 I began work on *The
Catholic Herald,* which was merged in 1935 with *The Catholic Citizen.* Since then I have been on the staff of the com-

bined paper, *The Catholic Herald Citizen* of Milwaukee. I kept on writing after getting back into newspaper work, getting a generous number of rejection slips and some acceptances. For some years, however, the newspaper work was too engrossing to permit much other writing.

Father Reiner told us about Theresa Neumann of Konnersreuth, and this led to my translating three of Friedrich Ritter von Lama's books on the Bavarian stigmatist. The Bruce Publishing Company, of Milwaukee, published these and two other translations from the German, one of them, *The Mantle of Mercy*, a biography of St. Vincent de Paul by Leo Weismantel. When I told one of the publishers I wished Weismantel had written a life of St. Francis of Assisi so I could translate it, he asked me why I didn't write my own life of the Little Poor Man. So I did, and *The Larks of Umbria* was my first book. Writing it was one of the most enjoyable, rewarding experiences of my life. And the thrill of having a book published is, of course, even greater when it is your own instead of a translation.

My second book (seventh if you count the five translations) was *The Great Friend: Frederick Ozanam,* which appeared early in 1946.

Now I am at work on a book about Theresa Neuman. I hope to see published some day my little history of little Luxembourg, my father's native land, and the manuscript entitled *Tall in Paradise*, the story of St. Coletta of Corbia.

I should like to write and see published something about early Wisconsin. My great-grandparents and grandparents came here as pioneers, and my mother was born here early enough to know log cabins and the Civil War.

Among the most gratifying things about being an author —even a part-time, only occasional and minor one—are the helpful kindnesses of editors, publishers, librarians, and others, the letters from readers, and the reviews and criticisms, which are always interesting, often stimulating.

Writing is hard work for me, even after more than forty years since the dream began, but I like it tremendously. The hard work of it is more than compensated for by the pleasure I get out of the necessary reading of sources, and of course most of all by the satisfaction of having a book published.

I have no theories about how to become a writer. For me there was the dream, which persisted in spite of everything. I am glad and grateful that it did persist, and that it has been realized to some small extent at least. For there were those who never lost faith and made loving sacrifices to keep the dream from being shattered.

EDITOR'S NOTE: Mr. Schimberg's published works include his life of St. Francis of Assisi, *The Larks of Umbria*, Bruce, 1942, and his biography of Frederick Ozanam, *The Great Friend*, Bruce, 1946.

GEORGE N. SHUSTER

I OWE MY YOUTHFUL INTEREST IN LITERATURE AND WRITING to Father Corbinian, of the Capuchins, who taught German at St. Lawrence College. At the time I knew practically nothing of this language, but at the end of four years I wrote and spoke it better than I did English, so inspiring and helpful was this truly great teacher. Meanwhile, the instruction we received in religion was in the best Franciscan tradition. It associated concern for the liturgy with a very real charity and humility.

But although I wrote some articles after graduating from college, and was given encouragement by Father Burke, then editor of *The Catholic World,* it was not until I returned from the army in 1919 and went to teach at Notre Dame that I really decided upon a "career." Of course army life at the front was hard, and the spectacle of death and suffering very trying. Going into Germany with the army of occupation aroused my interest in that country, but it was not until later, when I had a good deal of reading behind me, that making an intensive study of conditions there became one of my major interests. At Notre Dame I wrote *The Catholic Spirit in Modern English Literature*, and worked, at Father Daniel E. Hudson's request, as associate editor of the *Ave Maria*. Father Hudson was a very remarkable priest. Among other things, he taught me how to say something in an editorial paragraph.

Meanwhile the *Commonweal* had been talked about, but I left Notre Dame without any thought of being associated with it, intent only upon getting a doctor's degree at Columbia University and showing my bride the wonders of New York. But Michael Williams invited me to write editorials for the new magazine, and this I did weekly during several months. Then I was offered and accepted a place on the staff. The magazine was never without its serious problems, and there were times when its treasury was as nearly empty as it is possible for a treasury to be. Nevertheless, the hard work of helping to edit it—the hardest work I have ever done—was extremely rewarding, not merely because of the service we thought we were rendering, but also by reason of personal relationships. Henry Longan Stuart was as good a writer as Catholic journalism has ever known. Thomas Walsh was genial and poetic, and Michael Williams himself had genius.

Literary associations were rich. We had the friendship of G.K.C., the co-operation of Hilaire Belloc, and the constant personal assistance of Agnes Repplier. In the United States there was hardly an author who did not at some time turn to us, and abroad we had a wide circle of friends. Pope Pius XI was interested in our work, and I owe to the *Commonweal* the friendship of Cardinal Faulhaber. Sometimes this reputation led to fairly humorous consequences. Thus once, while abroad, I had an appointment to visit a certain member of the hierarchy. When I called with Mrs. Shus-

ter, the face of the Vicar General, who was to present us
to His Excellency, turned frigid. He was only with the
greatest difficulty persuaded to perform his duty; and
afterward he had fancied me a theologian and therefore
doubted my orthodoxy when he saw me arriving with a
beautiful young woman.

The magazine was often knee-deep in controversy, and at
one time we received more "letters to the editor" than all
the other "high-brow" journals of New York combined.
No doubt the most exciting of our ventures were discussion
of the campaign of 1928, when Alfred E. Smith was the
presidential candidate, and analysis of the Spanish civil
war. Mr. Smith was truly a great man. I came to have the
deepest admiration for him. But for General Franco I had
no comparable feeling, and nothing that has happened since
has led me to change my mind. It was in connection with
the Smith campaign that I wrote the *Catholic Spirit in
America,* which seemed to me my most original and worth-
while book, though it is far from having been the most successful. Some day I hope to revise it, leaving out passages
which have ceased to be of interest, and concentrating on
the broad trends as I see them.

In 1937 I left the *Commonweal* for two reasons. First,
writing an almost endless amount of copy for a weekly
journal over many years brings one eventually to a point
where one no longer has anything to say. Second, I had
been offered a very remarkable grant by the Social Science
Research Council and the Carnegie Corporation in order to
write a history of the Center Party and of the Weimar
Republic. This opportunity was made available by reason
of the joint good offices of two distinguished friends—Professor Carlton J. H. Hayes and Dr. Heinrich Bruening. I
had met the former German Chancellor while he was in
office. Subsequently I had been with him while he was
being hounded from place to place by the Nazis. The op-

portunity to gather material about a great period in history
seemed too good to miss.

Prior to this assignment I had spent periods of study in
Germany and had written *The Germans, Strong Man Rules,*
and *Like a Mighty Army,* upon which books such reputation
as I may have largely rests. They were all commentaries
on the significance of the Nazi movement. Now I had the
chance to talk with many former members of the German
government, to confer with exiles and churchmen, and even
to make secret visits to the Third Reich. Then we settled in
Vienna for a good while, and witnessed there the annexation
of Austria by the Nazi dictator. Perhaps an article I sent
to the *Commonweal* about the tragedy is the best single
piece I ever did. After my return to this country I wrote the
notes for *Mein Kampf,* and planned to work on my history.
But appointment to Hunter College seriously interfered
with this worthy purpose, but I did collaborate with Dr.
Bergstraesser in writing *Germany: a Short History.*

Little need be said about my ventures into fiction. But I
have always liked to write it, and at least once pleased a
great many people. *Brother Flo* has been the recipient of
many compliments, and I shall confess that I like these
because I am very fond of the man with whom the little
book deals. *Look Away,* the faults of which are obvious to
me, was written in a great hurry, but the point it sought to
make was that a marriage can be a sacrament. *The Hill of
Happiness* has long since been out of print, but it is remembered as a tribute to my friends the Capuchins.

It seems to me that if I had to start life over I should first
of all make up my mind to disassociate myself either from
teaching or from journalism. These two enterprises have
always gotten into each other's way in my life; and though
today I relish both and consider them of equal importance it
seems to me evident that no one man can manage the two.
The junction was especially difficult in the Catholic environ-

ment. If one has not tried it, one can hardly realize how trying it is to prepare adequately to give instruction to young people while attempting to do some literary work of one's own. On the other hand, a journalistic career is an onerous and sacrificial one, indeed, unless he who dedicates himself to it has some other prop to lean on. We need a great Catholic literature and press desperately. We can have neither unless some men and women are enabled to go ahead and see what they can do.

In conclusion I should like to say a word about certain feeble endeavors of mine to awaken familiarity with great Catholic literature. During a number of years I made a desperate effort to translate from the German in particular. The time needed had to be sandwiched in between other tasks; and sometimes, as in the case of Father Peter Lippert's truly great book, *Job the Man Speaks with God*, the ultimate results did not seem to justify the effort expended. Yet it is of this work that I am today proud, because it seems to me the only really helpful service I have rendered. Here is an endeavor which younger men and women might well carry forward, not for their own advancement, of course, but for the sake of the Catholic cause. For the Christian faith will reconquer the world only if it is always and everywhere conscious of the world-wide character of the Mystical Body of Christ.

EDITOR'S NOTE: Dr. Shuster has been president of Hunter College since 1940. His more recent books include: *The English Ode from Milton to Keats*, Columbia University Press, 1940; an anthology, *The World's Great Catholic Literature*, Macmillan, 1942; and in collaboration with Dr. Arnold Bergstraesser, *Germany: a Short History*, Norton, 1944.

RIGHT REVEREND
MATTHEW J. W. SMITH
by George Martin Ryan

MONSIGNOR MATTHEW SMITH REGARDS HIMSELF AS AN editor rather than as an author, although he has had five books published and for years has been gathering data for several others, all dealing with religious subjects.

His life story is one of long training for editorship, despite the fact that, in boyhood, he never had a thought of newspaper work. During early boyhood, he wanted always to be a parish priest; this ambition vanished during high school days and, after the usual schoolboy's indetermination, he fixed on authorship as his aim. He became involved in the newspaper business as the result of answering a want-ad for a proofreader on a daily newspaper, and he intended that journalistic experience should be simply a vestibule to life as a fiction writer. Instead, it made him a newspaper slave for life. Meanwhile, the vocation to the priesthood recurred. The young editor went into the seminary and at the age of thirty-two became a priest. He was im-

mediately put back into newspaper work, where he expects
to die. The writing of books, instead of being his chief job
in life, as he had originally hoped for, became incidental
in the grinding but fascinating work of editorship.

Matthew John Wilfred Smith was born June 9, 1891, of
Edward Francis and Annie (Feeney) Smith, in Altoona,
Pennsylvania, a purely industrial city, where his father,
later a railroad mechanic, was then a merchant. The an-
cestral background on both sides of the family was Irish,
although the future editor's parents were both born in this
country and he has two great-grandmothers buried in
Pennsylvania. The family now has its sixth generation on
U.S. soil.

His mother was well acquainted with the English and
American classics. She had a rare system of her own to get
her children interested in books. Matthew knew how to
read before he started to school and he was reading adults'
books when he was eight. The mother would buy two or
three books for every child at Christmas and would keep
urging the children to read one another's. In this way a
child would get through about fifteen or twenty a year. But
there were always other books around the house, which it
was taken for granted the youngsters would read. They
were never ordered to read, but suggestions were cleverly
made to indicate that no one would think of having books
around without reading them. They were encouraged to
lend and to borrow books and, when a book came through
this method from a neighbor's or a relative's house, all the
children in the family would read it before it was returned.
At times, when the school schedule permitted, it was common for the youngsters to read two or three books a week.
One summer twelve-year-old Matthew read fifty-two.

The family had to live on a workman's income, and there
was no money for an elaborate library, but books were kept
in handy closets and the supply of them was never-ending.

Movies had not yet come in. Both adults and children had
their chief entertainment in reading.

One of Monsignor Smith's first memories, in reading, is
of a history of England; another is of Charles and Mary
Lamb's *Tales from Shakespeare.* Popular works were not
barred. The boys read every book of Alger, Henty, and
the other juvenile authors popular at the time. They often
read the novels let lie around by adults; such as the sac-
charine tales of Mary J. Holmes. The parents, however,
kept dangerous books out of the home. The children were
gradually introduced to the classics, and the result was a
family in which every member could write. That there was
anything unusual about all this never entered their heads.

Matthew Smith was given his primary education by the
Sisters of Charity in the Cathedral school, Altoona, and
then was sent to the Altoona public high school, the only
high school in the city at that time. As a member of the
Mechanics' library, a public subscription institution, he continued the family habit of voracious reading all during his
high school course, although he carried a schedule of studies
that, by the time he took his diploma, which he could have
claimed long before, gave him enough educational credits to
be ready for the junior year of college, under the rules of
that era.

His collegiate training, however, was to be unusual. The
family income needed help and he went to work as a proof-
reader on the *Tribune,* a daily newspaper, where the editors found that the boy knew both language and literature.
The long years of reading told. The editors formed a con-
spiracy. They wanted to try out a method of their own for
the training of writers and they found young Smith a willing guinea pig. They taught him all the techniques of
journalism, with the aid of such texts as were then available, and they demanded that he read at least one book
from every English and American author who had made

the grade in lasting literature, with a heavy absorption of
the works of some of these writers. The editors guided and
tutored the law on this course; they also saw that he was
enrolled in college extension classes. The editor of the
Tribune, W. H. Schwartz, was an exceptionally well-read
man, who in addition to editorial work had been through
years of high school teaching.

Smith took almost no recreation, except for attendance at
two theatres every Saturday (his one day off), and he went
through a four-thousand-hour tutored reading course in the
classics, while he worked at every type of editorial task.
The system of literary instruction was that destined to become famous long afterwards at St. John's College, An-
napolis. At the end of the course, the editors succeeded in
getting a recognized Master of Journalism degree for their
pupil. Doctorates in philosophy, laws, and journalism followed later in life.

In 1913, Smith, because tuberculosis had been trailing the
family, joined his brothers, sisters, and father in moving to
Colorado. His mother had died at forty-one of "consump-
tion." After about a half year as telegraph editor of the
Pueblo Chieftain, a daily, Smith moved to Denver, where
in 1913 he became editor of the *Denver Catholic Register*,
a post he has held ever since. Not many young men twenty-
two years old would face the task of editing a diocesan
paper, but Smith had no qualms. He knew that he was a
trained journalist, and he had learned that any one who
reads always has plenty to write about. Maybe, he admits,
there was also a touch in him of the fool who rushes in
where an angel fears to tread. But Bishop Nicholas C. Matz
was willing.

The paper, which had been losing heavily, began to pay
its way immediately, although its total possessions at the
start were a mailing list, two old desks, two chairs, a $4,000
debt, and a typewriter so decrepit that the young editor

could not use it. When he asked for a new typewriter, the
owners held a weighty conference. Was the editor worth
the risk? The circulation was 2,800; Smith was to live to
see, early in 1945, when it was to pass the 660,000 mark;
but the climb was no mushroom growth. It represents a
life's hard work.

If you go back to 1913, you will find that the Catholic
press was not using genuine modern journalistic headlines
and makeup. Matthew Smith, more than any other individual, introduced them. Some people sarcastically called him
Hearst and some thought he was lacking in reverence to
make such innovations. Were not Catholic papers meant
to be dull? In 1917, when Smith went to a Catholic press
convention, he found that the total circulation of all the
diocesan papers of the country was barely 250,000.

The young editor had no easy time. Denver was no fine
city but a rough western frontier town. The battles and
lack of ethics on the part of the daily press were something
that one would have to live through in order to believe. The
first headline Smith ever wrote in Colorado was about a
cowboy who had just shot up the town of Craig, in the
northwestern part of the state. Politicians would not believe their ears when they found they could not buy editorials from the little editor. One powerful daily publisher
enticed the lad to his office and ordered him to open fire on
another editor as a bigot. Smith had been too long in the
business by this time not to know that little papers do not
have to crawl before big ones. He did have to crawl before
apathy in the Church of those days toward the Catholic
press. Time has since wrought many changes. Circulation
is today the editor's smallest worry. Denver also has become a much pleasanter town to live in since the public's
mental juvenility of past years has been outgrown.

While frontier days still prevailed, one editor called in the
Denver Catholic Register owners and said that either Smith

or he would have to leave town; Denver was not big enough
for both. Smith stayed and the editor left. It should be
explained that this was not because of the pugnaciousness
of Smith but because the daily editor lost his job as a result
of more than one display of neurotic judgment.

Meanwhile, seeing that he would never be happy except as
a priest, Matthew enrolled as a student of philosophy and
studied it assiduously for several years; then he went into
St. Thomas' Seminary, Denver, where, after the customary
course in theology, he was ordained June 10, 1923. After
ordination, he continued to attend theology classes and he
has been through the full course for the priesthood twice in
formal class work. All during this time he continued editorial work.

He established the *Register*, a companion paper to the
Denver Catholic Register, in 1924, and developed its National Edition late in 1927. Diocesan editions, now (1947)
published for thirty-two dioceses, began to appear first in
1929. The largest are those for St. Louis and Cincinnati.

There has never been a dull moment in Matthew's life.
He was the first newspaperman in America to use colored
pictures on page one and he has invented types of headlines
that have been copied all over the world. Lately he became
the first editor of a Catholic weekly to start bringing in the
news by telegraph typewriter. Blessings on his work have
come six or seven times from the Pope.

The editor of the *Register* has not solicited diocesan editions. They have simply come. Once Matthew and his
brother, Hubert, had such a unique idea on circulation that
the Post Office Department asked them not to reveal it lest
it should revolutionize the publishing business and the
second class mailing privilege.

Perhaps the most unusual part of the *Register* setup is a
full-fledged college that operates in connection with the
paper and that, in addition to teaching journalism by a most

practical method, carries on courses in English taught by
university professors, in philosophy taught by priests who
have graduate degrees in that subject, and the full course
of theology taught by professors from St. Thomas Seminary (with which the college is affiliated). The students
are laymen and priests of the editorial staff. It is common
to hear a layman discuss the profoundest phases of theology
when *Register* men come together. A lay editor was once
cornered by a visiting priest educator who tried to trap
him in theology. "I will answer," said the layman, "if you
define precisely what original justice was." The priest
scratched his head and walked away, sorely puzzled at what
manner of laic this could be.

The printing plant of the newspaper represents a half-
million dollar investment, housed in its own beautiful building.

Editor Matthew Smith, made a Domestic Prelate in 1933,
with the title of Right Reverend Monsignor, wears purple
only on ceremonies and works coatless in black shirt sleeves,
but never without the Roman collar.

He has never been a mere titular editor, content to have
his name on the masthead and some one else doing the
work. He spends a heavy week, every week, in writing,
proofreading, headline writing, news judgment, copy editing, and all other editorial tasks. A large and able staff
assists.

He lives in a convent institution, where he says Mass, but
his newspaper work is too strenuous to allow any pastoral
duties. In past years, however, he has had plenty of experience in pastoral work, teaching, and as vice-chancellor
of the diocese. For twelve years he has been a diocesan
consultor.

Looking back over the years, he says he has "covered"
everything from police court to canonization trial, and has

had interviews given to him for publication by every type from patrolmen to Pope Pius XII. There is nothing, he says, that he loves more and hates more, among things earthly, than newspaper work.

EDITOR'S NOTE: Msgr. Smith's books include: *Letters to an infidel,* Herder, 1925; *Great Controversies,* Herder, 1928; *Practical Ascetics,* Herder, 1928; *The Church Upon the Rock,* 1941; *Unspotted Mirror of God,* 1943.

ROBERT SPEAIGHT

I WAS BORN IN A HOUSE ON THE CLIFFS AT ST. MARGARET'S Bay, near Severn, on January 14, 1904. The first thing I can remember was the English Channel and the Ostende packetboat and the P. & O. lines, all lit up, moving down the straits on a Friday evening. Once I saw the German and the British Grand Fleets pass by within half an hour of one another, and of course we could very often see the coast of France. Sometimes, on a clear day, the spires of Calais were clearly visible through the telescope. All these signs of travel must have given me a taste for other countries, and in particular a love for France which has grown through the years, so that I now feel equally at home on both sides of the Channel. At the same time, my Kentish origins, so near to the pebbly beach where the Romans and afterwards Augustine landed, have given me an abiding sense of how my own people first became a Christian nation. The beginnings of the English story can all be traced on the Kentish shores.

When I was six we moved to Hatfield, an old country
town in Hertfordshire, some twenty miles from London.
We inhabited a fine Georgian house which my father had
restored. I was the eldest of three brothers and it was in
Hatfield that we all grew up. At the top of our hill were the
gates of Hatfield Park, where we used to walk with our
nurse. I still love to wander there, although it is many
years now since I lived in Hatfield. The aged oak trees, still
sprouting a few leaves, the gracious lime avenues, the
pheasants in the woods and the swans on the river, and
above all the great Jacobean mansion, built by Robert Cecil,
the chief minister to James I, and the Tudor Palace where
Queen Elizabeth was confined during the reign of her elder
sister—all these impressed me at an early age with a sense
of history and a love of nature. No other town in England
bears so proudly the marks of the Reformation and the
new Protestant aristocracy to which it gave birth. Nowhere
else, I should add, has it so redeemed its infamous beginnings. At the parish church on Sundays the Marquess of
Salisbury and his family sat apart in their private chapel;
at the station they had a special waiting room, built by the
third Marquess who was three times Prime Minister of
England; but their privileges were paid for by devoted
public service. This example of aristocracy functioning for
the general good has, I think, done much to make me in-
different to social equality. It has done much to convince
me that the hereditary principle has a valuable part to play
in a healthy commonwealth, and it has given me a distrust
for the rhetoric of democracy.

When I was nine and a half years old I was sent away to
school at Hare in Sussex. It was an excellent Preparatory
School of the old-fashioned kind, very scholarly and Spar-
tan. Generally speaking, I was not unhappy there. At the
age of fourteen I went on to Haileybury, a large public
school only nine miles from Hatfield. Here I gained a

scholarship and developed many tastes which were to re-
main with me afterwards. I won prizes for Elocution and
Shakespeare criticism, and played Mark Anthony in "Julius
Caesar" in the school play. Before I had left Haileybury,
I had determined to be an actor.

In 1923 I won a scholarship in History at Lincoln College,
Oxford, and before going up I was sent abroad for several
months to study German. M. Poincare's policy in the Ruhr
having prevented me from going to Frankfurt, I went instead to Zurich, where I lived *in pension* with several other
young people. I went a great deal to the opera and the play,
hearing many of the Wagner operas for the first time, but
I did not learn much German. In May, therefore, I went on
to Vienna with a few pounds in my pocket and two letters
of introduction, and lived for two very happy months with
a Doctor and his wife and their three little girls. I loved
Vienna, though it was then an impoverished city. I saw a
great many plays and heard a great deal of music. The
sister of my hostess was a singer and we came by a number
of free tickets. I have never been back to Vienna since, but
I met some of my old friends in Austria in the summer of
1936, and was disturbed by their open Nazi sympathies.

On returning to England in the summer of 1923, I played
Hamlet for the first time at a Shakespearean Festival
organized by my father at Anymering-on-Sea. My friend,
Martin Browne, now one of the best directors on the
English stage, directed it, and this began a collaboration
which was resumed later when we both had adopted the
stage as our profession. Also playing in "Hamlet" was
Gyles Isham, the current star of the Oxford University
Dramatic Society, who was to become one of my closest
friends.

At Oxford I read for an Honours Degree in English
Literature, but my heart was in the theatre. When the Oxford University Dramatic Society produced "Hamlet" a few

months after I came up to the University, Isham played the chief part and I played the Player King. In following years I played Falstaff (in "Henry IV," Part II) and Peer Gynt. Those performances were favourably noticed by the London critics, they brought me in touch with important people in the profession and stood me in good stead when I came to embark on my career. I left Oxford in 1926 after three deliriously happy years. It was the period of *Brideshead Revisited,* and those who have read Evelyn Waugh's book will know what that meant in terms of an easy and carefree enjoyment of the good things of life.

In the Long Vacation of 1926, I went up with Isham (who had recently become a Catholic) and another friend to stay at the Benedictine Abbey and School at Ampleforth. It was my first introduction to Catholicism in action and it made an impression upon me that I was never to forget. Immediately afterward, Isham and I went abroad to Italy for a few weeks holiday, passing through Paris on the way. We visited Milan, Verona, Mantua, Florence, Assisi and Perugia. Among these cities, each with its incomparable treasures, Assisi seemed to me the holiest place I had ever seen or could imagine. In August I went up to Liverpool to begin my stage career at the Playhouse, then under the direction of William Armstrong.

It was not a very happy year. Except for the first three or four plays my parts were not very interesting, and my fellow-actors were not particularly congenial. Liverpool itself stood in drab contrast to Oxford and Italy. Still I do not regret the year I spent there; it was a valuable experience to become part, even for a short time, of a life so totally different from anything I had known hitherto. The comfortable and rather Philistine bourgeosie, the cotton brokers, the Lascars in dockland, the hundreds of thousands of Liverpool Irish, the great Anglican Cathedral going up stone by stone, the north-country solidarity of the people—

all these were new to me. So were the demands, so exacting and yet often so humdrum, of my professional life.

In the summer of 1926 I left Liverpool and joined my brother in Paris for a two weeks holiday at the house in Neuilly where he was living as a paying guest. Now, for the first time I began to get acquainted with the great city, going a great deal to the theatre and the museums, and meeting a wide variety of people. I had decided to find what work I could in London, but my next employment was a season of Shakespeare in Egypt. It was not until a year later that I made my first success on the London stage in an adaptation of "The Brothers Karamazov." I played the part of Smerdyakov, the epileptic murderer and suicide, and for some time afterwards was doomed to be cast for this type of part. In 1929 I became known to a wider public as Hibbert in Sheriff's famous war-play, "Journey's End." This ran for eighteen months in London and in the summer of 1930 I went abroad by myself for a five weeks' holiday. After bathing in the south of France and walking in Corsica, I met a friend in Oberammergau for the Passion Play.

When I returned to London, I felt quite certain that I wanted to become a Catholic. I was received into the Church by Father Martin D'Arcy, S.J., on the eve of All Saints in the same year, 1930.

From now onward my interests outside the theatre grew rapidly—in religion, in politics, in art, in literature. After a season (1931-32) at the Old Vic, during which I shared the leading parts with Ralph Richardson, playing "Hamlet" in its entirety, I published my first novel (a very immature pastiche), *Mutinous Wind*. This was followed in 1934 by *The Lost Hero*. I find it hard to reread this now, but it was admired by certain critics at the time. My first literary success, however, was *The Angel in the Mist*, in 1936. This was followed in 1939 by *The Unbroken Heart*. This last is

the only one of my novels which I can still read with any
satisfaction. Meanwhile, in 1935, I had created the part of
Becket in T. S. Eliot's "Murder in the Cathedral," and between 1935 and 1938 I had played it more than eight hundred times in Britain and America. It was my biggest
theatrical success, and as a result I was asked to write a
life of St. Thomas A'Becket. This was published in 1938.

During these years before the war I contributed frequently to the Catholic Press and was in general sympathy with
the views of my friend Douglas Woodruff, editor of *The
Tablet*. But I disagreed with him over the Ethiopian War,
believing that, however reluctant we might be to quarrel
with the Italians, we ought to support the authority of the
League. I also thought he underestimated the immediacy
of the German menace. But I have never ceased to contribute to *The Tablet*, and I especially admired it during the
war when it steadfastly refused to be seduced by the emotional Jacobinism with which the British publicists de-
bauched the British people.

I paid three visits to the United States in 1938 and 1939—
once with "Murder in the Cathedral," which was played in
Boston and New York; once with "Five Kings," in which
I played Chorus to the Falstaff of Orson Welles—an ill-
starred but interesting venture; and again in the summer of
1939 when I gave a course of lectures in Modern Poetry at
the University of Notre Dame. I gave a further course in
English Literature from January to June 1940 and inaugurated a Summer Theatre on the campus in July. Few
memories are more precious to me than those weeks of ar-
duous work in which teaching Sisters made the clothes and
young students played the parts for "Twelfth Night," produced out of doors in front of the Commerce School. The
result was a genuinely Elizabethan evening; had Shakespeare been there he would have been proud to claim this
posterity as his own.

Early in 1941 I returned to England and spent the remainder of the war years on the staff of the British Broadcasting Company, first in their Home and later in their European Division. This work was fascinating, although it prevented me from either writing or acting. I had been broadcasting continually since my first year on the stage and was glad to be able to turn this experience to some political account. The only work of professional consequence that I was able to undertake during the war was to play the part of Christ in Dorothy Sayers' sequence of radio-plays, "The Man Born to be King."

In September 1944, I flew out to France just after the liberation of Paris and returned for three months in the summer of 1945. During this time I lectured for the British Council and sent home articles for *Time and Tide*, to which I am now a regular contributor. I travelled widely in France, both in 1944 and 1945, in the same capacity of lecturer and journalist. Meanwhile, I had returned to the theatre as soon as the war had ended and resumed partnership with Martin Browne in a season of new plays by poets at the Mercury Theatre. The most successful of these, Ronald Duncan's "This Way to the Tomb," ran for more than three hundred performances, and was presented at the Studio des Champs Elysies in Paris during the summer of 1946.

In 1942 I became a director of Hollis & Carter, Ltd., publishers, and in 1946 was elected a Fellow of the Royal Society of Literature.

EDITOR'S NOTE: Mr. Speaight's published books include *Mutinous Wind*, Peter Davies, 1932; *The Lost Hero*, Eyre, 1934; *The Angel in the Mist*, Eyre, 1936; *The Unbroken Heart*, Eyre, 1930, and Basilian Press, 1946; *Thomas Becket*, Longmans, 1938; *Acting*, Cassell; *Shakespeare and Politics*, Royal Society of Literature; *The Voice of the Vatican*, Sands, 1942, *Remember France*, Sands, 1943.

REVEREND FRANCIS
JOSEPH STANG

I WAS BORN IN BADEN, SOUTHERN GERMANY, THE SON OF John and Teresa Stang. My great-grandfather, Matthew Stang, had left his native Norway because of the religious intolerance prevailing there. With his large family he emigrated to East Prussia and from there to Bavaria and Baden in Germany. His family was soon scattered, and one of the sons went to Ireland, to County Down in the North, and there is, according to Dr. Magee, the Bishop of Down, a place in the County called Stang.

My parents were deeply religious. From my father I inherited the characteristic of facing any ordeal or hardship and bearing them silently, and his great love of the Church. From my fine intellectual mother—she was in the estimation of those who knew her a living saint—I inherited a great love for Our Blessed Mother, a devotion to the most forgotten souls in Purgatory, and a great love of books as well as the urge to write.

For ten years John and Teresa Stang had no children.

How fervently did they pray for this gift of God! They even went afoot on pilgrimages. And finally to the joy of this worthy couple Our Lord heard their prayers. A peculiar coincidence seems to be the fact that my parents were married on May eleventh, my sister was born on September eleventh, and I was born on November eleventh.

The home of the Stang family was truly a Christian home. The poor and afflicted always found their way there. Every Friday we children would go to visit six poor families and bring them food and financial help.

The piety of our mother was so great that she taught her children to be also a spiritual help to others. It was customary in our home parish that when some one died, the church bell would toll, even in the middle of the night. As soon as Frau Stang heard it she would awaken her husband and children. All would kneel down and say with her five Our Fathers and five Hail Marys in honor of the five wounds of our dear Lord Crucified, for the particular person who had just died and for all the dying.

I made my classical studies in my home city. Many of my school friends were non-Catholics, and more than one, frequenting my parent's house, were drawn into the Church.

John and Teresa Stang set an excellent example to their children. We were treated kindly, but an order had to be obeyed at once. Mother endured great physical suffering, but offered it up for the love of God, especially on behalf of her children. How often did we hear her say that she would rather see us dead than that we should offend our dear Lord by mortal sin. She wished that her children should make some special sacrifice for the love of God. It was not a command but a suggestion. But we promised it and keep it to this day. It was never to smoke, drink whiskey, or play cards. Although it is not wrong for people to use these things moderately, mother had a reason for wanting her children to abstain totally from them, and this proved to be a blessing.

Since childhood I had a great admiration for *l'Eglise de France*. I was thrilled when as a little boy I read how the saintly Cardinal Richard, Archbishop of Paris, had been evicted from his home and the Catholics of the city had carried the prelate, an octogenarian, through the streets to a new home, a little dwelling.

Wanting to be a priest and knowing the plight of the Church and her dire need for priests in France, I wished to be a priest in France. Rene Bazin in his book *La Grande mirère des prêtres*, describes the awful conditions prevailing there at that time.

The years in France, years of study and prayer, were the happiest of my life. How beautiful were the scenes in the magnificent churches on the feasts of Noel, Pasques, and la fete de Dieu.

I had the happiness of having very distinguished men as my teachers, among them Msgr. (later Cardinal) Baudrillart and Msgr. (later also Cardinal) Verdier. One of my benefactors was Canon Chauvin, director of l'Ecole Massillon. I often visited Msgr. Hirscher, Titular Archbishop of Laodicea, a linguist, also Abbe Lecanuet, author of a life of Montalembert, and Abbe Chocarne, biographer of Lacordaire. I learned to appreciate French thought and literature.

Political clouds in 1913 began to predict a catastrophe, a new world war. And in 1914 the situation grew worse. I came to the United States where I finished theology and was ordained by the late Bishop Koudelka for the diocese of Superior, Wisconsin. Then Bishop Schinner, who adopted me for the diocese of Spokane, Washington, loaned me to the diocese of Superior to help out for a year. There I was placed in charge of seventeen missions, all very poor.

Recalled to my own diocese, I was appointed assistant pastor of St. Gaul Church, Colton, Washington. The post proved to be a real novitiate. Summer and winter the hour to retire was 7:50 P.M. The rectory was locked at that hour. At 4:30 in the morning the pastor would call his assistants to his room for the daily meditation.

After the death of the pastor I was placed in charge of Holy Rosary Church, Chewalah, Washington. It was a small place beautifully situated, surrounded by mountains. The parish school was in such a condition that a new one was needed. To draw Catholics, I advertised the school, the country, and the climate in Minnesota, Iowa and Wisconsin papers, and soon the parish began to grow steadily.

There was no Catholic hospital in the territory covering two hundred miles to the north and sixty miles to the south. So, under the kind direction of Bishop White, I built St. Joseph's Hospital at Chewalah, which is operated by the good Dominican Sisters.

In 1937 my health broke down. After two years at St. Anthony I came to St. Ignatius Hospital, at Colfax, Washington, conducted by the Sisters of Providence, of Montreal, and remained there until 1947 when I removed to St. Mary's Hospital, Walla Walla, Washington.

My writing for several French periodicals was interrupted by the war, but I expect to recommence it soon. In Austria I wrote two books in German, one on Pope Pius XI and the other on St. Teresa. In English appeared *The Greatest Calling*, *Matt Talbot*, and *Margaret Sinclair*. I have other books in preparation.

In 1941 I was named a member of the Gallery of Living Catholic Authors.

EDITOR'S NOTE: Father Stang is a nephew of the late Bishop William Stang of Fall River, Mass., who, a great scholar himself, was largely responsible for launching the literary career of Canon Sheehan. Bishop Stang urged Rev. Dr. Heuser, editor of the *American Ecclesiastical Review*, to publish the Canon's writings serially in that periodical.

REVEREND LEO C. STERCK

I WAS BORN IN 1902, IN TERMONDE, BELGIUM, ON THE RIVER Scheldt, in the heart of Flanders. My father was a doctor, tall, dignified and handsome. I remember him vividly, yet it was my mother, tiny, blond Anna Catherine Dewit Sterck, who from the very beginning was the guiding influence of my life. She charmingly combined the most genuine deep-rooted piety with a very gallic spark of gaiety, wit, and worldly wisdom. I have no doubt that I owe my vocation to her prayers. After my birth she had a plaque placed on the wall of the church at Lourdes, petitioning the Blessed Virgin to make her son a priest. But I also indubitably inherited from her my fondness for society, good talk, good food, and the little elegancies of life.

I can see myself now, as a little boy, dressed in the best English manner, always more serious and correct than my brother Frank. He and my pretty dark-haired sister Simone, were the tomboys of the family. There was nothing they would not try once, while my sister Mary-Paule (the only blonde among us) and I, were more inclined to sit upon our dignity. At our summer villa in Ostende or at home in Termonde, I confess to playing the grand seigneur. I also played priest, with a perfect miniature outfit which included vestments and appointments for the altar; and the children of the neighborhood were thoroughly baptized, married, and buried, sometimes all within one day. The only naughty thing I can recall doing is stealing a peach from my grandfather's garden, whence perhaps my priestly sympathy for those who reach longingly after forbidden fruit.

I attended the Collège de la Sainte Vierge in Termonde, and La Petit Séminaire in Malines, and would have undoubtedly continued my studies at Malines had not the war intervened. I recall the distant rumble of guns which made the crystal chandelier in the white parlor tinkle constantly and the window panes vibrate. The food grew poorer daily. Nights the windows were covered with black paper and we listened to the drone of planes overhead. If only my father had been home, perhaps we should have been less apprehensive, but just before the war he had left to investigate business opportunities in America. Little did we then realize it would be more than six years before we saw him again. I wonder how he felt when my mother wrote him that our home in Termonde had been completely destroyed and that our country house at Heyst-opden-berg had been looted, the interior irreparably damaged, and made the headquarters for German officers. They treated us politely, if a little superciliously, and I still remember with something like envy the fluent brilliancy with which they played Bach and Beethoven on my mother's piano. In the same room, on a huge map pinned to the wall, they followed military movements and plotted actions with little flagged markers. Fortunately my mother had buried some of our

family heirlooms in the garden. But most of them we never
saw again.

In 1920 we joined my father in America. I enrolled at St.
Ambrose College, Davenport, Iowa. My father had chosen
Moline, Illinois, just across the Mississippi River, where
there was a large Belgian settlement, as our new home. It
was not easy. None of up spoke a word of English. As the
eldest child, I took all the responsibility my eighteen years
could bear, but as usual the brunt of it fell upon my mother,
and as usual she prayed her way through with amazing
equanimity.

The three younger children soon became totally Ameri-
canized, forgetting their mother tongue French, if not all
their Flemish. As for myself, I never quite lost my accent,
nor my continental outlook. The new world was a wonderful place to live. We could not get over the ice-water, the
swift elevators, and all the bananas you could buy in the
grocery stores, whereas at home they were a luxury for
Christmas and special feasts. But life in America was not
without its hardships. My father died suddenly in 1926,
and once more my mother was obliged to see us through.
She taught music and gave lessons in French so that I could
finish my studies at the Sulpician Seminary in Washington,
D. C.

The years passed quickly, and I found myself an ordained
priest in 1927. Once more I had to adjust myself to a new
and different life, but the life I wanted above all else. Then
came my appointment as an assistant at Sacred Heart Cathedral, Davenport, and a new blessing in my life in the
gracious person of the pastor, Monsignor Leonard. No one
could have been better adapted to polish the rough corners
off a young man still new in the priesthood. Suave, kind,
wise in the follies of men and the ways of Providence, he
looked at the world through his round dark-rimmed glasses

with the wisdom of a Chinese sage. He taught me to live
for the day, to relax, and not to be swept off my feet in the
rushing stream of life. Even death came to him gently in
his sleep. I found him thus, a rosary still clasped in his
hand, a rosary which has been one of my most precious possessions ever since.

I feel that Divine Providence has been particularly kind
to me in the contacts I have made throughout my life. Or
perhaps it is just my vital interest in other people and their
problems which has brought me into such close association
with interesting personalities. From each I have borrowed
something: a new interest, a deeper insight, a higher patina
of maturity. But whatever the cause, it has been my experience that whenever God subtracts one blessing, He adds
another, of a different nature. And so it was after the
death of Monsignor Leonard. I had the good fortune to
become the friend and protegé of Father Culemans, aviator,
philosopher, and savant, pastor of Sacred Heart Church,
Moline, Illinois. It was he who encouraged me to write.
French being my mother tongue, I was at first hesitant.
Could I express myself in what to me was still a foreign
language? I had been teaching for years, however. In my
classes in French and religion at St. Ambrose College, where
I have been on the faculty since 1927, I probably learned
more from my students than they did from me. I was beginning to think in English (even though to this day I still
count in Flemish ... which is no worse, I suppose, than
people who do their arithmetic on their fingers). Most
important of all, I had grown thoroughly familiar with the
American way of life. And so, gradually, I conceived the
idea for a book which would combine the American way,
the continental way, and God's way of life in a spiritual
cocktail for the refreshment of flagging human spirits.

Much time elapsed, however, before it reached the press

under the title of *For All to Live By*. In the meantime, while I was still in the seminary, I published a translation of a theological work, *Faith and the Act of Faith,* by Father Bainvel, S.J., as well as later on my own textbook for French literature entitled *Great Books of France: a Catholic Guide.* I was also made an honorary member of L'Institut Litéraire et Artistique de France and a life member of the Guillaume Budé Society, a classical literary society of Paris.

However gratifying this may have been, I was still dissatisfied. Parchment acknowledgments of merit and the letters you write after your name are hardly enough to warm the human heart. My work as chaplain at St. Vincent's Orphanage, where I have served now for eighteen years, has given me more real joy. Here I come in contact with children of all ages, mostly in unfortunate circumstances, and their problems and difficulties have become very clear to me indeed. I may, in my leisure hours, like to trace the intricate counterpoint of a Scarlatti sonatina, or toy with my collection of antique pill-boxes, but whatever their cultural value, they are merely the superficialities of life. I can in conscience enjoy them only in proportion to the knowledge that I have helped others, who may never have heard of such niceties, yet who are struggling for the very necessities of existence or seeking a solution to the basic problems of life.

For this reason, the concept of *For All to Live By* continued to germinate in my mind until I finally put it on paper. The book which resulted is an expression of my personal philosophy, based on the life and philosophy of the happiest, saddest Man who ever lived: Christ Himself. The fact that the Catholic Literary Foundation chose this work for their November 1946 selection gave me great pleasure because it enabled me to reach many more readers than would otherwise have been possible, and the bonds uniting my heart to the hearts of others the world over, will, in some small way, be multiplied and strengthened.

Writing for a much narrower public, I have also turned out a number of literary reviews and brief essays on art (another of my enthusiasms). Several of these have appeared in *Liturgical Arts* magazine. Other articles, reviews, the inevitable beginning of a play, and the first chapter of a novel, still repose in my file. My ideas are always having kittens: each one begets a half dozen more; and I only hope I shall have time to develop some of the more consequential ones thoroughly. At present, besides continuing to teach (the best antidote to becoming stuffy and fortyish that I know), I try to be a good master of ceremonies for Bishop Hayes, and the Registrar of St. Ambrose College. I have always deplored the fact that men with artistic and literary temperaments are considered, at the worst, unstable, and at best, poor business men. I am proving to myself that quite the contrary is true. In fact, administration suits me—for the present at least—if I may be permitted to have an occasional literary brain-child in the form of a good, red-blooded Catholic novel or another book on religion.

After all, I am first and foremost a priest, as Divine Providence, at every turn of my life, has always reminded me. To bring God to man and man to God is my primary work, and to this end I pound the typewriter, unscramble the credits of confused Freshmen, and say Mass every morning in the little chapel of St. Vincent's Orphanage. As a result, my forty-four years have been rich and full, each day bringing a blessing to offset every evil, and some new evidence of God's goodness. In my life, as in that of every priest, Christ has literally carried out the words of His priestly prayer for unity: "Those whom Thou hast given Me I guarded, and not one of them perished . . . and these things

I speak in the world, that they may have joy made full in themselves."

EDITOR'S NOTE: To provide interpretations, even in outline, of the highlights of French literature from the Song of Roland to Claudel, in seventy-five pages, is the feat accomplished by Father Sterck in his *Great Books of France*, Author, St. Ambrose College, Davenport, Iowa, 1941. Bruce published his *For All to Live By*, in 1946. His translation from the French of *Latin and the Act of Faith*, by Father Jean V. Bainvel, S.J., was issued by Herder in 1926. It deals primarily with the psychology of faith.

CHARLES WARREN STODDARD (1843-1909)

by

Reverend Arthur J. Hope, C.S.C.

IN 1864, WHEN HE WAS TWENTY-ONE YEARS OLD, CHARLES Warren Stoddard sailed out of the Golden Gate for Honolulu. He was sailing also directly into the arms of literary fame. An elder brother was ailing and the doctor had advised an ocean voyage. Charles would be his nurse.

Before boarding ship, the San Francisco *Chronicle* had given him a commission as a sort of roving reporter. Charles was to jot down his impressions of the islands he visited, send them back to San Francisco where they might be published. These letters are now known as the Idyls of the South Seas. When Stoddard composed them, he did not sign his own name. He was timorously sceptical of their merit. Later, when he understood that they were warmly received, his cautious soul was overjoyed. He was then ready, anxious even, to admit his authorship.

Perhaps it is not important now, but in 1864, when Oahu and Tahiti were only names on a navigator's chart, it was

quite something to be known as the author who surpassed
all others in conveying a sense of delicious languor, the
soothing drowsiness of the tropics, the feel of joyful living,
the utter contentment of body and soul. If these islands held
any hardship or inconvenience, Stoddard never notes it. His
letters speak only of gently swaying palms, exotic blooms,
the rhythmic crawling of the surf, unconcern about food or
clothing, the ecstasy, so understandable in Stoddard's sensitive personality, of finding himself loved by simple people.

Stoddard had a limpid, easy way of expressing himself.
On one of his trampings about the islands, he sees a water-
fall:

Its whole quivering length glitters and glistens with jewels, where
it hangs like a necklace on the bosom of a great cliff.

Maurice Francis Egan said of Stoddard's prose: "It is
the most plastic, spontaneous, poetical and personal among
contemporary writers." By nature, Stoddard was indolent,
yet independent. Perhaps these qualities best explain why
his stay on the islands was so agreeable to him. The un-
ruffled and carefree life of the natives, their serene unconcern about civilization, their friendliness and simple joys,
evoked in Stoddard a genuine sympathy.

George Wharton thinks Stoddard was a writer of letters.
In his more lengthy works, Stoddard is not so successful.
His best writing occurs in those shorter pieces where he
strolls pleasantly through his memory of places visited and
people seen. Without seeming to labor at it, he hits upon
the most exquisite form of expression. Seated in a little
nook near the altar, he tells us of the high Mass in the leper
colony at Molokai:

The solemn boom of the sea surf was fit accompaniment for that
solemn service; and the long low sough of the sea wind was like a
sign of sympathy.

Undoubtedly Father Hudson, editor of *The Ave Maria*,
read the *Idyls of the South Seas*. It was just the sort of

writing that would appeal to his sensitive spirit. It was not until 1875, however, that Stoddard came to know the magazine. He was in Rome at the time, and not very happy. One afternoon, he stopped at the American College, and in the little parlor, while he waited for a friend, flicked the pages of the latest issue of the *Ave Maria*. Who, he wondered, might this Hudson be?

It was not until ten years later that Father Hudson and Stoddard met face to face. In the meantime, however, Father Hudson wrote a timid note of appreciation. Stoddard replied unfeignedly grateful. This beginning of letters led to a voluminous correspondence covering nearly a quarter of a century. Stoddard found Father Hudson very *simpatice*. Indeed, it was the priest's quiet kindness to Stoddard that, later on when he had begun to write for the weekly, drew from him the remark, often repeated, that he wished to write for no other magazine in the country except the *Ave Maria*.

It was not only the striking beauty of Stoddard's style that endeared him to Father Hudson. During the author's stay in Honolulu, he had often crossed to the island of Molokai, and there, with reverence and admiration, conversed with one of the outstanding missionaries of the 19th century, Father Damien, the Apostle of the Lepers. It was Stoddard's pen that first made known to the world the sacrifice and labor of the missionary. Unknown to himself, Father Damien had drawn Stoddard and Father Hudson together.

Father Hudson listened eagerly to his story of Father Damien. He knew it would make a good story for the *Ave Maria*. In the fall of 1885, through six issues, runs the series called *The Martyrs of Molokai*. So great an impression did it make, it was later brought out in book form.

Stoddard had received very little formal education during his youth. As a child, his health had been delicate. More-

over, constantly he had been shunted from one relative to
another, interrupting whatever schooling he had. Just before he sailed on his first journey to the South Seas, he had
been employed as a reporter for papers in San Francisco,
and had tried his hand, unsuccessfully, at dramatics. His
ability to write was entirely a natural gift.

In 1884, Stoddard had fallen on hard times. Father Hudson, trying to be helpful, made a suggestion: "Would not
Stoddard be pleased to join the faculty at Notre Dame?"
Stoddard was over forty at the time, and it would be such
a novel experience. "You know," he replied to Father Hudson, "I am quite a Bohemian, and I may be quite a misfit in
the classroom." But because he was financially embar-
rassed, and because, at Notre Dame, he would be close to his
friend, he accepted the proffered post. In the spring of
1885, with many misgivings, he arrived at the university.

Stoddard had traveled around the world with a pencil in
his hand. He had dozens of little books in which he kept
note of the things he found interesting. When he felt well,
he wrote rapidly. His manuscripts were difficult to read.
He was conscious, too, of his proclivity to misspell words,
for sometimes he offers two or three versions. The meticulous wisp of a man who had to correct his writing frequently twitted him about his verbal fertility.

Stoddard must have made copious use of his notebooks in
1886. In that year the *Ave Maria* published two series of
articles entitled "With Scrip and Staff." For thirty issues,
Stoddard records in an easy, fluid style, his impressions of
the Holy Land and the Far East. It was a prodigious
literary effort. When one remembers that Stoddard was
teaching several classes at Notre Dame at this same time,
his output seems all the more remarkable. Seated in his
rocking chair, a gift of Father Hudson, he kept to his room,
high among the turrets of Notre Dame, sacred to literary
pursuits. The students, who liked him immensely, made

frequent assaults on his door. Little by little, he found himself unable to resist their friendliness.

At first, Stoddard was very happy. Father Hudson had made him as comfortable as one could expect in a boarding school of those days. There were times when he felt cramped. Indeed, by 1887, he definitely made up his mind that teaching at Notre Dame was for him quite unsuccessful. For forty years he had lived a life free of all discipline. Regular hours and punctual attendance at class, observance of little rules, the monotony of decorum—all these things irked the writer. So he left the university. But his friendship with Father Hudson remained unbroken, and his contributions to the *Ave Maria* continued in a steady stream.

In Covington, Kentucky, Stoddard stopped off to visit his friends the Clearys. The visit lasted a year. During that winter he was taken seriously ill. He was unable to write, but Father Hudson sent him some money "on account" to tide over the period of inactivity. Convalescent, he wrote to his editor friend:

I am bettering slowly. They take such good care of me here. I can lie in bed all day long if I like, and dainty meals will be served at my bedside, and the best of toddy in the shape of a nightcap. Before I am out of bed in the morning, the darky enters and builds a huge coal fire in the great (sic), which fire is kept burning until bedtime.

At the same time, Stoddard was visited by Mrs. Robert Louis Stevenson. They were old friends. She urged him to spend the winter in the Adirondacks with her illustrious husband. Had the season not been so inclement, Stoddard would have accepted gladly.

The mention of Stevenson brings to mind the *Open Letter to the Reverend Doctor Hyde*, a piece of ironic satire unequalled in English letters. After the death of Father Damien, Doctor Hyde, a Protestant clergyman, had pre-

sumed to cast aspersions on the moral character and worth
of Damien. It presented Stevenson with an opportunity to
defend a priest for whom he had high regard. How bril-
liantly he seized that occasion, the readers of the *Ave Maria*
discovered in 1890. Seldom has anyone received such a
literary lashing. Now this magnificent diatribe, whose
literary excellence is matched by its coherent logic, would
never probably come from Stevenson's pen had it not been
for Stoddard. For Stoddard it was who had put Stevenson
on the track of Damien.

Stevenson's step-daughter, Isabel Osborne, had married
Joseph Strong. And the Strongs went to live in Honolulu.
Stoddard, a neighbor, visited them often in their bungalow.
Enthusiastic over the apostolate to the lepers, Stoddard
went on endlessly about Damien. The Strongs began to
take an interest. After each trip to Molokai, Stoddard re-
galed them at length about the nobility, the sanctity of
Damien. So it was that sometime later, when the Steven-
sons came for a visit, Isabel and Joe told them about the
remarkable priest, the martyr for the lepers.

Thereupon Stevenson proclaimed he would go to see with
his own eyes. In the presence of humble effacement and
complete oblation, the gentle Stevenson was wrapped in
admiration. This first-hand evidence of Damien's devotion
made an indelible impression. Had Stevenson not gone to
Molokai, had he not conversed with Damien, it is hardly
likely that Dr. Hyde's calumnies would have seemed worthy
of his attention. And since it was through Stoddard that
the acquaintanceship began, some of the credit for that
famous letter must go to him.

Between Stoddard and Father Hudson, Damien was ever
a point of interest. From Covington, he posted an article
for the *Ave Maria,* in which he dramatically announces the
fact that at last, Damien had contracted the dread leprosy.
"Corpus Christi on Molokai" gives him a chance to recall

how Damien had carried the Blessed Sacrament on that occasion. He speaks of the missionary's efforts to distract and cheer the poor lepers, how he had organized a brass band of sorts. In a letter to Father Hudson, he suggests that the boys at Notre Dame might well ship their band instruments to Molokai, for which act the citizens of Indiana "may be doubly grateful!"

During the summer of 1887, Stoddard did twenty essays on the cities of northern Italy. Grouped together, he called them *Under Italian Skies*. At the same time, he wrote an imaginative piece about life and death in a Trappist monastery. "Brother Mansuetus," as he called his subject, bizarre and overdrawn, is almost comical. Stoddard was dead serious about him though. He had some glamorously emotional ideas of what a monk should be.

In the summer of 1888, Stoddard accepted an offer to act as quasi-tutor and traveling companion to a wealthy young man, whose parents were trying to get him ready for Harvard. The young man, his mother and Stoddard sailed for Europe. The association, lucrative though it was for Stoddard, irked him and prevented his writing. He did manage, however, to contribute two articles, one of which he called "Memories of Monte Cassino," the other, "Student Life in Rome," in which he described the international group of ecclesiastical students in the Eternal City.

In the fall of 1889, we find Stoddard at the Catholic University in Washington. Bishop Keane, then Rector, had offered him a position as professor of literature. Driven by sheer necessity, Stoddard had accepted, even though his previous experience as a pedagogue had been so unpleasant. His new post, lasting fourteen years, proved to his surprise both lucrative and enjoyable.

Stoddard had more leisure. He was free to write without interruption. This was ultimately beneficial for the *Ave Maria*, for during these fourteen years, Stoddard was able to contribute, every year, a goodly number of engaging articles for Catholic readers.

In 1903, Stoddard severed his connection with the Catholic University. He was tired of teaching and, too, he was ill. After a brief sojourn in New England, he returned to California. From his home in Monterey, he wrote frequently to Father Hudson. Not more than once a year, however, did he send an article for publication. His last described one of the legendary miracles of the Holy One of Assisi, which he called "San Francesco del Deserto."

On April 15, 1909, his scrawling hand sent Father Hudson the intelligence: "I am better and will write soon." Nine days later, he was dead.

EDITOR'S NOTE: Through the courtesy of *Ave Maria,* Father Hope's chapter on Stoddard is presented here. Scribner's published Stoddard's *South Sea Idyls,* and the Ave Maria Press issued his *Lepers of Molokai, The Passion Play at Brixleg, A Troubled Heart and How It Was Comforted* (in which he tells of his conversion to Catholicism in 1867), *The Wonder Worker of Padua: St. Anthony;* while his *Poems,* collected by Ina Coolbrith and edited by Thomas Walsh, were published by John Lane in 1917.

RICHARD SULLIVAN

I WAS BORN NOVEMBER 29, 1908, IN KENOSHA WISCONSIN, of mixed ancestry, Irish and German. My maternal grandparents and my paternal grandmother all were born in Kenosha county; my paternal grandfather presumably came from Ireland, though the record of his odyssey is vague. My mother's name is Rose (Pitts) and my father's Thomas Sullivan. I was educated in the St. James parochial grade school, the Kenosha public high school, the University of Notre Dame, the Art Institute of Chicago, and the Goodman School of Drama (a part of the Art Institute).

After my graduation from Notre Dame I lived in Kenosha from 1930 to 1936. I married a Kenosha wife, Mabel Constance Priddis, and my elder daughter, Jill, was born there in 1933.

In 1936, I came to South Bend, Indiana, as a member of the Department of English at Notre Dame. My younger daughter, Molly, was born here in 1938.

From 1932 to the present, I have been publishing stories: I would guess about thirty or forty to date, in perhaps a dozen or so nationally circulated magazines. Some of these stories appear now in various standard anthologies. I have also published a one act play, *Our Lady's Tumbler*, and three novels, *Summer After Summer*, *The Dark Continent*, and *The World of Idella May*. I have also done some radio plays and some thrillers which are better ignored. I also wrote the script for a Notre Dame promotion movie.

I am still at Notre Dame; still writing. And as far as I know, that is the complete story.

EDITOR'S NOTE: Mr. Sullivan's *Our Lady's Tumbler* was published by the Dramatic Publishing Company, of Chicago, in 1940. Doubleday issued his three novels: *Summer After Summer*, in 1942, *The Dark Continent*, in 1943, and *The World of Idella May*, in 1946.

FATHER TABB
(1845 - 1909)
by Reverend John J. Barry

THE LIFE OF JOHN BANNISTER TABB HAD ALL THE ELEMENTS that belong to fiction. His service in the Civil War as clerk on a blockade runner, his capture, internment in Lookout Prison, the loss of his family's fortune, his impaired vision —these events formed part of a tense and exciting background. After the war he had difficulty readjusting himself to the changed conditions. He studied music, taught school, and wrote poetry. A close friend, an Episcopalian minister, encouraged him to study for the ministry. After he had begun his studies, this same friend persuaded him to become a Catholic and study for the priesthood. Again he followed his advice and some years later the Church was proud to call him Father Tabb, poet and teacher.

Father Tabb came from an aristocratic Scotch-English family, one of the oldest and wealthiest in Virginia. In his veins ran the blood of the Washingtons and the Randolphs. The beautiful plantation, "The Forest," where he was born on March 22, 1845, was situated not far from Richmond. Here, in an atmosphere of wealth and culture, the children, three boys and a girl, received their early training from private tutors. John, the third child suffered from weak eyes. Noted oculists pronounced his case incurable, but not alarming if care were taken. He was a gifted boy, with unusual talents in music and drawing. Many of the scenes and characters of childhood he sketched with skill and accuracy. He prized in particular the drawings of his nurse, Nina, his tutor, Mr. Hood, and one of himself kneeling at his mother's knee, reading the Protestant Bible.

The Civil War brought an abrupt end to the peace and quiet of the Tabb household. Young men from the surrounding plantations were enlisting in the Southern army and the urge to join the colors was strong among the Tabb boys. The eldest, William, who was twenty-two, enlisted as a captain; the youngest, Yelverton, only fourteen, became a private. John, who was seventeen, tried to enlist but was rejected because of his poor eyesight. Undaunted by this rejection, he was able, through the influence of Major Ficklin, a close friend of the family, to enter the Confederate navy as a clerk on a blockade runner, the Robert E. Lee.

For two years this speedy boat ran the Union blockade. On a secret mission to England the crew was honored and feted. Here young Tabb attracted much attention with his clever caricatures of Northern leaders. An English periodical offered him a position on its staff as a cartoonist. He refused, stating he had a job to do and was determined to finish it.

On the return journey the boat was captured after a running battle with the larger and speedier Keystone State. The crew was imprisoned in Bull Pen, Point Lookout, Maryland. A sketch made by Tabb reveals the wretched quarters where he was confined. Here he met a young prisoner,

Sidney Lanier, who had served as signal officer on a captured blockade runner. Tabb writes of their meeting: "Here
in this shell-hole, while I was lying on my cot, ill with fever,
the distant notes of a flute reached my ears. I said to myself, 'I must find that man'."

Their association helped to pass many a dreary hour in
the old prison. Both were deeply interested in music and
poetry, and both were eventually to become leading poets of
the South. Lanier, who was a recognized musician, believed that music played a great part in poetry. His influence on Tabb's future work was very evident, especially
in the latter's "short swallow flights of song."

The long period of their imprisonment developed in these
two sensitive spirits a deep and lasting hatred for the
North. Both left prison broken in health. Lanier never re-
covered; Tabb's vision was greatly impaired by lack of
medical attention. On their return home they found only
ruin, starvation, desolation. Poverty stalked the once fertile
plantations; beautiful colonial mansions lay in smouldering
ruins; life was at a standstill. Valuable farm land sold as
low as fifty cents an acre. Long bread lines were daily kept
in check by Negroes, once the slaves of those who now stood
waiting patiently for a meagre supper of cornmeal.

In the gloomy period that followed, Tabb had great difficulty in readjusting himself. His family's fortune had
vanished before the onrush of the Northern army. After
studying music for some time, he became an instructor in
St. Paul's Protestant Episcopal school for boys in Baltimore. The rector, Rev. Alfred Curtis, thought a great deal
of the new teacher and they became close friends.

Five years later, encouraged by Curtis, Tabb entered the
Episcopal seminary at Alexandria to study for the ministry.
During this period Curtis became deeply interested in the
Oxford Movement and the part Dr. Newman played in it.

The latter's *Apologia Pro Vita Sua*, telling the story of his life and conversion, won the deepest admiration of Curtis, and he expressed his feelings in a letter. In the correspondence that followed, Newman invited Curtis to England. The latter accepted.

He returned to America a Catholic, having been converted and baptized by Newman. His first convert was Tabb. It took him two years to convince Tabb that he, too, should join the Church. Finally the latter went to Bishop Gibbons for instruction. "I," wrote the Bishop years later, "instructed him in the belief of the Catholic religion, administered successively to him the sacraments of baptism, confirmation, Holy Eucharist and holy orders."

When asked by his associates why he became a Catholic, Tabb replied: "I climbed higher, then higher and higher until I got to the top of the fence, saw the other side, liked it, and went over." He often admitted to friends that the old heresy frequently troubled him and that he preferred the King James Version of the Bible for the beauty of its language.

Two months after his conversion he entered St. Charles' College as a student. Three years later, 1875, when he was thirty years of age, he graduated and accepted a teaching position in St. Peter's School, Richmond. After teaching for a few years, he returned to St. Charles' College as an instructor in English and Greek. In September of 1881 he enrolled as student of theology in St. Mary's Seminary, Baltimore. He was ordained in the Cathedral on December 20, 1884. Soon after, he was returned to his Alma Mater as a teacher, and remained there until his death, twenty-five years later.

He made an excellent teacher. His sternness, nicely balanced by wit and humor, made him a favorite among the students. Although recognized as a fine Greek and Latin

scholar, he taught only English and Bible History. To aid
his classes in learning the fundamentals of English, he
wrote his own textbook, *Bone Rules: or The Skeleton of
English Grammar,* and dedicated it to "his pupils, active
and passive, perfect and imperfect; past, present, and future."

When his students were prepared, he was at his best;
when not, his wit turned to sarcasm that always carried a
sting. Sometimes he would make sketches on the blackboard
or write little poems to reveal how disappointed he was.
One day he drew a picture of himself lying in a wooden
coffin. Below it he wrote these lines:

> Here lies the old fool
> Who taught us in school
> To keep the Bone Rules,
> O Lord, keep him cool.

Father Will Whalen, one of his pupils, described him in
these words: "My poetic ideals were shattered when I
viewed the man—ugly in extreme, almost blind, a small
head with a scanty thatch, very thin and round shouldered,
and owning the longest arms I have ever seen."

One of the things the students always hoped for was to
have him recite one of his favorite poems and forget the
lines. At such times he would roll his eyes, grunt, "claw
around as if to capture the fugitive phrases," and then
swing his right arm like a windmill and soundly slap his
bald head with his long loose-jointed hand. No one dared to
laugh on these occasions. This was reserved for the playground. Father Tabb, standing at the window overlooking
the yard, frequently saw himself imitated. He enjoyed these
scenes, especially when the actor would swing his right arm
and slap himself on the head.

Many of his clever puns were copied on the margin of
text-books and became the heritage of the student boy. One

that became a favorite occurred when a new student made a remark about his dim eyes. Father Tabb turned quickly: "Who's talking about my demise? I am very much alive."

In spite of his many eccentricities the boys loved him as teacher and priest. They told of his kindness and generosity, especially to poor students. The stern rebukes in class were later softened when the offending student was called to the priest's room, "bare as famine," with only a little table and chair, and a "wee rug" by his bed. Here he received a bag of choice candy—round sugar marbles with a large nut in the center.

Some of the students who later became priests admitted that they owed much to the pious example of Father Tabb. His great devotion at Mass, his tender love for the Blessed Virgin, his nightly saying of the Stations of Cross—these were things that boys noticed. Many a night young eyes secretly watched the tall gaunt figure of the priest, carrying a little candle, set in an old tin holder, as he said the Stations. They told of his long pause at the Fourth, when Christ meets His Blessed Mother. Some said that the yellow glow of the candle revealed tears when he came to the Eleventh, where Christ is nailed to the Cross.

During his long career of teaching his pen was busy writing poetry. He was at his best in very short poems. The quatrain became a flexible instrument in his hands, with power, beauty, delicacy. "It is not without cause," wrote Alice Meynell, "that these complete poems are so brief. Sudden flights of song are they, and swift and far, but quickly closed, all complete."

In these miniature poems he reveals himself a master of words. He weaves them cleverly into his work, blending their sounds to draw out their beauty and power. Frequently he made cumbersome thoughts cast off their heaviness and dance on words of life and color. The music that

runs through his verse is only an echo of that deeper music
that surged in his soul. In "A Legacy" note the music and
delicate beauty:

> Do you remember, little cloud,
>   This morning, when you lay
> A mist along the river, what
>   The waters had to say?
>
> And how the many colored flowers
>   That on the margin grew
> All promised when the day was done
>   To leave their tints to you?

Some of his poems are light and frivolous. They were
deliberately written that way. To him poetry was a means
of expressing himself and he used it for many occasions.
Where others would write letters, he would rime a few
clever lines and print them with a pencil or pen on the back
of a penny postcard, sometimes accompanied with an appropriate sketch.

This light verse reveals a rare sense of humor. It has a
spontaneity and an unusual turn that provokes thoughtful
laughter. Note the following:

> To jewels her taste did incline;
>   But she had not a trinket to wear
> Till she slept after taking quinine,
>   And awoke with a ring in each ear.

Mr. Andrew Lang, the critic, once misspelled Tabb's name.
The latter replied in the poem "To Mr. Andrew Lang, Who
Misspelled My Name 'Tab':

> O why should Old Lang Sign
>   A compliment to me
> (If it indeed is mine)
>   And filch my final b?
> To him as to the Dane
>   In his soliloquy,

This question comes again,—
"2b or not 2b?"

In his serious work he tells much of his own life, his love for the human and divine, the little common things of life, the innocence of childhood, the beauty of nature in all her changeable moods. At times he sings with the sheer joy of singing and the hope that his verse may bring a little hope and happiness to those who could spare "only a few moments from life's busy whirl." At other times a strain of melancholy, delicate and tender, runs through his work and touches the emotions of his readers. In his poem "Childhood" he writes:

> Old Sorrow I shall meet again
>   And Joy, perchance—but never, never,
> Happy Childhood, shall we twain
>   See each other's face forever!
> And yet I would not call thee back,
>   Dear Childhood, lest the sight of me,
> Thine old companion, on the rack
>   Of Age, should sadden even thee.

He had reason for this melancholy strain. The lengthening shadow of blindness was drawing nearer and he anticipated the total darkness that was to shroud his life. With this in mind he penned these pathetic lines in "Going Blind":

> Back to the primal gloom
> Where life began
> As to my mother's womb
> Must I a man
> Return:
> Not to be born again,
> But to remain;
> And in the school of Darkness learn
> What mean
> "The things unseen."

Throughout this period he never lost his sense of humor. His philosophical nature and sunny disposition enabled him to make the best of the situation. He wanted no sympathy and he accepted none. This was his cross and he desired to carry it alone.

He became totally blind a year before his death. To one who loved life as he did, it must have been a terrible affliction. Not to view again the faces of those near and dear to him, the beauty of a spring day dancing across the meadow, the trees robed in the gorgeous colors of autumn. the stars set like jewels in a black velvet sky—these privations alone would be sufficient to produce a profound gloom. If they did, he never revealed it. At times he tenderly referred to his affliction in a line drawn from Francis Thompson's "Hound of Heaven," "the shade of His hand outstretched caressingly."

In spite of his handicap he continued his writing, and the thoughts and feelings of this lonesome period are recorded in a "Sunset Song," "The Image Maker," "Waves," and "Blind." A growing paralysis gradually hampered his activity and eventually left him quite helpless. Death came peacefully during the night of November 19, 1909.

The funeral took place from the college. His remains, in a black cloth coffin, was borne from the reception room of the church by six of his former students. Father D. J. Conor, who delivered the eulogy, said: "How powerless does death seem in a case like this to achieve a real victory. It was surely no violent transition by which the soul of Father Tabb passed from the temporal to the eternal. As an exiled spirit he seemed to tread the rough paths of earth where most of us are content to find a home ... His art was not an end, but a means. Poetry was with him not a substitute for religion, but an inspiration that made religion all the more necessary."

In the afternoon the funeral cortege moved slowly through a guard of honor formed by the students. As the hearse passed, each one said "goodbye" in the form of a prayer for the soul of Father Tabb, friend, poet, teacher.

EDITOR'S NOTE: This chapter appears in *The Book of Catholic Authors* series through the courtesy of the editors of *The Catholic Educational Review*. Father Barry, Ph. D., is professor of English at St. Francis Major Seminary, in Milwaukee. The full-length biography entitled *Father Tabb* (John Hopkins University Press, 1923), written by Dr. Francis E. Litz, includes a number of his uncollected poems; Dr. Litz also edited *Father Tabb's Poetry* (Dodd, 1928). The priest-poet's informally adopted son, William McDevitt, published *My Father, Father Tabb* in 1945. The book includes in facsimile the first publication of the longhand autobiographical sketch of Father Tabb, as well as other biographical and bibliographical material.

REVEREND FRANCIS BEAUCHESNE THORNTON

WHEN I LOOK BACK ON MY CHILDHOOD I FIND IT SO IMAGINA-
tive that it seems not my own. Gifted with violent senses,
their responsiveness lifted me up on thrilling sights and
sounds: the clear brilliance of the sun, the bright singing of
new grass, the smell of roses or bread fresh from the oven,
the drift of gold shadows under the elms, star glitter, the
touch of water and the scent of hay, make me almost a
pagan worshipper of Beauty. Out of these lovely things,
avidly drunk in, the mind created from their bright tissues
a world in which I moved and all else moved with thrilling
life.

The poet's world must be necessarily an expressive world.
I made early attempts. One of these brought trouble, but
it also enabled me to begin the process of setting my feet on
the ground; of learning the difference between the real
world and the imaginative one in my mind.

It was in the sixth grade that the revelation came. The
class had been assigned a theme on Autumn. When I had
finished setting down the descriptions, which came with
great facility, I had written a prose poem: not a good one,
perhaps, in the absolute sense, but surprising for my age
and grade.

Sister refused to believe I had written it. She gave me a
lecture on the sin of stealing from authors, and publicly at
that. By the time we had the matter cleared up, Sister and
I had become fast friends and I had found out I could write
and had learned the clean limits of my two worlds.

The seventh grade saw the beginnings of verse: long
narrative works of knightly romance in pure doggerel. This
mood developed during the high school course and graduation found me the first editor of the school magazine, *The
Iris.*

High school days had been happy ones. McDonnell
Memorial High at Chippewa Falls, Wisconsin, was a beautiful place, the School Sisters of Notre Dame intelligent beyond the average. My four years had been a time of some
discipline and omniverous reading: everything from dime
novels to Dante.

There were several years of teaching and writing and a
period at the Paulist House of Studies in which I contributed copiously to the Paulist magazine for children, *The
Leader,* under the pen name of Jean Doré.

After the failure of my Paulist vocation, I entered St.
Paul Seminary, St. Paul, Minnesota. During my course of
studies I sold several poems to *The Commonweal* and
America, and it was a great thrill when one of them was
selected for the poetry page of *The Literary Digest.*—Half
the pleasure of writing is finding an audience.

At ordination in 1928, I was stationed as curate at St.

Luke's in St. Paul. Archbishop Dowling was always encouraging me to write, and he was almost as pleased as I
when my first book of verse, *On Wings of Song,* was published in 1928. The reception it received in St. Paul encouraged me to write and publish a second book of verse,
Bitter Wine, in 1929.

Then I was off to University for graduate work: years
of learning, thinking, writing. At Notre Dame, Columbia
University and Oxford. A background of beauty, an atmosphere of witty conversation, travel to France, Switzerland,
Italy, Spain, Germany and Austria; sights, sounds, beauty
pelting the mind with the stuff of dreams.

In addition to a scholarly monograph, *The Bases of Pope's
Essay on Man,* I fabricated a big book of mature poems. It
is still unpublished, though many of the verses have appeared in *The Catholic World, Blackfriars,* and *America.*

Graduate teaching at Duquesne University brought out a
spate of magazine articles and poems. In addition to my
teaching work, I was in charge of student publications and
learned considerable by training my faculties of analysis
and criticism.

The complete writer is one who brings the greatest possible number of faculties into play in the creation of literature: to be analytical and critical as well as imaginative,
emotional and creative, is to start the process which will
produce good work. Chesterton and Belloc did not learn
their trade overnight. They dashed nothing down in a
hurry: the discipline of the faculties, long thought, and the
detection of the pattern for communication are the necessary preparation for authorship. The rest is the grinding
work of setting down that which is already complete in the
mind.

These were some of the thoughts which came to me from
working with the students on their publications.

A course in the Catholic Revival which I gave at Duquesne University in 1937 started me on the work which has
taken up all my free time in the years as an Associate editor
of *The Catholic Digest* and as Chaplain in the Canadian
Army. While the course on the Catholic Revival was being
given, it was driven home to me that most of our high school
and college libraries have not the resources which would
make such a course worth while. There were plenty of good
histories of the Revival, such as Calvert Alexander's, but
there was no adequate text.

To an author a task is a task, and I resolved to attempt
to create a text to fill the need. That there is a need no one
can deny. Our Catholic college students are only too often
apologetic and struck with inferiority in launching themselves on a career in the modern world. Perhaps if they
could once make a survey of their riches and link this with
the main stream of continental culture, they might begin
to take pride in Catholic achievement, and so face the world
as complete Catholics.

The task is almost finished. A two-volume "directive"
anthology, covering the whole course of the revival of letters
in England, Ireland, France and America, will be published
by the Bruce company in the near future. It will be titled
Return to Tradition.

Though this sustained task has taken me out of the creative world, I can now return to that beloved world with
added pleasure. I have planned a book on reading, and one
on Gerard Manley Hopkins and Alexander Pope. They
should be finished within a year and a half.

Becoming a writer is a happy chance. It means becoming
alive in the fullest sense that a man can be. And yet it is
without personal pride since, we all know like Topsy, "we
just growed."

Learning to write, to speak, and to think are one. You
cannot speak well if you do not teach yourself to think;

you cannot learn to write well without storing up the bright
stuff of ideas which, by logic and the mind, are patterned
into beauty from which others may receive refreshment.

EDITOR'S NOTE: Father Thornton's books include: *On Wings of Song*,
1928, The Wanderer; *Bitter Wine*, 1929, id.; *Return to Tradition*,
1947, Bruce.

REVEREND GERALD VANN, O.P.

THE TRAVELLER WHO ARRIVES IN ENGLAND BY WAY OF DOVER, and then takes the train for London, finds that his journey takes him through the orchards and hopfields of Kent. It was in Kent that I was born, in August, 1906; and its orchards and hopfields are among the things that I remember best of childhood days. Especially the hops. We used to go, my three elder brothers and I, in the summer, and help with or hinder the picking: the hops are trained up a high trellis-work of pole and twine, and the bunches hang thick and fragrant; when you've been picking, the fragrance clings to your hands. There were the strawberry fields too; when the picking was over you could go in and take anything you could find left over. My elder brothers once, in their early teens, had a brilliant idea, and earned a considerable sum of money and my mother's deep displeasure (my father died a little before I was born) by collecting quite a large quantity of these strawberries, borrowing (surreptitiously) my perambulator to carry them in, and hawking them through the streets. They have not, in later life, become the captains of industry that one may have supposed.

There was a convent school, run by some French nuns, some four miles away; and to this we went in our early days as weekly boarders. I was five when I went there; my brothers having by that time left: I remember a very delicious dish the nuns used to provide at lunch sometimes in the summer, consisting of strawberries and raspberries in a tumblerful of (presumably very diluted) red wine, about which I used to be very high-hat during weekends at home, where wine was not included in the menu. I remember the horror of the nuns at my accent when I was made to talk French, and the long blue pencil with which the nun who taught the piano used to point out mistakes. I remember with horror having to recite at a concert, and I remember the pleasing thrill of being brought downstairs in the middle of the night and having cocoa and bread-and-lard (their war-time substitute for butter) during the air raids of the first World War. It was in those days, too, that my brothers invented or learned a secret code-language which they used to use, to my indignation, when they thought it better that I shouldn't know what they were saying; fortunately, I managed to get "the hang" of it after a time, and listened in with, I suppose, a sickening expression of wide-eyed innocence on my face.

My mother had, from her childhood, known many of the English Dominican Fathers. She was born, and lived until her marriage, quite near the Noviciate House at Woodchester, in Gloucestershire; and though she was now far away in Kent, some of them continued to correspond, and to pay occasional visits. One Father, I remember, appeared in church during one of these visits, in his white habit, and

was seen by an old Irish woman, who promptly spread a
rumour around the parish that the Pope in person had descended upon it.   I cannot remember when it was that I
decided that I wanted to be a Domincian myself; but, at any
rate, it was decided that when I left the convent school I
was to go to the Dominican school, which was then at
Hawkesyard, in Staffordshire.

Hawkesyard had been the property of Josiah Spode, of
pottery fame, who built himself a mansion on Strawberry
Hill lines, with unbelievable stone onions spouting from
the corners of the roofs and conceived in so grandiose a
scale as to seem to be weighing down the somewhat squat
house beneath them.   Not that any such criticism occurred
to us in those days.   It had been left, together with the park
and woods, to the Dominicans, who in time had built close
by a priory and church.   The school had begun its history
at Bornhem in Flanders in penal times—the actual date of
its foundation by Cardinal Howard was 1600—and had
come to England in the nineteenth century.   For seventy
years or so it was housed at Hinckley in Leicestershire;
from there it was moved to Hawkesyard in 1898; and in
1924 there was yet another removal, a bigger house being
necessary, to its present address at Laxton, in Northamp-
tonshire.   Though we were, of course, a separate establishment, we saw a certain amount of the life of the Priory:
sometimes there were Priory versus School matches, for
example, and the two communities tended to mingle somewhat when the English winter provided enough snow and
ice for tobogganing and skating.   We went every day to the
Church for Mass in the morning and sang Compline in the
evening; and on Sundays filed into choir in white cassocks
and surplices for High Mass.   (We used, moreover, to have
to serve the High Mass; a terrifying experience, for the
sanctuary seemed vast, and one had the impression that
hundreds of eyes were glaring condemnation at one's in-

efficiency). I suppose it must have been during this period that I began to have literary ambitions: certainly I remember (with some embarassment) founding a school magazine, called *The Hawkesyardian,* and contributing to the first number an interminable "ballad" about something or another, which I hope is no longer extant. I was also guilty of starting an affair called the Art Club, which endeavoured to concern itself with questions of aesthetics, with doubtful success; and I remember, as one of my few outstanding achievements, persuading the headmaster that it was right and proper that on the feast of St. Cecilia, the patroness of music, the boys who learned the piano (myself, of course, among them) should be allowed a half-holiday while the rest toiled and moiled among their books. At the end of the summer term the School used to give a concert, to which the Priory was invited; and it was through these that I discovered I loved acting,—there was a play in which I appeared as a witch-like old crone and thoroughly enjoyed myself.

I was seventeen when I left school, and after the long summer holidays, I went on at once to the noviciate at Woodchester. I had never been to Gloucestershire before; and I was eager to see it, not only for its own loveliness, but also because of its associations with my mother and her people. (My grandfather was a somewhat romantic figure in my eyes, because he had run away to sea when a small schoolboy and after a life at sea had eventually settled down here. He and my grandmother had both become Catholics late in life, and very devout ones: one of the stories I liked hearing about him was how he used to pace up and down the garden as though it were the deck of a ship, saying the rosary quietly to himself as he thought, though in reality, being very deaf, he would be shouting it out at the top of his voice.) There were very few lay-brothers during that year at Woodchester; and the novices had their full share of housework. I remember working in the laundry, and hating blankets; I remember cooking for the community for a fortnight or so, and making appalling soups, though I was said to have a very light hand with pastry ...

After the year at Woodchester, one went back to Hawkesyard to study philosophy, and, in those days, theology. Actually, at that time Father Bede Jarrett had begun his foundation at Oxford; and I was among the group who went from Hawkesyard to the solemn opening and became the first Blackfriars community.

For my last year's theology, I went to the Dominican house in Rome, the Collegio Angelico. It is an international college; and so it happened that except for one very aged and infirm Father, I was the only Englishman there at the time, so that I was deeply grateful for the stimulating society of the contingent from the States, and threw in my lot (such as it was) with them. Indeed, I fell into their arms from the start. The journey out had been rather a taxing one: I travelled from Brussels to Rome without stopping except to change trains; and, as I was travelling third, and as the change took place (I think through my own stupidity) at Bale in the dead of night with some hours' delay, I finally arrived at Rome in a somewhat woebegone condition. There I managed to get hold of a *carozza*,—a very ancient horse-drawn vehicle on which one sat perched up at a ridiculous altitude as though to receive the jeers of the crowd—and so found myself at the forbidding portals of the Angelico. There was an American on the doorstep, and he came forward to greet me. But alas, I was past coherent speech; and for some days he made considerable capital out of the story of how I had gazed in mute dismay at the scene before me and then murmured in an all too English voice, "Well, really ... " (I had a genial revenge later, on St. George's day, when I made them all stand and drink the health of the King in good red wine.) Those were the days when

Mussolini was establishing himself; the streets had never been so clean, people said; on the other hand, I remember that once, when I was talking to another Dominican, not an Italian, I ventured some remark derogatory to the regime and was astonished to see him fly to the window and fashion it with a bang for fear of eavesdroppers, though we happened at the time to be well up on the fourth floor. It was with my American friends that I sat at the feet of Pere Garrigau-Lagrange, had an audience of the Pope, saw something of Rome, and exchanged vocabularies. It was with one of them that, having taken my degree in theology, I travelled part of the way back to England, via Florence, Bologna, Milan, and the haunting loveliness of Venice. We parted company finally at (I think) Geneva; and his parting gesture consisted in leaving me, just before my train started, ensconced in a third-class carriage crowded with people, and returning just in time to thrust into my embarassed arms an enormous bottle of beer.

Back in Oxford, I began reading for my B.A., a three-year business. Before leaving for Rome I had already done a certain amount of writing, sometimes for American periodicals; it was in this period after my return to Oxford that my first book, *On Being Human,* was published. It was then, also, I think that I made my first occasional attempts at lecturing and public speaking.

The three years over, I was sent to join the teaching staff at the school, now at Laxton. Not long afterwards, the second book, *Morals Makyth Man,* appeared; and the others followed at intervals. Meanwhile, I had begun the work of giving retreats, study circles, and lectures; an interest in social and international problems led me to the Catholic Council for International Relations, and to take part in its meetings, at The Hague, St. André in Belgium, and Dublin. I had been much exercised, too, over the problem of the morality of war, and had written a book on the subject;

and, feeling the threat of war, I had, in 1927, founded a
Union for Peace, which was intended to join members of
the various nations together in common prayer for international justice, charity and peace.

The war came, with all its misery; we are through the
war, but not the misery. As one goes on in life; as the
world changes, and one's understanding of it, so one's pre-
occupations, the emphasis in one's writings, change also.
The Heart of Man was published during the war; *The Divine Pity* just after it; and if there is a common train of
thought behind both of them it is, I think, the appalling
tragedy of the loss of Godgiven greatness of destiny, the
loss of divine life, and so the loss even of *manhood*, to which
humanity seems to be rushing inexorably. To reject God is,
in the end, to reject man as well: to lose both the sense of
height and the sense of depth, to end in the void. We are
witnessing, in Berdyaev's phrase, not merely a crisis *in*
humanity, but the crisis *of* humanity. But behind all the
disintegration and the horror there is undying hope, and
it is for the Christian to assert it; for the heart of man,
however unaware, however scornful, is watched over and
sustained by the gentle power of God's pity.

EDITOR'S NOTE: Father Vann's published books include: *On Being
Human*, Sheed, 1934; *Morals Makyth Man*, Longmans, 1938; *Of His
Fullness*, Burns, 1939;   *Morality and War*, Burns, 1939; *St. Thomas
Aquinas*, Benziger, 1940; *The Heart of Man*, Longmans, 1945; *The
Divine Pity*, Sheed, 1946; *Eve and the Gryphon*, Blackfriars, 1946;
His Will is Our Peace, Sheed, 1947.

SISTER M. IMELDA WALLACE, S.L.

WHEN ONE IS INVITED TO WRITE A SKETCH OF ONE'S LIFE sundry problems arise, the worst of which is: "Now just exactly am I not going to say?" All of one's own life is very interesting to one's own self—alone.

My father (may God rest his stern and noble soul) was a North Arizona pioneer, a Scot and a son of pioneering Scots. His forefathers settled in Connecticut and carved a farm out of the primeval forest prior to the Revolutionary war; but, being Tories, they left immediately afterwards and struck out into the wilderness, now the Province of Ontario, with the United Empire Loyalists. By the time my father, Daniel Wallace, had grown to manhood, farming in Ontario must have become too soft and easy a life for the type of man who seems born to struggle with the elements. At any rate, he moved into the forest lands of Michigan, and began the toil of felling trees, tearing out stumps, and forcing wild fields to bear the discipline of plow and harrow. But Michigan was only a tarrying spot. He sold that farm as soon as it was really under cultivation, and went to the "Last Frontier," Northern Arizona.

My mother (may the angels of peace bless the day that gentle maid-child was born) my mother was a scholar, a poet, a frail and dainty lady who brought with her fine linen and rare china and books with gilded bindings and pictures of Scottish moors and castles half-lost in ivy, even when she followed her husband, obediently as a good wife should, out to the "Last Frontier."

Now as for me, while father and mother were still in Michigan—the sixth day of September, 1884—God gave them their fifth child, a small, frail, crippled girl. Mother wanted me to be named Laura Isabella; but father said that the name was too heavy for so tiny a midget to carry; and so he chopped it up and nailed it together to form the name "Lorabel." Mother was too busy rubbing, rubbing, rubbing; even when memory begins to come fluttering in and out as baby memories will, she was always rubbing my feet until she made them straight.

Mother was a dreamer, but she had a will to power that could drive her frail body to accomplish things. Oh I know, all pioneer women did similar things. But for example:

One day down on the Verde River, my elder brother rode an eleven-year-old renegade. No, not on a dare! He rode because he thought he could conquer that broncho and he could buy some comforts for mother and his little sisters at home if he earned the extra money offered.

Perhaps three minutes afterward, the men gathered around the bruised and crumpled boy, and the round-up boss said: "Go up to town. See to it you get Dan Wallace and tell him we judged the mother must not see her boy. Tell him we will bury his boy here—oh come sundown, I guess."

But that is not the way it went. Father was sleeping. It was mother heard a horse coming, hard-ridden, from down Verde way. She was at the gate hailing the rider with the blunt question: "Is he dead?"

"Er, why no, I mean when I left, he wasn't, but—"

"Get a buckboard and be here in twenty minutes."

"But you can't. Even a buckboard can't get down the—"

"Get the buckboard and be back in twenty minutes."

And he did. And mother went, Father accompanying her. The boy had not died at sundown; and he did not die, either. With nothing but her two hands, cold spring water, and beef soup mixed by the cowboys over the camp fire, she fought death for six weeks and won.

So what has all this to do with autobiography? You know the psychologists will always argue as to which has the more effect on character, heredity or environment. Well, from these rough jottings, you may know my heredity, and my environment during the formative years from three to twenty-four.

To be exact, the twenty-one years should stand minus three. Mother went back to Canada three times and took me with her, so the years of seven, twelve, and fifteen were not spent under the shadow of the San Francisco Peaks in Northern Arizona, but in the ultra-refined, most-sweetly-and-absolutely-Victorian little city of London on the Thames (Ontario, Canada), and in its environs. That also had its effect.

Up till fourteen, I was just like every other child on the Mogollon Mountains. Simply fed, simply clothed, simply educated, we were a jolly crew, climbing craggs, poking around the ruins of lost civilizations in the canons, riding horse-back—and, of course, working when we had to do so.

Then came the day—every soul has a day on life's calendar marked "that day."

By one of those small circumstances which "just happen," but are really the plan of God's providence fixed before He spun the stars and set them whirling, on "that day" I "just happened" to go to Mass. It was the funeral of somebody or other.

I am not going to try to explain what happened. To non-Catholics no explanation can be made; I tried it for ten years, and I know. Even now, so many long years after there is not yet one of my loved ones living who understands. Of course, those who have passed over "The Great Divide," they understand now.

To Catholics there is no need to explain. They do not understand, exactly; for that matter, neither do I; but they know what happened. Almighty God in His Goodness, in His absolute and adorable freedom, gave a mighty grace to one little girl in Northern Arizona "that day."

On "that day" I went to the Catholic Church to Mass; and I do not think that I had a thought in my head more serious than, oh perhaps, going for a horseback ride, or for a burro ride if no horse were available. I had no interest whatever in the Church; it stood in my mind about on a par with Mohammedanism—utterly false, and somewhat more silly than false. My father called the ideas of Catholics "positively blasphemous"; they saw a piece of bread and worshipped it as God. Mother said less; but she was certain they were wrong.

So, on "that day" I went to Mass a born-in-the-bone Protestant; but I came from that Mass a convinced Catholic.

Sometime, during that Mass, when everything was still and all around me people were kneeling, suddenly I knew that the Bread was not mere bread, but Jesus Christ, the Lord God Almighty. I knew I must kneel and adore Him; and I did. I knew the Church in which He dwelt must be the one and only true Church. I knew that I must go out, find what the Church taught, learn it, believe it, live by it.

I knew all that as clearly in that moment as I know it now.

I went out, knowing with fair clearness, though still hoping it would not be so, that from "that day" forward to the end of life there would be a bar between me and my people. My love would always be going from me over the bar to them; but their love would strike on the bar, at least for years.

The bitterest thing in my pain was seeing father suffer— shamed by me as if I had done something criminal; and there was mother's suffering—blamed for my "going wrong" because she had never been so strict with her youngest as with the others. Oh well, what of that? Long, long ago Our Lord smoothed out their sorrows. He explained to them—I have no doubt of it—and then their sorrow was their greatest joy. God's ways are not our ways.

God has been very good to me. The joy of the Faith is worth infinitely more than the sorrow of "that day" or the years immediately following. He brought me into His own house; and I have been a very happy Sister of Loretto.

Many years have gone by, teaching in Catholic schools. Often I have had the joy of preparing little children to receive the Bread of Angels.

Eleven years have gone into my small part in forming the *Living My Religion* series. If the little books help children to love God more, how very happy I shall be only Our Lord Himself knows.

EDITOR'S NOTE: Besides the catechetical series on which Sister collaborated with Msgr. M. A. Schumacher, she is the author of a stirring Arizona romance, *The Lure of the West*, Meier, 1924, and of *The Outlaws of Ravenhurst*, first issued by the Franciscan Herald Press, in 1923, and now available from the author, Loretto, Nerinx, Kentucky. This dramatic historical novel depicts the last stand for the Faith made by the Gordons of Scotland in the early days of the Protestant revolt.

REVEREND GERALD
GROVELAND WALSH, S.J.

I MADE MY FIRST BOW ON THE STAGE OF LETTERS AT THE AGE
of six. It was a cold, raw day in September in the year of
Our Lord, 1899. There in a small classroom adjoining the
auditorium of the Academy of the Ladies of Loretto in
Hamilton, Ontario, a young Sister hung up a large chart
with the letters of the alphabet. I can still remember, with
a kind of horror, the dread moment when she said: "Take
your slates and write *g*"—that printed, lower-case g, mind
you, with the twiddle at the top and the baffling juncture of
the upper and lower halves! I wanted to renounce this
whole business of education and return at once to my home
in Connecticut on Long Island Sound, and take up fishing or
farming!

Things were still worse that afternoon. My sisters were
boarders; but my brother, Maurice, and I lodged with Mrs.
Beech on Herkimer street. She was entertaining some

elderly ladies to tea. Very unfairly, so it seemed to me, one
of them asked me: "What does c-u-p spell?" She might as
well have asked: "How do you spell Cholomondeley?" (pronounced in Canada, of course, like Chumley). One of the
nicest of the ladies came to the rescue. "C-u-p is a thing
you drink out of." Just at that moment the eldest of the
group, finding the scalding tea too hot, delicately tilted her
cup, poured tea into the saucer, cooled it with her breath,
and began to drink. Thinking I was still in class, my hand
shot up and I shouted in lisping triumph: "C-u-p, . . .
thaucer!"

From letters I passed to literature. Maurice, three years
my elder, was a minor theatrical prodigy. He had already
played, with what the Montreal press called "phenominal
success," the title role in *Little Lord Fontelroy*; and they
used to dress him up in a dozen different costumes and make
him recite in public. I liked him best in his tartan and kilts,
acting the duel scene between FitzJames and Roderick Dhu
in *The Lady of the Lake*. Long before I could read I had
the whole thing by heart; and long before anyone told me
the difference between prose and poetry I loved the rhythm
and the rhymes.

My father, who taught me more than any of my early
teachers, believed that, in education, tasks should be well
above one's talents. When I was eleven he stood me at the
end of a very large room, put a dictionary and note-book on
the table before me, placed in my hands a copy of Newman's
Loss and Gain, and told me to read aloud. Whenever I hesi-
tated over a strange word, he would say: "Consult the dictionary." Of the various meanings given, I would have to
pick out the one most suited to the context. When a decision
was made, I had to write the word in column one, the
selected meaning in column two, the Latin, Greek, or other
root in column three, and the meaning of this root in column
four. I still recall my resentful bewilderment in handling

rationale. But the habit remained; and before I was fourteen I think I had mastered all but the technical words in
that fairly large standard dictionary.

When, at the age of twelve, I was packed off to go through
the six forms of an English school, I was given a good deal
of paternal counsel; but on no point was there more insis-
tence than on the duty of writing long and carefully composed letters in reply to all that I received. It was this
letter-writing, I think, that first made me fall in love with
writing.

It was facility in writing, more than anything else, that
won me my ratings in the nation-wide Oxford and Cambridge Local Examinations which were taken in the fourth,
fifth and sixth forms of most of the English schools: first
class honors in all four tries; top place, three times, in economics; the national award of the Royal Geographical Society; third place in history; and high places on the distinction lists in English and French.

My first venture into journalism (apart, of course, from
the school magazine, of which I was editor) was a long
letter to the public press in defense of "free-trade" as
against "Imperial preference." I was already planning
(though only sixteen) to follow my brother to Cambridge,
read economics, and become a famous professor. A year
later I embarked on an ambitious article on "The Political
Economy of Friedrich List." I sent it to the editor of the
highly exclusive *Westminster Review.* It was accepted and
published.

In the meantime—without the remotest prevision that the
Jesuits were going to get me—I wrote an article on the
Society of Jesus for the *Catholic Home Journal.* It was
only when I had read Francis Thompson's *Life of St. Ignatius,* in my last year at school, that I felt I had a religious
vocation. Without hesitation, but likewise without the
least sense of heroism or histrionics, I changed all my plans.

Normally, I would have returned to America; but by this
time my father had read himself out of the Faith—to which,
by the mercy of God, he later returned. So I bought a ticket
to London and knocked at the door of Manresa House, Roehampton ... It was only much later that I learned that, before I was born, my mother used to sit on the verandah of
our home near South Norwalk, look across the fields toward
Keyser Island where the Jesuits spent their vacations, and
pray that, if it should be a boy, he would grow up to be a
Jesuit.

Even from the purely academic point of view I could not
have made a wiser choice. Father Charles Blount, besides
being (as I thought) a saint, belonged to one of the oldest
and most distinguished of the English Catholic families,
had come out top in his year in Classics in London University, had been a professor of theology, a regular writer
on the staff of *The Month* and, for many years, the Prefect
of Studies at Beaumont College. As a Junior I was taught
to write Latin and Greek by Alban Goodier, the future
Archbishop of Bombay, and I cannot believe that there ex-
isted anywhere in the world a more inspiring teacher. And
then for Philosophy at Stonyhurst there were scholars like
Michael Maher, John Rickaby, and the rest. Among my
fellow novices, along with James Broderick, the future biographer of Bellarmine and Canisius, and Thomas Roberts,
who was to become the Archbishop of Bombay, were Edward Heloham and Edward Enright, who had come out top
of the lists in the University Local Examinations, and
several others who had followed close behind them.

I was still *in statu pupilari* at Oxford when I wrote the
article on the Comparative Study of Religion which Father
Keating published in *The Month*. But what helped me most
during these years was a vast amount of writing that was
not meant for publication. I still have five large volumes
of an "intellectual diary." It is filled (among other things)

with book reviews, of a most miscellaneous sequence of works. For example, in one short period *Romola*, *The Queen's Tragedy*, and *Lorna Doone* were followed by *The Mill on the Floss*, *John Inglesant*, and *Barnaby Rudge*, and these by *The Cloister and the Hearth*, *The Deemster*, and *Marzia's Crucifix*. In between these works of fiction came Montalembert's *Monks of the West*, Vacandard's *Vie de Saint Bernard*, Livingston's *Greek Genius*, Vaughan's *Life of St. Thomas*, and the *Magna Vita Hugonis* in medieval Latin,—not to mention the steady diet of St. Thomas, Suarez, and the philosophical textbooks. During each year's eight-day Retreat the diary becomes more personal; and, of course, there was any amount of unpublishable verse. It now seems to me all very unequal, uninspired, unmusical, ill-defined, mixed-up and vague; but I am sure it taught me a good deal about writing prose. Some is purely descriptive, as in "November";

> The leaves fall down and the cold wind,
>   Whirling among them, frore and sere,
> Whistles, with low murmuring, a kind
>   Of dirge song for the dying year...

Some is purely imaginative, like "Iceland Mother":

> I looked for the ship, far over the sea,
>   The ship that would sail no more,
> While the waves were lazily licking their lips,
>   Lapping along by the shore...

There is much of a half rhetorical, half genuinely pious emotion that all beginners in religious life are bound to yield to:

> Oft times, my sandals set aside,
>   Over the shard
> Sharp shattered, and through briars strewn—
>   My flesh all marr'd
> I passed; and often I have hewn
>   Steps in the hard
> Rock, reaching for my Bride.

The longest piece was "Skylarks in a Cage." They had been stolen from a nest and put into a cage hanging from the branch of a tree. The mother bird "chirped at the bars feeding her young, flying to teach them to fly."

> From perch to perch, weak, callow things,
>   They hopped, they spread their small,
> Full-stretching, futile, flapping wings,
>   To 'scape from barrèd thrall . . .

It made me think, of course, of "my fledgling thoughts and my callow desires" and of the mother-soul:

> Solicitous, despairingly,
>   She tempts to flight with "Hence!
> From barrèd insufficiency
>   And cagèd impotence."

Apparently, it was all in vain, and so it ends:

> Yonder blue of the sky is Love,
>   And Poetry the air,
> But never desire of mine, above,
>   Nor thought wings higher, where
> Song touches my lips and God my heart
>   Unconstrainedly,
> But caged by brutal bars they smart
>   In strait humility.

My best training in writing came from my Oxford tutors, Mowat of Corpus, Weaver of Trinity, and Jalliffe of Keble. They were remorseless in insisting on a combination of substance and careful composition. The Oxford system is to heap up the sieve with an immense mass of reading and then let the dross fall through, leaving only the nuggets of significant facts and ideas. "Just two facts and one idea, Mr. Walsh; but choose them wisely," one of the dons used to tell me. When the system gained me first class honors, the Gibbs Scholarship, and the Marquis of Lothian Prize, I knew it was a good one.

My first published book was *The Emperor Charles IV: A Study of Holy Roman Imperialism* (1924). It was based on

an immense amount of research in fourteenth-century primary sources and did something, I think, to redeem a great
ruler and a good man from the contempt of the *Machtpolitik*
historians. The footnotes of the manuscript were mercifully omitted in the printed work. The most Oxford-like epi-
gram was the one about the Holy Roman Empire being, in
the fourteenth century, something more than a notion, while
Germany was still something less than a nation.

During the next fifteen years I wrote a great many articles and reviews for *The Month* in England, *The Catholic
Historical Review*, *Thought*, *The Historical Bulletin*, *The
Modern Schoolman*, *America*, and *The Messenger* in America and the *Gregorianum* and *Studium* in Rome. Of the articles, the most original was, perhaps, "Dante's Matelda,"
the deepest was no doubt "Dante's Philosophy of History,"
but the one I liked best was "Dante as a Medieval Human-
ist." This last became the nucleus of *Medieval Humanism*
(1942). It was reviewed in the *American Historical Review* by no less a scholar than E. K. Rand, was picked as
"the book of the week" by more than one Protestant
journal, and was put on the list of essential reading for
Freshmen at Princeton.

In the meantime, the book I had wanted to write for
twenty-five years was *Dante Alighieri, Citizen of Christendom*. It was finally to have been written during a sabbatical
year in 1934; but in that year I was called by the General of
the Society of Jesus from my professorate at Woodstock
College to teach in the Gregorian University in Rome.
When I returned to America to start a Department of
Italian Studies at Fordham in 1937, teaching and adminis-
trative duties kept me too occupied. It was worse still
when I became the editor of *Thought* in 1940. However, an
invitation by the Trustees of the Lowell Institute to lecture
on Dante in 1945 forced me to get my ideas onto paper.
The book contains a great many original contributions to

Dante scholarship, but they are introduced so unobstrusively that few readers or reviewers, apart from the specialists, were aware of the fact. So far, the most quoted words appear to be the description of Dante as "laughing citizen of Christendom, loving nature, people, poetry, and prayer, and, above all else, the power, the wisdom and the love that moves the sun and all the stars."

Among much other writing, I suppose the most important must be reckoned a chapter in *The Catholic Philosophy of History* (1936), one in *Faith for Today* (1942), and one in *Great Religions of the Modern World* (1946). But what, I hope, will give me more chance of getting into Heaven is the thankless job, as editor of *Thought,* of having translated article after article from French, German, or Italian ,and of having given final shape to thousands of pages that were supposed to be written in English.

EDITOR'S NOTE: Father Walsh, who earned a doctorate in both theology and philosophy as well as a B.A.(Lond) and an M.A.(Oxon), includes in his published works *The Emperor Charles IV*, Appleton, 1924, *Medieval Humanism*, Macmillan, 1942, and *Dante Alighieri*, Bruce, 1946.

MARY R. WALSH

SKATING, SLIDING, AND TRIPS ON SNOWSHOES MADE THE LONG
winters zestful during my childhood in Maine. But it was
best of all in the later afternoons when the great pine on
the knoll had turned to velvety black against an amber sunset to come in to the warmth of home and the delights of a
book and an apple before an open fire.

At the Convent of Parisian Sisters of Notre Dame de
Sion, I learned at four to read and write in French. Mother
Etheldreda there was a majestic personage full of kindness
and wisdom. When I stayed at the convent before my First
Communion, there was something unearthly about the high-
pitched cry of the nun in charge, wakening me to the white-
ness of my curtained cubicle. "Loué soit Jésu Christ," she
would chant, and we would reply from our chaste little
heavens, "Loué soit Jésu Christ!"

After grammar school and one year at high school, I
moved with the family to Boston, and again entered a world

of black-uniformed pupils and sweet-voiced nuns. This was
at the Convent of Notre Dame de Namur in Roxbury. Ge-
ology was mysterious and fantastic with its giant animals
in periods with resounding names, but algebra was my favorite study. Sleeping with the book under my pillow, I
could do a problem, like a crossword puzzle, the first thing
in the morning.

There were walks in the park-like "meadow" where we
strolled in small groups centered by a Sister, some walking
beside her and others walking backward before her. It is
too bad I can remember little of those conversations, sedate
or gay, beyond our subdued amusement one day at the remark of a sober little nun who was meticulous about community ownership. Feeling a little chilly, she murmured,
"*Our* toes are getting cold."

My father's death had been a great blow, but I was almost
equally devoted to his brother, Louis S. Walsh, who was
consecrated Bishop of Portland at about that time. There
was a Maine pine tree on his seal, and the motto, In Justitia
et Pace. He is remembered by many for his zeal and his
achievements, but my strongest memories are of his intense
love for the beautiful in ceremonial, in music, and in every
art. How he loved to sit at the piano, and finding a few
chords of accompaniment, roll out the old songs, "I stood
on the Bridge at Midnight, as the Clocks were Striking the
Hour," or "Jerusalem, Jerusalem, Hark how the Angels
Sing!"

Four years in Trinity College in Washington were far too
studious, though brightened considerably by my brother and
his friends at Georgetown. I gave no time at all to athletics
—seeing no use in them—but was persuaded once to run in
a meet. I took a hot bath just before, reducing myself to a
state of languor, but ran the course and was astonished to
find myself alone at the finish. There had been an error

at the start, and I was a loser when I tried to repeat. In dramatics I did better, playing Shakespearean clowns at Commencement plays.

After college, my mother and sister and I and our two brothers, with two school friends and the mother of one of them, set out on a travel year that was a milestone in all our lives. In England, Ireland, Belgium, Germany, Switzerland, France, and Italy, we revelled in new sights and ways of life, separating sometimes and rejoining each other with happy celebrations in various capitals of the world. One of our group of eight good companions was beautiful Alice Kock of New Orleans, now a Religious of the Sacred Heart. She studied that winter with my sister and me at the Convent of the Trinitá in Rome.

Comparative literature was perhaps a natural field of study for me next. I took a degree of M.A. at Radcliffe after courses with Baker on Drama, Kittredge on Shakespeare, Odell Shepard on Lyric Poetry, and Copeland on Writing, all bright stars of the Harvard faculty. Shorthand and typing were needed, however, for entrance into the business world, so I attended Bryant and Stratton for several months.

On my first job, at the Atlantic Monthly Company, however, my shorthand rusted away unused, as it was discovered that I could write selling letters. One of my good angels, May Toy of the Boston Public Library, had supplied me with a book from which I gleaned that you must "catch, convince, confirm, and compel." So I did, in my letters, and quickly sold out the ponderous two-volume *Letters of William James,* with commendation from Ellery Sedgwick. Teresa Fitzpatrick was and still is the dynamic manager at the Atlantic. I asked if I shouldn't get the book again and learn some more, but she begged me, with a twinkle, to keep on as I was going.

Then came another trip to Europe. My mother and I
spent a winter in Paris, on the Riviera, and in Savoy, at
Aix les Bains, where mother took the baths for her arthritis,
and I took them to keep her company. It was the custom to
have a maid carry your clothes back to the hotel, and when
the treatment was finished each day, your long white woolen
robe with its hood was removed from a hot oven and spread
over a sedan chair. It was folded up over your feet when
you got on, and tied firmly at ankles and throat, then a
covering was let down from the roof of the chair, windowed
with a little spot of isinglass. Husky porters took up the
poles and jogged through the streets to your hotel, and up
to your rooms, where they lifted you into bed and pulled up
the covers, with a warning to stay there. I used to untie
my feet as soon as they went, to go into the other room to
make sure that they had brought me back my own mother.
When the Germans reached Aix a few years ago, I used to
wonder if they were taking the baths with any of the old
crew in attendance, and whether some of the Nazis, securely
trussed, might not land in the green waters of lovely Lac
Bourget.

When many of the processes of the Atlantic book business were taken over by Little, Brown, I joined the staff of
Houghton Mifflin Company, also in Boston, and attended so
many conventions for the Library department that I came
to be known as Miss Houghton Mifflin. But my most interesting work for them was as Editor of Children's Books.
After about a dozen years I left to open my own literary
agency, and since 1940 have been placing the books of many
writers, and counselling them on the organization and revision of their manuscripts. Contracts are usually with New
York firms, but one novel, *The Mass of Brother Michel*,
was placed with the Bruce Publishing Company of Milwaukee.

Probably the most interesting thing about any author is

how she came to write her books. So I will pass over my joy in landscape painting and two recent painting trips to the Mojave Desert and to Mexico. Only two books have appeared under my name, though I have assisted in the writing of others. Both are children's books, brought out by Alfred Knopf, and are about Ireland a hundred years ago, when the grandparents of many Americans were living there. Thousands were forced by persecution and poverty —and often when they were little more than children—to leave their homes and go alone to a strange land. We owe them our good fortune in being Americans; we owe them our faith. So my books are a small repayment in love and gratitude for our debt to the Patricks and Michaels and Marys and Norahs who embarked weeping on those small vessels in Irish ports. Whatever happened to them in America, as my grandmother used to say, "You couldn't knock the faith out of them with an axe."

The stories are drawn almost wholly from what I remember of the sayings of my two grandmothers. One was a Mangan married into the proud old family of the O'Donnells. She was severe and reserved, teaching her children to be "civil and strange." The other was tiny, white, and frail, with such sweetness in her tender smile and in her childlike blue eyes that she seemed all spirit. She is the Little Grandmother in *The Mullingar Heifer*.

The stories in *Molly the Rogue* of the old beggar woman who pretended she couldn't walk, and of Malteezer, the talking cat, have been told for generations in my family. But I didn't realize that I knew far more than a few odd bits about Ireland, until there came a request from Knopf for an Irish story. After trying three other possible authors, I decided to do it myself, and placed the story in County Kerry where I had visited the birthplace of my grandmother O'Donnell.

One of the wonderful things about writing is that we don't know what riches we may find in our minds and memories until we sit down with paper and pencil to tell readers what we feel most deeply about, and would like to share with them.

EDITOR'S NOTE: Knopf published Miss Walsh's *Molly the Rogue*, in 1944, and her *Mullingar Heifer*, in 1946. And by the way, the R in the author's name stands for Regina.

MAISIE WARD

(Mrs. Frank J. Sheed)

I WAS BORN AT SHANKLIN IN THE ISLE OF WIGHT, ON JANU-
ary 4, 1889. My mother had come to Shanklin on account of
its mild climate: returning to her home at Freshwater when
I was about six weeks old she exhibited me proudly to the
poet Tennyson who remarked: "She's exactly like Henry
VIII."

My parents moved to Eastbourne when I was two, and
there we came to know Professor Huxley and his wife and
played with their many grandchildren, of whom Aldous and
Julian are today well known. We lived at Eastbourne and
were educated by governesses until I was twelve when my
parents bought a permanent home, "Lotus," near the town
of Dorking in Surrey. Here my sister and I went daily to
a small convent nearby, until at sixteen I was sent to Cambridge where the Mary Ward nuns had an excellent school.
Under their care we attended lectures and had the privilege

of hearing Monsignor Robert Hugh Benson preach the sermons that today may be read in his *Religion of the Plain Man,* and *Christ in the Church.*

Leaving school at the end of 1907, I had a very interesting life with my parents. My father was editing *The Dublin Review,* my mother had just published *Out of Due Time* and was writing *Horace Blake.* Hilaire Belloc lived in Sussex not very far from us, and we came to know Chesterton and many other men famous in letters and politics. I travelled a good deal in those years, visiting Constantinople where my uncle was Ambassador, going often to Paris and to Brittany and spending some unforgettable weeks in Florence studying the glories of medieval art. My only writing during that period was some book reviewing for *The Dublin Review* and a short biography of St. Bernardino of Siena, written for a series that Father (later Archbishop) Goodier was editing.

When the war broke out in 1914, I became a Red Cross nurse. My father died in 1916, and my mother shortly afterwards sold our home in Surrey. My brother had inherited a house in the Isle of Wight and my mother and I lived sometimes in London and sometimes with him in *The Island* (as we Islanders always called it). "Vectis" was the Roman name, and they left maps of it that are still reproduced. It is forty miles long and seventeen broad with heather hills and green downlands; the waves break perpetually against its white cliffs or run between them into sandy bays and up deep narrow gullies which are called "chines." Seldom has so much beauty been set by God in such narrow bounds.

In 1919, the Catholic Evidence Guild came into being in London—a society for explaining the faith in public parks and at street corners. A scrubwoman and I were the first two women speakers. This Miss Cozens had read her way

into the Church while scrubbing floors for a living and I
learnt a great deal from her. I had just finished writing
a short biography of Father Maturin, the great Anglican
convert, but for the next fifteen years I wrote no more. I
spoke constantly, reorganized the Catholic Truth Society
Lending Library, and divided my time between these two
activities.

In 1920, a young Australian visiting England discovered
the Guild, and took the post of Organising Secretary to the
Catholic Truth Society. Henceforward, Frank Sheed and
I worked together. With the help of Miss Cozens and
others, and under the guidance of our Director of Studies,
Dr. Arendzen, we reorganized the training method of the
Guild and published a first slim edition of *Catholic Evidence
Guild Training Outlines* with the Catholic Truth Society.
Six years later, Frank Sheed and I were married, and short-
ly thereafter we founded the publishing house of Sheed and
Ward.

We were fortunate in the fact that a great burst of Catholic literary activity had followed the war, not only in England but on the Continent, so that a multitude of books
awaited only translation. We were also to introduce to the
English-speaking world many foreign writers hitherto unknown and also to promote the study of those already
known but of whose works but few had been translated
into English. The names of Przywara and Prohaszka, besides those of Gilson, Maritain, Karl Adam, Henri Gheon,
Paul Claudel, remind one how widespread was the stirring
of the Catholic mind at that moment. Reading Adam's
Spirit of Catholicism, Gertrud von Le Fort's *Hymns to the
Church*, Claudel's *Satin Slipper*, and Gheon's Saints' lives,
all meant unforgettable experiences. With all these books
we were amazingly fortunate: Claudel declared that Father
O'Connor's translation was better than his own original.
But the problem of first-rate translation remains *the* prob-

lem in Catholic publishing if it is to be worthy of the title catholic or universal.

The very first book we issued was Belloc's attack on Wells, called quaintly a *Companion to the Outline of History,* and both Belloc and Chesterton, although already involved in contracts with other publishers, gave us warm support in our venture. Father Martindale made us the present of a book as a wedding gift and thereafter published with us almost all his work. Christopher Dawson was rising into fame as the greatest of modern historians: he and Edward Watkin, already our friends, became our authors. It was a period of great excitement and stimulation. With the birth of my first baby imminent, I would sit in Battersea Park correcting the proofs of Father Hugh Pope's *Layman's New Testament,* or reading manuscripts, hoping to discover a new Chesterton on the horizon.

We had taken a tiny flat overlooking Battersea Park and close to the former home of the Chestertons who were now living in the country. Here, on St. Luke's Day, 1927, our first child was born and we gave her the name Rosemary Luke. After her birth I almost died from phlebitis resulting in a clot of blood that settled on my lung. For weeks I lay between life and death, but the unceasing prayers of the Evidence Guild and my other friends were answered by a complete recovery. Three years later, our son was born on St. John's Day, and christened Wilfrid John Joseph. G. K. Chesterton was his godfather.

Meanwhile we had left London and I was again living in Surrey, this time in the village of Horley. Here we opened an auxiliary chapel for the parish church four miles away. An old stable was turned into an attractive little chapel and a Catholic congregation sprang up rapidly. The priest would come down from London at the weekend and stayed in our house—a great privilege for ourselves and our children. My husband taught the congregation to sing one or

two simple Gregorian Masses: we found that by teaching
them first the sound and the sense of the Latin words, by
having them read the Gloria and the Credo while we translated and explained, we were soon able to get them to sing
Latin as loudly and happily as their own language. Even
the Catholic boys from a mental hospital nearby would be
heard chanting the Gloria as they dug or weeded the garden.

We were very happy at Horley, but the journey to London, not only on every weekday but also on Sundays for
Park speaking, became very heavy for my husband. Twice
we returned for a year to London but our little house and
the chapel drew us back to Surrey again.

My first visit to America was made simply for a lecture
tour: my husband and I went together, leaving our children
with my mother. It was the eve of the depression, but we
made so many friends that three years later we decided on
the venture of opening a branch of our publishing house in
New York. March, 1933, saw the official opening of 63
Fifth Avenue which still remains our publishing address.
The generous welcome and wholehearted hospitality we
have received in this country remains to us a source of lasting gratitude. I have known much happiness in the United
States.

We did not, however, yet live here. We "commuted" over
the Atlantic for many years, and we had added to our com-
mitments at home a farm which we attempted to run in
connection with the Catholic Land Movement. Our farming was an unqualified failure, and soon after we started
our New York house, we were glad to lease the land to a
practical farmer. The effort to practice the unfamiliar art
of farming had so strained our resources that it was only
money left me by my mother when she died at the end of
1932 that made our American venture a possibility.

My mother's death awoke in me an intense wish that the
memory of her and of my father should not be lost for

future generations. I had given up all idea of authorship long ago, but now I felt a strong urge to write, and I completed my first volume *The Wilfrid Wards and the Transition* (The Nineteenth Century) in time for Chesterton to review it on the radio before his death. It was published in 1934. I was still at work on the second volume, *Insurrection versus Resurrection*, when Chesterton's death in 1936 caused his wife and his adopted daughter, Dorothy Collins, to look for a biographer for him. His own approval of my work led to their selecting me. I began the book as soon as I had completed *Insurrection* and worked at it with many interruptions—lecture tours, publishing, etc.—until 1943.

Each visit to New York now meant the making of new friendships and the discovery of new authors. I remember especially the thrill of reading the manuscript of Father Feeney's *Fish on Friday*, and the discovery that we had an author in our own office in the person of Mary Perkins who was writing *At Your Ease in the Catholic Church*.

After the war broke out in 1939, my husband and I came over here once more, travelling across Europe and taking ship at Lisbon, returning by Naples and Rome, a few weeks before the fall of France and the entry of Italy into the war. But already travelling had become so difficult that we felt we must never again while the war lasted both leave our children at the same time,—or indeed, leave them in England at all. The New York house was doing a rapidly increasing business and it seemed best to respond to the invitations of our many American friends by bringing our children over here and "commuting" from this side of the Atlantic instead of the other. In the event only my husband was able to procure permits and transportation. I have remained in the United States except for fairly frequent visits to Canada. For three years we lived in the lovely suburb of Philadelphia, Torresdale, where a Convent of the Sacred Heart—Eden Hall—was within walking distance of Rosemary's education, and where the presence of a group of old friends made it possible to combine writing and leisure very pleasurably. A garden of lovely flowering shrubs made spring glorious, and in spite of my letters from blitzed England and my husband's frequent visits there, I could be only happy in such surroundings. The letters were so memorable that I drew them together in a little book called *This Burning Heat*. For more permanent a fruit of the blitz is Caryll Houselander's *This War is the Passion*, which my husband brought back from England at about the same period. Our London office was completely destroyed in the blitz, but fortunately no lives were lost. My husband was in England at the time and rented a new office on the following day.

The month after the publication of *Gilbert Keith Chesterton* in this country we moved to New York,—October, 1943. Here we are now living and here I wrote my latest book, *The Splendour of the Rosary*.

EDITOR'S NOTE: Books by Maisie Ward (Mary Josephine Ward Sheed), all published by S & W, excepting the first two, are *Father Maturin: A Memoir*, Longmans, 1920; *St. Bernardino*, Herder, 1914; *The Oxford Groups*, 1937; *The Wilfrid Wards and the Transition*, 1934; *Insurrection versus Resurrection*, 1937; *This Burning Heat*, 1941; *Gilbert Keith Chesterton*, 1943; *The Splendour of the Rosary*, 1945; and in collaboration with her husband, *Catholic Evidence Training Outlines;* she also edited Sothern's *Chosen Races*, and a series of studies in English sanctity entitled *The English Way*.